Please direct correspondence to:
Post Office Box 158841
Nashville, Tennessee 37215
U.S.A.

Order this book online at www.trafford.com/08-0880
or email orders@trafford.com

Most Trafford titles are also available at major online book retailers.

© Copyright 2009 Rita Clare Whitmer.

All rights reserved. No part of this publication may be reproduced, stored in a retrieval system, or transmitted, in any form or by any means, electronic, mechanical, photocopying, recording, or otherwise, without the written prior permission of the author.

Cloud Photos by Rita Whitmer
Dr. Erickson Photo by Nora Garcia
Memorial Day Photos by Katy Cooper
Layout, digital imaging and production assistance from Pat Whitmer
Barnwood Cross by Tom Whitmer, Montana

Holy Bible verses from King James Version

Note for Librarians: A cataloguing record for this book is available from Library and Archives Canada at www.collectionscanada.ca/amicus/index-e.html

ISBN: 978-1-4251-8255-7

We at Trafford believe that it is the responsibility of us all, as both individuals and corporations, to make choices that are environmentally and socially sound. You, in turn, are supporting this responsible conduct each time you purchase a Trafford book, or make use of our publishing services. To find out how you are helping, please visit www.trafford.com/responsiblepublishing.html

Our mission is to efficiently provide the world's finest, most comprehensive book publishing service, enabling every author to experience success. To find out how to publish your book, your way, and have it available worldwide, visit us online at www.trafford.com/10510

Trafford
PUBLISHING

www.trafford.com

North America & international
toll-free: 1 888 232 4444 (USA & Canada)
phone: 250 383 6864 ♦ fax: 250 383 6804
email: info@trafford.com

The United Kingdom & Europe
phone: +44 (0)1865 487 395 ♦ local rate: 0845 230 9601
facsimile: +44 (0)1865 481 507 ♦ email: info.uk@trafford.com

10 9 8 7

The events related here are true. The people, places and times are real. No names have been changed except in one instance when the name was not known.

Angel Talk

Rita Whitmer

PSALM 26

That I may publish with the voice of thanksgiving, and tell of all thy wondrous works.

Dedicated To

Dr. Dale Erickson
Dr. Lawrence Spingola
Dr. Barry Maron
Robert B. Watson

and to the loving memory of my beloved Mother,
Marilee Calk Whitmer

for their unselfish and devoted efforts to save
that most precious miracle of all... a human life.

THE WEAVER

God only knows
Of all the old souls
And tapestries woven with time
Embroidered with treasures
From heavenly pleasures
And pageantries flowing sublime.

God only shows
To some of His souls
The threads and the patterns to find;
The weaver rejoices
And dreams through his choices…
Miracles left behind.

Rita

Table of Contents

	Prologue	1
1	The Wonderful Servant, 1963	5
2	Knocking On Heaven's Door, 1970	16
3	From Daylight To Dawn, 1974	32
4	Calling Down The Rain, 1975	93
5	Blessed Are The Believers, 1976	100
6	Going To The Sun, 1976	108
7	The Cow In The Corn, 1979	121
8	Once Upon A Lifetime, 1980	131
9	The Navajo Angel, 1980	142
10	Promises To Keep, 1980	148
11	The Blizzard, 1983	160
12	The Birthday Party, 1984	171
13	Angel Fire, 1985	177
14	The Investor Angel, 1985	183
15	The Wheelchair, 1986	189
16	The Camper, 1987	200
17	The Mexican Serape, 1989	206
18	The Rijksmuseum, 1990	215
19	The Cowboy, 1992	226
20	Gladys Baker, 1994	233
21	The National Cemetery, 1994	240
22	The Christmas Coconuts, 1994	251
	Epilogue	262
	Acknowledgements	268

Prologue

Hebrews 1

14 Are they not all ministering spirits, sent forth to minister for them who shall be heirs of salvation?

Oh, indeed they are! They are Divine Messengers, Guardians of all who live, Keepers of Heaven's Light, elusive yet constant messengers of love—that most powerful foundation and everlasting expression of Almighty God. And when they are at work, they minister through miracles…and they carry the name of "Angel."

They come to us as whispers in our dreams, as unseen hands that set tragedy aside before our eyes, as incongruous bearers laden with life-saving nourishment, as silent guides who mark a path of safety through hopelessness—all to enlighten our human lives. They are flickering stardust in the night and light our time as mortals with a special awareness that when realized, casts a dazzling and undeniable new meaning to the word "life."

For we as humans—the ultimate species of life on this planet—are the cherished children of God Almighty. We have been blessed with qualities and capabilities that have baffled the logic of analytical human thinking through ages of history and civilization. But, that same curiosity of the unknown has walked hand in hand, century by century, with as many inexplicable, unimaginable and unforgettable moments of earthly truths.

History has already written its own story, but knowledge—words that mark the capacity to share and expand learning—has been intentionally preserved for future worlds in the shimmering truths of papyrus, stone, and ancient scrolls that live on and on. All of it, every letter, every figure is augmented by the unwavering nudges and solicitous attentions of the Angels of God.

More than three decades have passed since I encountered my first admitted miracle of God and His Angels. Since then, They have been with me everywhere granting constant protection, safety, and reminders to me of Their nearness all the time. These precious moments—and they have been just that, moments—have insured my unwavering faith and trust in God, and have dominated my daily living with continual awareness and communication to Him in His Heavenly Order.

Constant prayers, gratitude and acknowledgements of Their presence rest in my mind and on my lips throughout every waking moment, anytime, anywhere. I pray for a child riding his bicycle on the street, for a kitten that dashes from beneath a car, for the firemen in fire engines rushing to rescue someone, for every telephone call I receive from someone I have been thinking about. Through these days, I am constantly reminded of the magnitude and, in the same breath, minuteness of our human mortality, the fragility of life, ever pushing me with the need to share these stories of special knowledge and enlightenment I have gleaned through the whispers of Divine Intervention. After years of pondering these wonderful gifts, I realized these events were whispers that needed a voice—I could be that voice!—a voice that perhaps even God and all the Angels would smile at, hearing of Their own miracles!

So, these are some of the stories of those special moments, special things, special gifts at the hand of God. While these experiences are unique only to me and the people involved, similar examples of Divine Intervention occur every day to people everywhere, in every country, under every imaginable circumstance. The loving attention of God and His Angels is there for those who ask for miracles and receive them, for those who need and do not know they received, and for those who demand and never hear the whispers over their own voices. Most especially, these gifts are for those who whisper back in prayer, sharing again through lives filled with serenity, compassion, new-found benevolence, and unquestioned giving to life on this wondrous planet.

The precious whispers of Divine Messengers become the positive energy and treasured source of expanded human knowledge and enlightenment. Divine Intervention is intended to improve our lives and allow us to help others improve theirs, for we must realize that our human purpose is to learn and to grow and to share. Each effort is separate, but each is bonded to the other through the infinite, everlasting power of love. While love is intangible, non-material and immeasurable, it takes its form and its worth is established only through sharing. So it is by giving more that we receive more, for love compounds itself beyond our mortal limitations and reaches into forever, leading our souls toward the precious expanses of Heaven.

Indeed, They are ministering spirits. And the searching spirit of my soul shall forever celebrate the kindnesses of God and all His Angels. I pray that through these, my own gentle whispers of love, the enlightened souls of mortals everywhere will seek and hear the loving sounds of Angel talk.

1

The Wonderful Servant, 1963

PSALM 96

12 Let the field be joyful, and all that is therein; then shall all the trees of the wood rejoice.

Angel Talk

Montana basked in the golden glow of a good harvest that summer. Spring rains had swept across her borders in giant storms and poured down upon the wheat fields, preparing them for the yield that promised to be a bumper crop. It was a rare success to the ever-hopeful farmers who, after enduring countless seasons of drought, blight and misfortune, now prepared their machinery for harvest of the vast waving fields of grain.

Such a prospect of an undisturbed, bountiful harvest spread happiness across the country. The little school section where my family and I lived was no exception. By the graces of God, we were jubilant, too, for our wheat fields flourished, the spray planes had defied gravity and the grasshoppers, and even the creeping guinea had seemed to wait for another year to overtake the growing wheat. It was time "to bring in the sheaves." Combines began appearing in the fields as the great harvest moved into full swing.

Little more than two years had passed since we left the ranch. My twin and I were now twelve years old, middle children among seven others. With Mother's unwavering support, Daddy had recovered enough from his heart attack to help her direct and instruct us as we became teenagers. Though his shattered health brought new and strange lessons of health, we slowly rebuilt our lives—parents and nine children—and looked forward to a successful harvest with much gratefulness.

Daddy chose that summer to have custom cutters—men with machinery and workers who harvest the crops for a fee—harvest our crops that year. Anxious to begin cutting, they had pulled one combine and grain truck to the field to cut a round and see if the fields were ready. Some were, some weren't. Some Daddy decided to swath so the wheat would at least be lying safely in windrows on the ground should an unexpected rainstorm appear. At least the tender wheat stems would not be damaged and the precious crop lost. So, we moved into harvest with high hopes, not knowing it would be one of the best—and worst experiences—we would ever know on the farm.

The Wonderful Servant

It was a glorious day, warm sun shining, clear skies, no chance of rain. The golden fields waved gently in the wind, waiting. Daddy sent Terry Brown, one of the custom cutters, to the north field with our little brother, Rex, who was nine, to share in the adventure. After only a short round, Terry reported the wheat was so tall and thick they would not be able to leave short stubble or cut the wheat close to the ground. Threshing too much straw took too much time for the combine to thresh it. Instead, they would leave a taller stand of stubble on the field to be plowed under back into the ground later for summer fallow.

Our brother, Clinton, who was leaving for college in a few weeks, was in another distant field getting our sister, Betsy, situated on the tractor to begin swathing. Already some of the beautiful windrows of wheat lay in a foot of stubble where they would be safe until the combines came through.

All was well as Daddy surveyed the two distant scenes of activity from the house, watching as Terry and Rex stopped to unload the combine. But in an instant, our world changed when a column of black smoke billowed from beneath the truck they were loading. Daddy knew what it was...it could be nothing else. Shouting like a charging general, he hollered, "You kids, come on!! There's a fire! Come on! Let's go!! Let's go!!" Four of us scrambled from all parts of the farm running toward him for his next order. He kept shouting, "Get shovels!! Get gunny sacks!! Let's go!! Let's go!! Bango! Bring the water truck! Let's go! Let's go!!"

In an instant the whole beautiful summer day of pristine blue skies crashed into a desperate frantic rush to save the wheat fields and whoever might be caught in the fire. Daddy ran to the tractor with the plow hitched to it, and at full speed, tore out of the farmyard. Suddenly time was our enemy as he headed across a windrowed field seeking the shortest route to the fire.

Mother rushed from the house, leaving our sister, Patsy, with our two-year-old baby sister, Barbie. Running

Angel Talk

with shovels and gunny sacks, we leaped into the car as Mother drove us toward the growing cloud of black smoke. Desperate and grief-stricken, we watched the terrible scene in the distance and wondered if we would be in time to stop the destruction of our world.

Though speeding down the ditch road, the car seemed to inch instead of fly as the ominous smoke climbed higher and blacker. Clinton had seen it, too, and left Betsy to windrow. Now he, too, was in his pickup speeding across the field of freshly mown windrows. So from four directions we rushed to save the fields—four outfits: Daddy with the tractor and plow, Bango with the truck and water tank, Mother in the car with three daughters, and Clinton alone in the pickup. All of us rushed in a desperate dash to get to the field before the fire could spread to the standing wheat and across the entire countryside.

But tragedy seemed to immediately start finding its victims. Bango took a turn on the ditch road too fast and watched in horror as the 500 gallon tank slipped off the flatbed and slid with its precious cargo into the ditch! There was no way to retrieve the giant tank—the water was lost! Shattered at his mistake he stood stricken by the truck waiting for us in the car—a thirteen year-old boy trying to do his best only to fail. He could not know that losing the water tank was just another obstacle in the mounting drama unfolding on all corners of the farm. Without a thought nor word of the loss, Mother stopped for him and sped on toward the threatening cloud of smoke beyond.

Daddy was behind us crossing the summer fallow field. Slowed by the rough furrows, he dared not go too fast for fear of breaking the hitch to the plow. Losing the one tool that alone could plow the fire guard would be disastrous. He couldn't risk it.

We raced closer, watching Daddy inch his way to the fire. Now the combine was moving away from the burning truck and we could see Terry fighting the eager flames with his fire extinguisher. Suddenly the smoke dissipated almost to nothing, only white wisps in the air! Maybe

The Wonderful Servant ☦

Terry got it out! Maybe it was over! Maybe everything was going to be all right!!

Still the combine kept moving toward us, away from the fire toward the house we left behind. Then we realized in disbelief that only Rex could be driving it! A little nine year-old boy? Impossible! But it could be no other! No one else was with Terry! But then in the same instant of amazement, our wonder was replaced by new horror as great pillars of black smoke billowed skyward, fresh and menacing. Now our tears became something else to fight.

Clint slid the pickup to a stop a short distance from the burning truck just as we pulled up. We leaped from the vehicles into action, beating the flames with our gunny sacks, smashing shovels into the ground for dirt to bury the red, hot enemy. Good Heavens! How the flames gobbled up the golden wheat, turning it instantly from gorgeous grain to black ash! It was impossible to stop! We shoveled, we beat, then watched in another horror as the grain truck cab erupted in flames, fire whipping into the truck box half filled with wheat. Fearing the gas tanks would explode, Clinton and Terry aimed all the fire extinguishers at the truck—it was useless. It was all too much, too fast, too hot and too late.

Quickly, too, the wind seemed to become an evil thing, flying from only a breeze to a churning wind. Flames leaped through the dusty chaff and stubble like gunpowder on a campfire! Where was Daddy?! He seemed a lifetime away—would he reach us in time to keep it from reaching the standing wheat?! We had no water—the flames were hot—the wind was hot—the fire was getting away from us!! Our crop, our world would be lost in minutes if we didn't contain it!! By now the flames had burned from under the hood into the truck cab, leaping around the windows, burning the sideboards. But Daddy was near, almost to us! Coming steadily across the field, in moments he would be near enough to drop the blades and begin plowing the fire guard through the wheat! We might stop it yet!!

Angel Talk

Suddenly someone shouted, "The pickup's on fire!" The horror would not end! There, where the pickup sat out of harm's way from the burning grain truck, we stared in disbelief as new flames burned beneath it, crawling upward through the grease and chaff around the engine and exhaust pipe. Confused at how it could have started without us seeing it, Clinton jumped inside to drive it to safety—too late! Already the ignition wires were burned off! The spreading flames burned so hot and furiously beneath the truck we could not get close enough to push it away! No fire extinguishers were left, it was hopeless. We turned our attention to the field and let the pickup burn, now fighting the fire with new despair.

Each moment seemed to get worse. Yet, we knew Rex was still driving the combine farther and farther away—at least it would be saved!! Now Daddy was plowing the wheat down in deep furrows—enough that the flames couldn't jump the fire guard into the other fields. Then someone shouted breathlessly, "They're coming! They're coming!"

One glance was enough to see help was on the way! Far away on the road, giant trails of dust rose behind cars and pickups racing toward our farm! Every person in twenty miles must have seen the smoke across the level prairie—no mountains existed to hide it. Word had spread like the flames themselves as farmers from miles around were racing to help us. Would they be in time? Would we lose our fields but save the countryside? Who could know...

But we couldn't stop beating the flames; we couldn't rest, we couldn't slow down just because help was on its way. Greedy flames only seemed to sweep faster through the wheat; winds from the burning trucks blew the sparks and fire even farther into the field! Lord in Heaven, could we control it until the neighbors got there?! On and on we beat the flames, more where the last one ended, even as Daddy plowed the beautiful wheat down. But the neighbors came closer and closer. In the distant field, Betsy was going around and around, still swathing. Later we learned she didn't know how to stop the tractor and could only sob in horror as she watched us fighting the fire. Helpless, she kept going around and around, sobbing and swathing in her own private despair.

Suddenly, the army of neighbors—men and women alike—leaped from their vehicles without word or question and dived into the fight. With their own shovels and gunny sacks, grim courage and determination, they attacked the demon flames with a fury. It was enough.

Finally, the brave combination of Daddy, Mother, kids, Terry Brown and neighbors smothered the last determined flame. Black smoke changed to soft white puffs rising from the blackened wheat, charred gunny sacks hung limp and scarred in exhausted hands. It was over. The neighbors' fire extinguishers put out the last flames on the trucks. The last shovel of dirt fell on a threatened clump of stubble. Daddy silenced the tractor.

We all stared at the rescued wheat field—not shimmering waves of magnificent golden wheat anymore, but instead, black and gold. Men, women and children stood exhausted in the blackened stubble, a grimy army thankful that their efforts had not been in vain. A tragedy had been averted. Not only had our fields been saved, but the whole country had been rescued. Had the fire escaped, the prairie, fields, pastures, farmsteads in every direction for miles could have been gobbled up in the ruthless fire. Now it was over, everyone was safe, the combine was safe. The truck, the pickup and a few hundred bushels of wheat were lost. But the battle was won.

The neighbors stood in somber groups talking quietly to Daddy and Mother and to each other. Then our neighbor, Ruth Harris, turned to me with long strands of her dark hair straying in the wind, her apron flapping gently against her dress. Her eyes were clearest blue against the blue skies around us and she softly said, "Fire is a wonderful servant but a terrible master."

My heart jerked with the profundity of her words; sad tears sprang to my eyes. Suddenly the whole desperation of the day overwhelmed me. I wanted to cry and cry that it was all over, that the fields were safe, that my family and Terry Brown and the neighbors were safe and the wheat was safe. I wanted the blackness of the burned stubble to be gone and the trucks to not look so terrible in the brilliant sun and the beautiful day. I wished my child hope that the whole terrible day had never happened.

Assured that not a flicker of fire lingered, our parents invited everyone to the house for refreshments. Clint took another truck to rescue Betsy who was still going around and around, and surely still sobbing, in her field. Driving in caravan back to the house, Mother parked the car at the well and started for the house. Rex and Patsy and Barbie greeted us; we put Barbie out of harm's way in the front seat while we splashed water on our faces. How wonderful the water felt! We were literally trying to wash away that terrible ordeal. But it was not over yet...

Suddenly Mother screamed from afar, "Get Barbie! Get Barbie!" Stunned at her desperate cry, we whirled from the water trough to see Barbie smiling, innocent and darling, standing on the front seat with her arms spread across the back cushion. Her little pixy haircut framed her chubby, pocket-gopher cheeks as smoke rose in gray menacing wisps around her! The car was burning, too, and Barbie was in it!! Horrors we thought were done rushed back again! How could it be?! How could any day still continue to be as terrible as this?! A glance showed flames creeping through the floorboards inside the car, closer and closer to our tiny little doll! Desperate all over again, we snatched her to safety and quickly doused the flames!

A quick inspection proved that, just like the truck and pickup in the field, the tall stubble had wrapped around the hot exhaust pipe. Igniting the chaff, it was a repeat of the nightmare we had just fought and won!

Finally, finally, positively in control of the last threat to life and livelihood, we returned to the house, sober and pensive. Mother instructed us to never tell Daddy that his little helper had been in danger. We promised. He went to his grave never knowing of that last awful moment on that terrible, terrible day.

Our attention moved from the fire and the fields to serving the thirsty, exhausted neighbors. Mother sent me to the well for a bucket of water and there, leaning against the telephone pole near the path, was Rex. I set the water bucket down and looked at him, a little boy with dark curls and gentle green eyes looking back at me with an ancient, wise agony. I realized he felt the same way I did. I put my arms around him and we stood there, two little children in the sun with the blue sky all around, and we cried as though our young tender hearts would verily break. But all the tears in the world could never be enough to take away the sorrow.

Finally, we walked slowly up the hill with memories that would never let us be the same again. Soon Daddy and the other men returned to the field to assess the damage and re-evaluate the afternoon's events. It was then, standing there in the field and to everyone's shock, that they discovered a new truth. Some may call it happenchance, some would say it was irony, but most of us would simply call it Divine Intervention.

When Terry had shouted to Rex to get the combine out of the field, take it to the house and call the fire department, the little boy had done exactly that. Though this was his first ride on the combine, he had scrambled to the cab, shifted the gearshift into position as he had seen Terry do, and had driven the giant machine calmly away. Surely his brave little heart was pounding as he steered it toward safety as though he had done it a thousand times.

Farther and farther from the fire he drove until the drainage ditch loomed ahead. It separated the field from the road and the house; it separated him from safety. But God loves children, too, and Rex continued on his way. He simply drove to the narrow chasm, crossed it and continued to the house. Now as the men followed the tracks of the combine, they stood at the ditch looking down. There at the edge of the ditch, the tracks ended. Across the chasm, a short deep gash showed in the dirt where the header scraped before reaching the opposite side. The tracks appeared again and led to the house. It was then they knew that Rex had, by the grace of God, floated over the ditch to safety!

Impossible! The men knew the width of the header could not have allowed the combine to clear the ditch without tipping over or tearing off the header. But the tracks did the talking. The combine was sitting at the house where its little driver had parked it. It was true! Rex had driven straight to the ditch into nothing, then crossed to the other side and continued down the road!! It was as he said: "I just floated over the ditch!"

With the honest words of a child, who needs the clinical observations of stunned farmers?! Simple truth belied God and all the Angels watching, guiding, protecting the little boy on the giant machine...So, the tragedy that started the day ended with a wonderful gift from God!

Astonishing facts stood for what they were. Silent acceptance was the only acknowledgment of Divine Intervention needed on that heartbreaking day. Without a doubt, if once again we take reality in retrospect, considering the portent of those moments, we must assign credit to the kind ambivalence of Divine Intervention. For, what passing Angel could have viewed such a scene and not taken pity on the helpless players below?

With the trucks in flames, the winds spreading fire all around, Daddy rushing with the tractor and plow, the neighbors racing ahead of their dust trails down the roads, there was also a tiny, little boy, shaking and alone atop a giant harvesting machine. Straining through the bars of the steering wheel to see where he was going, and worse, totally unfamiliar with anything in the strange cockpit, he knew only to get it to safety. And safety waited on the far side of the ditch...

As we know, miracles do not always happen only to those who ask for them. They also happen to those who need them and have no thought of miracles or Angels at that moment. Rex thought only of doing what he was told: save the combine. He thought nothing of his own life or the danger he faced in doing what he was told. So, his child eyes were guided down a blind path; his anguished heart beat with courage, his little fingers touched the right levers, and the ditch became only part of the road that he "floated over" to safety.

So it is to the innocent, with such unassuming courage in the face of deadly odds, that the gifts of God are bestowed in the presence of His Angels. And, it is to all of us, in believing such gifts, that we receive the greatest gift of all, for, blessed are the believers.

2

Knocking On Heaven's Door, 1970

PSALM 8

4   What is man, that thou art mindful of him? and the son of man, that thou visitest him?
5   For thou hast made him a little lower than the angels, and hast crowned him with glory and honour.

Knocking On Heaven's Door

The years had passed slowly on the farm, suspended between good crops and no crops. We lived through too much rain and not enough rain, building a home, and succeeding and failing at understanding the tragedy of our father's illness. Seasons drifted by to plunge us into heavy schedules of farm work, school work and part-time jobs as we adjusted to each other and the new roles we lived. All of it was now a world of responsibility and work as we changed from children to teenagers to young adults.

Not only had Mother and we children changed, but our father had changed, too. Fraught with the lingering terror of another heart attack, he became a shadow of himself. His gaze somber and sad, he was surrounded only with memories of good health and strength. No longer were we the little black-haired children who squealed to see him coming home. Gone were the years when his every word and thought was the foundation of our world, when his physical strengths, intellect, character and our Mother were all we needed. Now we were grown, in school or at work, and he was left alone to get well.

But he had Barbie, who was his constant companion. As his energy vanished before our eyes, she became his "helper" and loved being at his beck and call, happily fetching things for him and doing his bidding in his loving presence. Now before his eyes, he watched us leave our child days behind and become old before our time—working, thinking little adults.

My own tall, thin form had also changed, and my life, too, had become a shadow of the days I had known before. In my thirteenth summer, I became a quiet reflective ghost of the tomboy riding horses and adventuring in the outdoors with such a passion. But my alteration had not come with the devastation of an unknown silent heart attack like my father's. Mine was by my decision, my choice—an impulsive childish whim that changed my life forever. Now, I suffered, too, like my father, but my agonies were not from fear. Mine were physical, a constant torment, and they never let me rest.

Angel Talk

It had been a beautiful almost autumn day, nearing the beginning of school. Rex and I played atop the haystacks with gay abandon, rolling in the warm straw. I challenged him to jump to the haystack below; he wisely refused. Undaunted, I leaped with a childish urge to fly! But I knew nothing of flying—I only knew wanting. My leap was not hard enough—I missed the waiting haystack and fell straight to the ground with full weight smashing my left foot into the ground.

From the moment of impact, I knew how badly I was hurt. Instantly, from toe to knee my leg burst into black and blue blotches, swelling as wide as my thigh in a second before my eyes. Rex slid from the haystack to me where I sat swearing like a sailor. The pain was unbelievable, absolutely excruciating. Trying not to cry, I held my leg off the ground trying in vain to ease the pain, trying not to pass out. Clint and Boone came running, staring dumbfounded at the ghastly black and blue leg that a moment before had been normal. Quickly they carried me to the house where Mother knew in a glance the leg was broken. As they carefully put me in the car, I had no thought of the seven years of suffering that lay ahead, and that I had changed my life forever.

To everyone's surprise, the x-ray showed no visible break. While looking for a normal break, the town doctor had seen none. In fact, however, the entire ankle joint had been shattered into more than a dozen pieces, pieces yet to break free from the bone. He had not x-rayed it again, but simply wrapped the leg in long elastic bandages, told me to stay off it for a while and sent me home.

Weeks on crutches passed until the swelling gradually diminished. Anxious to be normal again, to do my share of work, I set the crutches aside. It would be a terrible mistake, and just in time to interrupt the healing bones. Placing weight on the ankle broke the fragile knitting over the weeks. The bone chips were ground in the joint to be joined later by calcium deposits. Years of suffering had begun.

Already so grievously affected by our father's long illness, I was stricken with more guilt at not carrying my share of the load at home. Now crippled—who knew for how long?—I struggled to act normally at home and school. Like so many injured and ill people, I was anxious to do the things I had before. I pretended my leg was better, that I was fine. But the lie was futile.

Alone in my room, I watched my face in the mirror, practicing facial expressions so I would know what my face looked like in pain or placid and non-revealing. Emotions—happiness, surprise, horror, pain—crossed my face until I made certain no one would know my true feelings. Such naive attempts at being normal did nothing to help my leg heal as I tried to believe I was better.

At first I limped around slowly, stunned at the pain. It was excruciating, unbelievably excruciating. If this were to last a long time, I would be in for a whole new side of life for sure. But apparently this was what recovery felt like. The x-ray had showed no break, so this must be how an injured leg healed. Gradually as time passed, I placed more and more weight upon my ankle and resumed some semblance of pre-haystack behavior.

Every step was like walking on razor blades. Pain became a day and night, constant unbearable ordeal. My only priority was finding one more quick place to sit, get my leg elevated, look normal and try to ease the agony. Still embarrassed that my folly had created a hardship to my family, I tried to not complain. My siblings were especially kind and considerate, not letting me carry water buckets or other heavy loads. They were, as much as I was, always aware of the swelling, which varied according to how much time I walked. The more swelling, the more pain.

So, Fate would let me know how my father felt in his silent world, one not so different from mine. I became a silent, tolerant, agreeable teenager, walking less and less, playing the piano more and more, studying, writing poetry and trying not to let anyone know how badly I hurt.

Angel Talk

Three and a half years of grueling twenty-four-hour-a-day agony passed until I could take no more. My leg remained swollen throughout the years, though I favored it constantly and kept it wrapped in bandages. At last, Mother took me to a chiropractor who did electric shock treatments to relax the muscles, presumably the cause of the pain and swelling. After six unsuccessful treatments of being plugged into the wall socket watching my leg bounce off the table, the doctor took new x-rays. At last the offending bone chips were revealed and my true condition realized. The chiropractor referred me to the local doctor who without ado, announced a specialist had to do surgery immediately.

"What kind of pain have you been going through?" he demanded. Not interested in admitting what a fool I had been, I only replied casually, "Well, quite a bit." He looked at me as though he knew completely what I wasn't saying.

Days after my sixteenth birthday, a renowned orthopedic surgeon in Billings, Dr. Perry Berg, performed the operation, a daring one for 1966. After removing the bone chips, he reconstructed the tendons and ligaments and seemed hopeful for a good recovery. His skill was remarkable and I looked forward to being normal again. After months of recovery in a cast with crutches, I was able to walk without the relentless pain that tormented me for so many years. I thought I was home free.

But relief lasted only two years. Unfortunately, the bone chips Dr. Berg removed also had calcium deposits around them, which, upon removal, left holes in the joint which the body naturally refilled with more calcium. Though the operation was considered a success, the condition returned and brought the pain with it. The ankle joint filled again with calcium deposits and I faced that old, tragic truth: walking would forever be agony.

I would never be free of pain. My childhood dreams of becoming a nurse had died with the injury, had rekindled after surgery, but now fell by the way and were gone forever in the reality of the future before me.

Knocking On Heaven's Door

Life for young women in the late '60's held few options—one either became a nurse, a hairdresser, a secretary or a wife. Nursing was out—couldn't walk. The thought of messing with someone's hair all day was appalling, and I had no interest in being married when my obsession "to see the world" had not even begun. And, too, since the fateful leap, I also felt constantly compelled "to hurry up and live." So, it was easy to make my decision. I would go to business college, become an executive secretary. Not only was this career my fastest ticket to the world, I could also sit at my desk and type all day—who had to know how badly I was hurting?

That nagging feeling to make every minute count in life stayed with me through high school and to college. I even asked the college administrators if I could hurry through my classes as fast as I wanted. Recognizing my urgency, they agreed, allowing me to blitz two years of college in six months. Maybe somehow I could see the world and make my dream happen before an early death! It was worth a try!

So, business college went quickly and successfully, leading to a service rep position with Mountain Bell in a tiny Montana town. Nearly a year later, I was transferred to state headquarters in Helena, the state capitol. It was a move that not only changed my life but also started me on a lifelong stroll down Heaven's road with Angels everywhere.

Helena lay deep in the heart of the Rockies. It was February when I arrived, in time to share in all the snow and cold of a real mountain winter. Cold shook me to my bones, escalating the pain in my ankle until I could bear it only from moment to moment. The lovely old Victorian YWCA was home where I had a tiny room across the street from the Mountain Bell building. Though work was only a short block away, the walk became a brutal gauntlet in sub-zero temperatures—an endurance course I dreaded with every day that rose.

I was only twenty years old. My life was supposed to be before me, but instead I had become again immobile, hardly able to walk. My future as a cripple was more than bleak as I recalled dreams in the life I had known before. All the lively youthful activities my siblings and friends enjoyed were hopeless to me in the darkness of my suffering. I could not imagine what my life would ever be.

During working hours while seated at my desk, waves of pain swept up my leg so suddenly and sharply that I would nearly faint from shock. Who knew how long I could stand it? *I* certainly didn't know, but I had to endure it—my job was all I had to look forward to. But the world was at my fingertips, somehow my dream was worth suffering for--surely it was worth it.

My reaction to the pain in the mountains was no different from struggling all those years on the farm and through high school. I tried doggedly not to let others know what I was going through—it was nobody's business. It was something I did to myself and I had to face the consequences.

As the weeks passed at my new job, my efforts to isolate myself failed with a man from another department. Frequently, Ken Yahvah visited my office and almost invariably, our shop talk would lead to an invitation to church with him and his wife. Unfamiliar and uncomfortable with church and religious involvements, certainly not feeling sociable, I always politely declined.

Finally though, after two long months of suffering through relentless snow and freezing cold, I had had enough. Desperate, I confided in a friend at the Y, "Michael" Conkey, a recently widowed, middle-aged woman, and devout Catholic. I told her of my agonies and actually asked her for help. She immediately offered to drive me over the mountains to a famous orthopedic surgeon there. Soon we were on our way to see Dr. Ronald Losee in Ennis, a tiny town near Virginia City.

Michael wore a cross every day of her life and wore her own design of tunics in the shape of a cross. Her animated thoughts and conversation covered countless subjects, all of which were woven with loving references to God. Her constant talk of divine revelations and God's presence left me feeling strange and uncomfortable since my own religious education was comprised of a few schoolgirl visits to church with friends.

As we drove through the mountains, I was hardly prepared for the intense references she shared about the power of God Almighty. Though I believed completely in God and Heaven, and had read considerable books on spiritual awareness and cosmic planes, my lack of formal religious education left a nagging void within me. That void disappeared quickly, though, as we crept over the treacherous, snow-covered roads. Michael breathed an unselfish prayer out loud, "Lord, please help me, please deliver us safely for I have precious cargo!"

I had never heard anyone pray for me—just me. I had never heard myself referred to as "precious cargo" nor heard anyone say I mattered so much that they would actually ask for Divine Intervention to keep me alive! Now on the snow-covered mountain road, Michael's simple prayer would be my introduction to Heaven. But I wondered, were God and all the Angels really listening?

We arrived without ado at Dr. Losee's office, but the results of the historical visit were not to be so uneventful. After inspecting my ankle and Dr. Berg's handiwork, he seemed pleased, proclaiming the operation appeared most satisfactory. As he examined new x-rays, he was both surprised at the extent of the original injury and the further injury three years of stress produced. I was completely unprepared for his irrefutable diagnosis.

Without hesitation, Dr. Losee unceremoniously pronounced that I would require surgery immediately and again at least every two years to remove the calcium deposits that had formed in the ankle joint. With a tender tinge of regret, he added softly that I would be a hopeless cripple within two years if I stayed in Montana. A change in climate to a warmer environment would help ease the pain. In short, my condition was irreversible. My life would be, for certain, solely controlled by pain and my ability to deal with it.

Angel Talk

I was shattered. In total disbelief, I imagined my life—what would it be? I was only twenty years old!!! My whole life was ahead of me!! What about my dreams?! Now this doctor—this great and famous doctor—was telling me that a life of pain, crutches, operations were all I had until medical research developed new solutions! And all of it was still years down the road! Choking back tears, I bravely asked if moving to another part of the country, like Albuquerque where my sister lived, would make a difference. Would it help me at all?

Dr. Losee said matter-of-factly it would definitely be less painful in the desert weather. Yes, the warm climate would be highly recommended for someone in my condition. Overcome with hopelessness, I asked if he would write a letter to my boss for the need to transfer to New Mexico. Without a word, he reached across his desk, snatched paper from a basket and in his strong distinctive penmanship, wrote the words that would change my life.

The promise of less pain and suffering offered no consolation to such a youthful broken heart. The blackness within me seemed everywhere and impenetrable. I left Dr. Losee's office in a fog of pain—this time including my heart—and told Michael of his diagnosis. The letter binding my fate was a banner of sorrow as we started our way back over the mountain in bleak silence.

In an effort to lift my spirits, Michael stopped the car in Virginia City, a wonderful deserted ghost town and Montana's first Territorial capitol. Winter had enveloped the Old West buildings in total silence. Like white corridors back to yesterday, the silent streets piled with snow drifts seemed to wait for its residents who had walked away and never returned. Beyond the frosted windows of the shops and houses, dishes still rested on tables, chairs still stood beside pot-bellied stoves. An eerie stillness rose above the streets as we strolled through the haunted town in the fading light. It seemed that the cowboys and miners and townspeople should appear at any moment and light the lanterns waiting behind the doors. At last, as darkness fell, we wound our way home in silent sadness.

Next day I gave Dr. Losee's letter to my boss and announced my intention to leave in two weeks. There was no point in delaying. Staying longer would guarantee nothing except more suffering; I may as well suffer in the southern sun as on a freezing mountainside. Shocked at my revelations and the somber proof of Dr. Losee's letter, he kindly extended his support, promising to arrange a transfer to the Marketing Department in the Albuquerque office. Hardly aware of the magnitude of this decision, I was only relieved at the prospect of a world warmed with constant sun and surely less pain.

Money was no incentive. Being near my long absent sister was of no interest. Not even the adventuring I had long dreamed of mattered. I was numb—numb with pain, inside and out. More so, though, I was numb to the possibility that such heartbreak could precipitate a Heavenly event that would change every thought and every goal I would ever have for the rest of my life.

After Ennis, my health was also jeopardized in another way. The snowy stroll through Virginia City's deserted streets brought on a cold which soon worsened to pneumonia. I was deathly ill, too ill to care for myself. Word spread quickly through the "Y" that I lay ill in my little room. The grand old ladies in our wonderful old house hurried to my aid, arranging schedules among them, taking turns bringing soups, juices, blankets, and cool cloths. With all the love of doting grandmothers, they tended me until, finally, after nearly two weeks, the worst had passed and I returned to work.

Only days remained before my departure, time enough to train my replacement and finalize my responsibilities. Again, Ken Yahvah stopped at my desk, asking if I would like to attend church with him and his wife that night. Sick and anguished with the bleak, painful future before me, I considered I had nothing to lose and accepted his invitation.

He and Mrs. Yahvah drove me down the old crooked streets to a tiny little chapel on Last Chance Gulch. Assuring me that I would enjoy the service, they explained

Angel Talk

the church was non-denominational, that sometimes people spoke in tongues, everyone joined in singing hymns, and after the service gathered at a simple social time afterward. It was a special place.

They were right. I had never heard of speaking in tongues before and listened, intrigued, as several parishioners were compelled to such expression. An informative and uplifting testimonial of a drug addict accepting the will of God to restore his life, stirred a wonder within me. I watched and listened with growing interest at the serene drama around me. Never had I heard people talk publicly about such private and unfortunate matters, and had never heard people speaking in foreign and unworldly languages. When the group was led in singing, accompanied by gentle ramblings from worshipers, I was more apprehensive about the evening ending normally. Little did I know that "normal" was to be the last thing the evening and I would ever be.

While the congregation seemed relaxed and communal, the atmosphere within the tiny chapel, too, seemed fresh, serene and welcoming as the service drew to a close. But one more surprise awaited me when the minister announced, "Would those wishing to be healed please come forward for the laying on of hands." Ken turned to me instantly and said, "Rita, would you like to go forward?"

I was astonished. He didn't know of my injury. I had never told him, nor even that I was in pain. How could he know I needed healing? Few people knew why I was leaving; I had simply said I was transferring. With Ken's query, the bleakness of my future flashed before me. What did anything matter? I no longer cared what he or anyone else knew about me or my anguish. Again I reasoned, what do I have to lose? and said, "Yes."

Ken never hesitated. He and his wife led me to the altar where two other suffering people stood, each attended by two supporters. Ken stood on my right, his wife on my left, each taking a hand, placing their other hands on my shoulders. We bowed our heads, eyes closed. The minister began to pray softly for our healing.

Knocking On Heaven's Door

How quickly our lives can change! An hour before, I was a devastated hopeless innocent in a freezing world. Now I stood at the altar of God where in a few breathtaking, spellbinding moments His love would send me walking down Heaven's road for the rest of my life.

As the gentle, beseeching prayers of the minister drifted through my mind, I became aware of a deep, soft warmth at my feet. At the same moment, a soft, pure, white light, coming from a distance, drew near, filling the darkness of my closed eyes with growing brightness. Soon it surrounded me, enveloping me in its breathtaking beauty with an incredible sense of utter safety and *love*. Brighter and brighter, whiter and whiter, the light grew. More and more intense it became, totally encompassing me to the very depths of my being in such absolutely pure and beautiful whiteness that I was awed to a near faint, though captured in prayer with closed eyes.

In unison with the increasing brilliance of the light, the warmth increased, rising from my toes in such intensity that I was shocked. Climbing slowly, the warmth reached my knees, cloaking me in its fabulous comfort and safety, ever climbing up and up and up, growing warmer and warmer. Intense but not burning, it engulfed me together with the exquisite, exquisite white light of love!

The warmth reached my fingertips moving to the top of my head until I was totally wrapped in its power. Together the wondrous warmth and dazzling light enfolded me totally in their absolutely pure, pure glory, holding me, protecting me for an eternity that was surely only minutes. It was the most beautiful thing I have ever known, the most wonderful feeling I have ever known. It was the most spectacular gift a mortal could ever receive...

No longer aware of Ken and his wife at my side, I seemed to float; my feet no longer seemed to touch the floor. Suspended, levitating in my mind—or was it in truth, reality?—my conscious disconnected from the chapel, voices, space. I was aware only of the spectacular, intense loving white light and the deep, deep, wonderful warmth wrapping me like a beloved package!

Angel Talk

The power of the light and the warmth was everything that could possibly be in this world—no darkness, no pain, no worry. My heart and soul were no longer mine. Suspended, protected, comforted, loved by the glorious white light and warmth, I knew I was being blessed by God.

Everything I had been became something new. Now I was an innocent, ignorant child gifted with an unforgettable moment in time that would stay with me forever.

I floated at the altar suspended in rapture for two or three minutes—long, loving minutes. Was that all I was allowed, minutes? Then, gently, slowly, the gorgeous light and warmth began to recede, flowing downward. Heaven was leaving me...

Almost as though reluctant to release me, the light and warmth lingered, protecting me, sharing their glorious gifts until at last at my toes the warmth was gone. Still the white light lingered around me in purest gossamer glory. Then slowly, slowly it moved farther and farther away until it was gone.

Though my eyes were still closed, I suddenly became aware of the floor! My friends still held me, their hands on my shoulders. My body was buoyant, warm, almost youthful and happy. Seemingly separate from my mind, my body felt totally comforted with the reality of what had happened. Unquestionably, I knew I had *lived* a miracle—*something* was different, *a lot* was different. Though all I had known was light and warmth, I also knew to my very soul that God and His magnificent love had blessed me.

Silence filled the tiny chapel when I opened my eyes. Ken and his wife gazed at me with unspeakable love and adoration. In an instant I knew they knew what had just happened! How did they know? Had they seen the light? Had they felt the warmth? Had my hands warmed their hands with their Heavenly warmth? Had the light been only in the depths of my being—my soul—or had it joined the worshippers at the altar, in the chapel pews? Had the glory I had felt and seen in the darkness of my closed eyes been for my heart and soul alone, or did they know, too? Had such rapturous blessings resounded through the serene little chapel until everyone knew? I am certain they had.

His own face calm and loving, Ken asked softly, "Does your ankle hurt, Rita?" Stunned again that he referred to the precise source of my agony, I wondered, "How did he know?" Carefully I moved my ankle, and for the first time in seven long, agonizing years it did not hurt. Not even slightly. Again, more vigorously, up and down, to and fro, I moved it. No pain. I was healed.

Still with a look of total love, Ken added, "Rita, your ankle wasn't the only thing that was healed. You had problems with your left knee, your right hand, your liver, your heart, lungs and throat. They were healed, too. They won't bother you anymore."

Surprised at his blunt medical evaluation, I accepted his matter-of-fact pronouncement as his own kind of truth, his own reality. After all, what could he possibly know about my health? My only health problem was a shattered ankle, not a shattered body. But tonight, what could it matter?! Nothing mattered except rejoicing and thanking God for His blessing!! I had gone down Heaven's road, knocked at Heaven's door, and God and the Angels had opened it...

Ken and Mrs. Yahvah led me from the altar down the aisle to the chapel basement where refreshments were served. People came to me with love and rejoicing in their faces, congratulating me in awe for my miracle. How did they know? What had the little chapel looked like while we all stood at the altar? But that didn't matter either. Only the wonder and glory of God mattered. It never faded as the evening ended.

I asked Ken and Mrs. Yahvah if I could please walk home. It was a long way, a cold walk, but it had also been so long since I had walked without pain that I wanted to be alone without it. I wanted to feel what it was like to not feel it anymore. I wanted to see if walking a long time would make it hurt again. I was sure it wouldn't, but

Angel Talk

I wanted to make sure I was sure. Freedom was a new word in my life.

They left me with my miracle, alone in the night on the silent, empty snow-covered streets. The long, long way to the "Y" was short, filled with laughter and swinging on the streetlight poles in the snow. At last in my room, rejoicing still left me sleepless. The night was filled only with my prayers of gratitude and hallelujahs that lasted long past dawn. I was healed. I was healed. I was healed.

Now returning to work seemed a lie. Now I had no reason to go away; I could stay. My reason for leaving was gone. Though anguished over reversing my decision at work, it took little to decide how wrong it would be to disrupt so many people's lives again by saying I would stay. Wondering what the deserts of New Mexico could offer, what a warm climate would feel like, a hundred other questions soon made my decision for me. Adventure and a whole lot more living was just around the corner... with the grace of God and His divine presence in my life, I was certain I would be safe. But I never thought about happy.

Years after the miracle on Last Chance Gulch, I still wondered why Ken Yahvah had said I had problems with other areas of my body. It was not until nearly five years later that I remembered his words. By then, Ken Yahvah was right, but in the future, not in the past.

By 1975, I had, in fact, suffered injuries to those parts of my body. An automobile accident in late 1974 proved fatal to me; I would be a DOA at the hospital. Obviously though, I was resuscitated, but every area of my body that Ken said was healed, was, indeed, destroyed or traumatized in the accident.

In life we learn things, we have enlightenment that is beyond reproof. There is no doubt in my mind that I would never have survived those terrible injuries had I not had the benefit of God's blessing in the little chapel so long before.

Today, more than three decades have passed since my visit to the little chapel on Last Chance Gulch. Walking is no different than it was when I carried my miracles out the chapel door. I have suffered not a twinge of pain in the ankle since that moment to this day. New breaks to both my feet cause new agonies, but they are different from my ankle. Oddly, though swollen still, my ankle seems exempt from any pain, any injury.

Though time, circumstance and anguish have wrought different tolls on my heart, body and soul, nothing has diminished my absolute belief and trust in God and His ever-present awareness of us, humans on pathways to our souls. Heaven's road was paved in miracles, right up to the doorstep.

From Daylight To Dawn, 1974

PSALM 88

15 I am afflicted and ready to die from my youth up;
    while I suffer thy terrors I am distracted.
16 Thy fierce wrath goeth over me; thy terrors have cut
    me off.
17 They came round about me daily like water; they
    compassed me about together.
18 Lover and friend hast thou put far from me, and mine
    acquaintance into darkness.

DAYLIGHT

Memories of the little chapel on Last Chance Gulch and the glorious blessing I received there never diminished as weeks and months passed. Each day floated in a world of light not unlike the pure shroud of bliss that surrounded me that unforgettable night. I told no one—not even my family. I never even told my twin! Fearful of ridicule, being called crazy or ostracized for being different, I held my beautiful mind-boggling secret within me. Joyous for being so gloriously gifted, at the same time I also grieved for believing I could not share the truth. After all, who did I know who had received a miraculous healing like mine?!

Shortly after the blessing, I transferred to Albuquerque with Mountain Bell. There, another gift came into my life: walking without pain. Now I stepped with new confidence, new freedom. No longer did I worry how much my ankle would hurt, how long could I stand, where could I sit. The questions were gone. Never again did I wonder if the pain would recur. I knew it never would—nor has it to this writing. But still, every day I wondered, "Why did it happen to me? Why did God heal me?"

Of course there is no answer to such a question, short of being blessed with still yet another Heavenly visit to explain the why's in human context!! But my days became a post script to bliss without answers. Life was hours filled with endless gratification and overwhelming humility as I thanked God for His Divine Intervention in releasing me from those long years of endless pain.

So it was. I knew no one with an experience such as mine. Now I was left with fulfilling my new and awesome responsibility toward life with my own new life that was changed forever.

Living became a truly profound process of adding meaning to each day, thinking matters through carefully, making solid decisions for the benefit of everyone I was involved with. Everywhere I went I sought serenity, peace of mind and worthiness for my miracle. Determined to be the best kind of person I could in the eyes of God, and now at the benevolent Hand of God, I immersed myself in work and people with an even greater zeal and increasing love and regard for living.

Time passed quickly in Albuquerque. My sister and her husband rented a room to me, but just as quickly, she resumed her old big-sister bullying from our childhood. Immediately I became the live-in maid, but it didn't matter. I was used to helping my family and enabled her laziness without realizing her constant demands as a specter of abuse. When her husband co-signed on a loan for my first car, saying, "You're going to have the kind of car I want," I never contemplated the other meaning of his words. Too naïve and innocent, I was grateful to them; they were family. I felt obligated to keep my mouth shut and help them. I had a new lease on life, a life that was becoming everything I had hoped it would be.

No doubt about it, dedication, commitment and respect for life were more important than recreation and play. No one I knew had the lessons of life driven home as I had. I was determined to learn something from everyone and everything I did, and show my appreciation to God for my miracle.

Leaving my mother and sisters and brothers behind had not been easy; I missed them more than I could say. But life promises change and one day a substitute for loneliness presented itself. A man saw me dining with friends. In one glance, he decided to have me. He put the first hooks in my heart and started me down a road of pain and terror that would last for years. Only God and all the Angels would be able to save me.

All human beings—children, teenagers, adults—seek love and fulfillment. With the challenge of loneliness and heartache, we consciously and subconsciously search to fill the voids in our lives. Too often, however, we learn that the way before us is not always the right way or the honest way. Sometimes the easiest way becomes the hardest way. Sometimes the person leading the way does not always know his own path, and, sometimes he does not care about the ones he is leading. Such lessons in life help us learn about ourselves and our purpose for living. In every generation, we face lessons through family, growing up, through work, the unexpected challenges of Fate. Most importantly, we learn through the agonies of our hearts and emotions. Somewhere on that path, we realize that each lesson of our lives was meant to be.

The greatest of all lessons is love, which is the greatest of all powers, greatest of all healers, and the greatest gift to humanity. We are here to understand love and the feelings and changes it creates. We must realize the power it gives, the treasure it is, though these human lessons are the most elusive and difficult to learn. How odd to know that the truth we need to learn the most is also the most difficult to recognize.

So, at only 21 years of age, healthy, eager to live and now with Heavenly stars in my eyes, I was targeted by a stranger who wasted no time in forcing his way into my life. Because our father refused to allow us to date, I had no preparation for devotion from men, no knowledge of sincerity or true intent. I was a lamb in the wolves' den. His name was Tom Anderson*, and he calmly told his banker's secretary, "Modelle, I've met a girl and I'm going to bring her down."

His selfish oath became a cruel fact that marked my fate from the moment he saw me. He pounced on my innocent soul like new prey. Instantly he discerned I was inexperienced and naïve, kind and considerate, ill-prepared and no possible match for the well-honed charm and control he had mastered decades ago. More than twenty years older than I, he barreled into my life, determined to control my time, my thinking, my money, my soul. He wanted it all. I became his victim—not of drugs and alcohol—but of the terrible past he had already lived. Decades of rage he saved inside exploded when an innocent girl from Montana appeared and became the one he could control and destroy.

---

*Also known by nickname

Everything he was contrasted with the goals of my heart, the longings of my soul. He brought the worst of humanity into my life: rage, cynicism, jealousy, abuse, irresponsibility, alcohol, cursing, ex-wives, unloved children, greed, envy. He slammed them all into my world, tipping the scales of decency and respect and love in my life toward all the evil within himself.

But he did not know of my miracle, my faith, my love of God, my respect for life. He did not know my belief in God was greater than any evil he would cast on me. He could not make me reject God and all I knew Heaven was. But his efforts were enough to press my life to its mortal limits and throw me broken, again and again, at the feet of God.

He phoned; I hung up. I ran; he followed. He waited around every corner, watching, lurking in the parking lot, outside my office, by my car at the grocery store. I wondered when he worked, what happened with the life he had before he saw me.

There was no escape, no "somewhere safe" from him. My only rescue was my miracle, the sole basis of my unwavering faith in God who needed me for something. My life had a value to Him that no human could destroy, regardless of who tried and what happened to me. My life belonged only to God—my life was in His hands. I was a puppet on the strings of Heaven and I would survive or I would die by the will of God, not some living human.

I had no clue of what I was up against in Tom Anderson. But he had no clue of what he was up against with my Savior. As time went on, both of us would learn a great deal more about the awesome Power of my Heavenly Protector.

After my sister moved away with her family, I was left completely vulnerable and alone to fight Tom. Another older sister, Patsy, came to live with me, becoming a true shield from Tom's aggression. Indeed, he was careful to not let her see the worst in him when she was present. But even she knew my emotional commitment, the naive caring and responsibility I had developed toward

Tom. That old Montana solve-the-problem, get-it-done attitude was alive and well in me. She knew any advice or intervention she might offer would be useless to me, a young, inexperienced, naïve girl who knew nothing about men and less about emotions. When she, too, moved away, I despaired that the worst was yet to come. I was right.

Two things happened: I learned Tom was a liar, a married liar, and my father unexpectedly passed away. Tom had listened to my stories of my father's legendary courage and strength; now he was suddenly free of the one man he knew would protect me. He waited two weeks after the funeral before beginning a new routine of drunken abuse followed with beatings.

Now desperate to escape, I tried to break away and convince him he had to leave me alone. He was unfazed by my desperate need to have my own life, to be free. I was the one person he could control—a source of food and comforts. He would never let me go.

Unable to get away from him, I agonized anew when even Fate became his friend in need! A new drama was added to Tom's trials when his fourteen-year-old daughter became pregnant in Dallas. The child's mother had died shortly after her birth and Tom's mother raised her, albeit with her own naïve trust in teenage behavior. Upon hearing the news, I reluctantly drove with him to Dallas where, after two weeks of useless discussions and pointless options, he succumbed to his mother's wishes for the teens' wedding. Taxed to the limit by the entire ordeal, we returned to Albuquerque, exhausted and ready for a welcome rest. It was not to be...

Tom left me at my doorstep in the dark hours of the morning for his home in the country. As I unlocked my door, I stepped inside to find nothing in the room except my piano. No furniture, no dishes, no clothing...nothing. Everything was gone. Gone.

Fate had found my landlady next door—an old woman who decided during my long absence that I would not be coming back. She had simply rented the house to someone else. Though the rent was paid and I had given no notice, she had recalled my plan to move out later that year and simply decided this was the time. Furthermore, to accommodate the new renters, she also decided to move my possessions into her house. There, to my horror, everything I owned was stacked wall to wall, ceiling to floor in paper sacks in a spare bedroom! Too old and confused to understand her intrusion, she dumbly admitted, "If I had known you had so much stuff, I never would have moved it."

Too tired, too weary of endless conflict after conflict, the thought of fighting the old woman's illegal meddling suddenly seemed futile. She would never understand that she had not just moved me out of my home, but into the black, brutal captivity of a man I tried to escape from for months. Now I had no place to go, no one to go to. All my friends had husbands and lives that did not need the nightmare of me and my insanely jealous, cruel suitor added to their calm equation. I absolutely could not in good conscience ask a single one of them for a haven.

Next day, homeless and broken-hearted, I called Tom and described the new nightmare I found the night before. Jubilant to the point of euphoria at my dilemma, he declared, "Of course! Of course, come here! No other place to go except my house!!" He rushed to town to move me, cracking jokes and laughing, ignoring my tears and regretful remarks. Oblivious to the gloom and doom I saw in my future, he crowed, "Damn! The Man Upstairs is lookin' out after me!!" As he stowed the last sack in the truck, I said, "This is the day our troubles begin."

Without a second glance, he drove away, laughing. But I sobbed the thirty miles to the country knowing without a doubt that whatever lay ahead with Tom would be terrible. I did not know, though, that it would be years--many long, agonizing years--before I would ever find again some of that original, happy self I had brought to New Mexico.

Nothing in the following months made me glad to be with Tom. He had me. Insane jealousy before I moved to his house was nothing compared to insane jealousy afterward. Possessiveness, rage, anger—whatever emotion he felt towards me before was augmented countless times over, and it wasn't love. He wanted me in his sight every minute, demanding that I be with him with everything he did. Watering the alfalfa fields, feeding the dogs, sitting on the couch—he had to have me in his sight. The kitchen and bathroom were the only places he did not follow me. If I were out of his sight, he bellowed my name over and over until I responded and appeared. My only escape was work. Thankfully, at least there I had eight hours of peace and calm, a place Tom tolerated only because it was a money source he didn't have.

So, time became the black nightmare I had feared. Mental brutality escalated to spontaneous beatings; rape, morning, noon and night and coffee breaks in between. His evil exhibitions of control and oppression were caused by anything he did not like or want. His attacks could be caused by responding too slowly to a demand, not moving fast enough to do something for him, my retort to a curse, arriving from work five minutes later than I said I would. He was keeping his word to Modelle. There was nothing he did not say nor do to destroy the living, breathing independent soul in me...he was bringing me down.

Tom's past with its problems became my problems, too. Demands, certainly justified, from his ex-wife and two sons in Albuquerque—the life before me—became phone calls for money and plans for the boys to spend the weekends with us. Girlfriends called day and night. Of course no arrogant abuser can deny himself the challenge of another conquest. I was the one he wanted, but not even I was enough.

Ashamed at my life, my behaviour was a constant factor as I agonized at how I let myself get into such a hideous situation. How could I have done such a thing? I never knew people lived such lives. I had never seen a bottle of beer in our refrigerator when I was growing up. Now I was in a mess with no ending, not counting a happy ending.

The children directed their own anger at me as an intruder but Tom protected me from them with more curses and shouting. He needed me to help care for them, but he also knew I cared for them. They were innocent victims in a life they could not change. So it was that the double standard Tom lived by affected everyone in his path.

After a year of virtual captivity and isolation from friends, escape was all I thought of. Finally pushed to my limits, I quit my job and fled home to Montana. Days later he called from the tiny local airport. Threatening to kill my siblings and their children, to burn my mother's house if I did not return with him to New Mexico, I was plunged into a new effort to save my family. So, of course, to protect them, I left with him, returning to an even more terrible life of evil control and repression.

By 1974, my battle with the first evil human I had ever known had lasted for over three years. In that time, I struggled to understand his intentions, the endless double meanings of his words, his behavior. But finally I had had enough; I didn't care any more. I knew I had to get away.

Evil does not make room for the Power of God. The evil of Tom's mind and heart and soul could not see the courage I found each day in my faith in God, my never-ending gratitude for His miraculous gift to me. Tom never knew that the candles I lit had prayers breathed before the flames flickered high. He never knew that my nights were filled with prayers as he slept, or even as he raped me again and again, that God would hear me and deliver me from the hell I was in. Tom had brought me to his level; he had made me an adulteress, a liar, but he could not make me forsake God.

I was the one with the miracle on Last Chance Gulch. God gave me that miracle for a reason and I knew it was not to live through the horrors of Tom Anderson and his evil world. I prayed for deliverance and knew it could not last forever. It could not.

The first messenger of change arrived on a beautiful day in May, 1974. The glittering days of Spring had turned the winter mesa and fields to green. When the splashing sun brightened the miserable world I stumbled through, it seemed that Nature's beauty and goodness could restore the shattered pieces of my life. I longed, more than ever, to live happily in communion with the world I knew before I met this terrible human.

One day as I puttered in the kitchen, pondering my life, I gazed out across the alfalfa fields. Suddenly Tom's sons burst through the door shouting, "Rita! Rita! Come quick! Come quick! Come look at the owl!"

All the Montana in me jumped at this thought of seeing a visitor from the "wild kingdom!" Such a wonderful bird of prey was often seen in the northern territories, but knowing they avoided populated areas, I had never glimpsed one during my years in New Mexico. Hurrying to the front door, we stepped outside where they pointed, "Look! There he is!"

Silence hung across the yard. The two German shepherd dogs lay still, not moving on their chains in the drive. Not a breath of wind blew. Nothing moved. I turned where they pointed and my heart thudded in my throat. There on the hood of my car sat a small brown owl. At the instant I saw him, he turned his head toward me and looked straight into my eyes. His own great yellow orbs wide, unblinking, he stared at me as though he were saying something out loud.

Stunned at the owl's calm, steady gaze, my mind buzzed with the realization that surely the dogs should be barking! Surely he should have flown away when the boys rattled the door and called out to show me where he was! But he didn't...he never moved. He never took his eyes off me! He had flown out of the blue, rested on my car and waited. He waited while the boys rushed to find me, and he waited until I saw him. Then he turned his head and stared straight into my eyes as though he knew who I was. Now he waited, still looking at me, making sure I knew he was there. Then he slowly lifted his wings and disappeared into the sky.

Shaken by his magnificent gaze, I went inside as the boys ran off to play. But all day long, the owl was with me, his eyes holding my mind like something I should recognize or know. Why had he come so far from his habitat to find me? Why had he sat on my car? Why had he waited for me? There was something about an owl from my past that nagged at me, but I couldn't recall what it was. For days thereafter I thought of the owl until one day with a jolt, I remembered...and my heart was chilled through and through.

"I Heard The Owl Call My Name". It was the television show of the priest sent to minister to natives at the Indian village in the wilderness, unaware that he was dying. There with the Indians, he learned their legend that he who is to die will hear the owl call his name. That was it. My owl had come to tell me that something was going to happen to me. Not only had he called my name, but he brought his message to my door. Suddenly, as I recalled the movie, another flash from my childhood brought the memory of another owl, long, long ago in Montana...

In September of 1963, my twin, Wanda, and our brother, Rex, walked to school from our farm to the one-room schoolhouse on the hill. As meadowlarks sang atop cedar fence posts and flocking blackbirds swept up and down in the giant skies, we breathed great sighs of autumn air as we walked down the dusty road past the stubble fields. We were children, held by time, and only wondered through our schoolbooks about the worlds that lay so far away from our home. Seldom had we been more than a hundred miles from the farm. Now we lived the lives our parents set for us in the only world we knew existed. We did not know, though, that those days would be memories of an old life we would want to keep forever.

Wanda and I were in the seventh grade; Rex was in the third. Four other neighbor kids from down on the river joined us in the old schoolhouse. The older boys, Larry and Jerry Dempsey, were reared on a farm near the Missouri River where they spent much of their time tramping through the river bottom hunting and fishing, trapping beavers, raccoons and other wildlife.

One bright morning, the Dempsey boys waited for us, lounging on the school steps beside their old car where the trunk lid stood open. As we neared, Larry hollered,

From Daylight To Dawn

"Look what we've got! Look what was in one of our traps this morning!" They jumped down to the car and before our astonished eyes pulled from the cavernous trunk a spectacular, giant horned owl!

His great wings spread helplessly apart as he stirred against his captors. He was alive!! Still breathing, he looked at us soberly, almost with an ancient wise tolerance of the unspeakable insult he was suffering. His perfect, round golden eyes watched us like harvest moons in daylight! He was a huge king of the wind and unbelievably beautiful!!

Triumphant, the boys displayed their prize, dragging one magnificent wing on the ground as they waited excitedly for us to echo their thrill of the hunt. Speechless, we stood gaping at the wonderful creature as he breathed steadily, his unblinking eyes watching us, silent and brave—a captive only a breath away from flying to freedom! All our lives, he and his kind had been rare fleeting glimpses in the dusk and dawn, tantalizing us as they slipped into the distance with their gentle "hoo-hoo" behind them. Now he lay before us, a gorgeous master of the air—not soaring silently from tree to tree in the moonlight—not resting stonily on a telephone pole studying the darkness for prey. Instead, he lay a crippled victim, dumped cruelly before the horrified eyes of school children, calmly facing whatever terrible fate yet awaited him.

Another glance showed one of the owl's legs hanging free of the hunters' grasp, one that had found the teeth of the trap. Bloody and torn, long arteries dangled loose, lost beneath the downy feathers. In his struggle to escape the trap, the yellow skin was stripped away, exposing the fragile bone in a silent scream of agony.

Suddenly aware of my own recently shattered ankle, I saw the torture in his beautiful eyes—we were living things suffering the same agony! Instantly I screamed at Larry and Jerry, "How could you?! How could you do this to him?! He's hurt! We have to help him!" The stunned hunters were not only crestfallen at the failure of their glory, but confused at why ever we should help an old

Angel Talk

owl that would probably just die anyway. Instantly taking charge of my partner in pain, I commanded them to carry their trophy inside, pushing past the teacher who weakly protested that we remove the bird. One glance at my raging face silenced her objections and she watched as the medical trauma unit was set up.

I never considered her wishes, not that school should be in session, not even that she was in charge. Surely she must have thought how her contract did not include operations on wild birds and beasts, and I am sure she was further dismayed that her school term was so quickly getting off to such a dubious start. I didn't care. I didn't care about her or her school or our lessons. I only cared about that magnificent, beautiful owl lying so still on the counter and suffering so terribly. With no idea what to do nor where to start, I only knew I was going to do something to help that wonderful owl.

With my twin as assistant, I poured water into the tin basin and tried to think of what Nurse Sue Barton, my hero in novels, would do. I gathered items from the first aid kit, watching the owl as he watched me and began my operation. Though he must have been in unspeakable pain, he lay quietly. The only sign of life was his splendid, huge unblinking yellow eyes. Hopefully by then in shock, he lay without a flutter of his velvet wings, breathing evenly and steadily, his gorgeous eyes not missing a movement as we worked over him.

Crooning softly, I dipped a cloth in the cool water and began to clean his ragged wound. Motionless, he waited as I snipped the severed veins and arteries. They were useless to my novice surgical techniques and had ceased bleeding. Then I carefully smoothed the cleaned skin back in place, covered the entire wound with the only salve we had and bound his leg with gauze. His course skin felt like an old man's hand, rough and uneven, but his trusting orbs watched me with immobile, unprotesting calm. His eyes looked into the depths of my soul and I was devastated at the pain he must have been feeling. He was beautiful and I loved him.

From Daylight To Dawn

For the rest of the day, my owl lay quietly, occasionally moving his magnificent wings as though to lie more comfortably. Though we placed water and bits of our lunch near him, he refused to open his beak, preferring instead to simply lie still on the counter, awaiting his fate.

At the end of the day, once again I commanded the boys to take him home and take care of him until he was well and regained his strength enough to fly. They made no effort to override my directive and seemed remorseful and reflective of this strange turn of events, so different from what they had expected. Several days later they came to school saying he had healed considerably and they had freed him. He had simply flown away into the trees along the river and disappeared.

That year was our only year in the one-room schoolhouse. Next year we went to town school and later rode the bus to high school with the Dempsey boys. Occasionally they would mention they had seen "my owl" sailing on the wind, surely distinguishable because of his remarkable size, and perhaps, too, because of a difference in the way he rested on a perch or flew because of his old injuries. Though I thought of him often and whenever I saw an owl anywhere, I never saw him again. Unable to forget him, I loved the memory of him. The bond between us was formed as his gorgeous yellow eyes trusted me as I crooned and tried to ease his suffering. But I never thought the day would come when one of his kind, far, far from Montana would bring a message to me. Perhaps he came to see me in the desert to return the favor I had done for his forbear so many years before.

So it was that years later another owl stared at me and I stared back. His message was clear: the strain of the desperate conflict I was in would take its toll. Something was going to happen. This evil man, his demands, alcoholism, brutality, caring for his children, farm work, job, emotional uncertainty...it was all too much as I careened down a chasm of exhaustion and despair.

Pondering the poignancy of my owl from the past and now the desert owl, I could thank my new friend for flying into my life with his early warning. For, in the days and weeks and months that followed, I thought of him often, but now because his warnings were followed by others that came in my dreams.

Immediately after the owl came to visit, vivid dreams began occurring in my sleep, dreams of me with my father who had passed away two years before. In each dream we were seated in chairs in the clouds. He would ask how my mother was, how each of my brothers and sisters were, what each was doing. I, in turn, would tell him the latest accomplishments and issues regarding each. Solemnly he would nod his head, listening intently to my report. I would wake then with the astonishing clarity of the dream still fresh. Then I would remember the visit from my owl. Perhaps I was hearing a death knell, because after all, the only way I could visit with my father in the clouds was if I were dead as well.

For months the dreams of my father would come, night after night. There were others, too. Sometimes brief, sometimes long and detailed, always in color, they were always vivid with a lingering impact on my waking hours. I wrote letters to my sister, Patsy, in Ohio and described the dreams to her in hopes she could help clarify them for me. Perhaps she could ease some of the foreboding I could not dispel. She could not.

One recurring dream was of me lying in a bed in the darkness with blinking lights all around, like the cockpit of an airplane. It was senseless, but I could not purge it from my mind. When I woke, I was reminded of the possible message from my owl.

And, the days brought reminders as well. One day at the office, I heard myself say to a friend, "Something is going to happen and I'm not going to be able to move into the new plant with you guys in January." I was as stunned to hear my words as was she! Laughing to diminish the ominous threat, I hurried on with other things, all the while wondering wherever such words came from, thinking again of my owl.

From Daylight To Dawn

On another day as I sat at my desk, a friend stopped by to share several minutes of talk about the Bible. She quoted a lovely verse from Psalms. Thinking how it applied to me, I quickly rolled a piece of paper into my typewriter and typed it out. Long months later, the scrap of paper was returned to me among the papers from my desk at the office. Psalm 88:15, 16, 17, 18.

So, the long tormented months of spring rolled into autumn, then winter. My job was a haven from the nightmare at home. But, at last I was unable to bear it any longer, and fled to the safety of a friend at work, Evelyn Winkler. Evelyn was a divorced older woman who had known her own terrors from an abuser and whose name I had never spoken to Tom. She hid me in her home where, for just a few days, I was safe, able to rest and recover some sanity in peace.

My efforts were futile. Tom's fruitless efforts to find my hiding place only drove him to the front doors of my workplace. Days after my escape, he sat in his truck at the entrance doors sobbing as people streamed out for lunch. My friends told me he was there, waiting for me to go out. Humiliated and ashamed as I had never known in my life, I listened to their terrible news. Then, in a split second, I made my decision.

I was through trying to escape, to be free. No longer could I endure the ceaseless torments, harassment, embarrassment and conflict he had caused. I gave up. There was nothing else I could do. No laws existed to help or support victims and no police had authority to intervene in domestic affairs. No one was there to help me. I was done.

We drove away from the office building and I told him I would marry him on Sunday, four days hence. And I did. Thereafter, for five short weeks, I had peace, questionable and dubious peace, in my world.

But it was a world I saw in numbness at the finality of my decision. Was I a fool? How long could I have lasted? What could I have done differently? What did I do wrong?

Why could he not respect my wishes and let me go on with my life without him? What made him like this?

Any question had only one answer. His sick mind was committed to destroying me. I would never be like him, but I did the best I could do with what I knew, what I could do, what I could change, what I could understand. I knew truth, and I knew my future absolutely could not be only Tom and his evil world.

The life I dreamed of after my miracle on Last Chance Gulch was now destroyed. Today I had only doubt, fear, terror, but I also had God. I would never be that girl from Montana on a thrilling adventure again. My future would not be happy and filled with loving embraces and gentle words from a man who admired and respected and adored me. If I continued fighting Tom or tried to leave him, his jealousy would prevail. He would feel justified in any violence he wanted to commit against me, including killing me and the ones I loved.

Though I had no hint of happiness in the future, no trust, no guarantee that the evil nightmare I was trying to escape would not recur again, I also knew that my life surely could not end with marriage to a maniac. I could not believe that God had given me a miracle on Last Chance Gulch only to end up like this, in a marriage for years and years to a near-insane man. The brutality would start again, surely, but I knew there had to be more to living than waiting for another barrage of cruelty every day. So, as the quiet days after marriage passed, I thought of my dreams of death. I thought of my owl, and I prayed that God would deliver me from evil. And He did.

From Daylight To Dawn   ✝

DUSK

Five weeks. Five weeks of questionable and dubious peace. And when December 10th, 1974, rose cold and clear to become a beautiful bright day, I did not know I had only a few more hours of the morning to live. It was also the last day of my life as I knew it.

My appointment with the doctor had gone well; I was in excellent health. As I drove down the four-lane highway toward Albuquerque, I glanced at new photos I had picked up the day before. Distracted from my driving, I put them back in the envelope and set them on the car seat, saying to myself, "Whitmer, that's a good way to die."

I was on my way to meet Tom for lunch. The time was 10:10 a.m. I rounded the curve. Then suddenly the old red pickup truck ahead of me whipped into the right lane. A station wagon was stopped dead ahead in the highway. I slammed on the brakes, twisted the wheel and everything in my life changed forever.

They said she had been stopped in the highway "for a long time," more than five minutes. They said the man driving the old red pickup truck pulled over and walked back to my car. He looked at me trapped and dying in my car as rescuers tried to extricate me and said, "I was almost in that wreck." Then he walked back to his truck and drove away.

They said she was an occasional driver, an elderly woman with her grandson. When she stalled her car in the intersection, she didn't get out to warn people. She didn't engage emergency flashers; she didn't lift the hood. She didn't do anything. She was just an old woman who didn't know what to do so she just sat and waited. As stunned drivers yanked their cars around her, hearts thudding to realize she wasn't moving, she waited until finally, it was time for someone to die.

But I had time to hit my brakes and twist the wheel. When the frame of my car met the frame of her car, her car was pushed 200 feet down the highway instead of both cars exploding in a ball of fire. The miracles began.

Angel Talk

At impact, the bolts holding my car seat broke, the seat plunged forward, crushing me over the steering wheel. With no seat belt restraint, I was saved from a seat belt, but broke the windshield with my head and hand. My shins caved in the dash. The split second of turning the wheel sent the car off the road into the front yard of a house where it stopped against a tree. The right rear tire was one inch from the gas meter. First miracle.

People rushed from everywhere, struggling in vain to extricate me, seeing only a girl with long black hair babbling incoherently as her near-severed hand flailed in mid-air. Almost no blood issued from the injuries, confined internally to the crushed abdominal cavity, but it was evident to everyone that my injuries were critical.

Twenty minutes became thirty, then forty as they struggled in vain to free me. State Police officers took notes; paramedics waited; rescuers strained to cut the seat free. No "jaws of life" were available. I was hopelessly trapped in the four inches between the steering wheel and the car seat. Life was ebbing, time was running out. Nearly an hour and a half had passed, Then, suddenly a tall, well-built man pushed his way through the crowd.

His voice was soft and loving as he whispered, "Rita Baby, Rita Baby, it's Bobby Baby!!" Joining the struggle to free me, he worked desperately against the clock. At last he said, "We can't wait any longer! She's dying! We've got to get her out of here!" Ignoring the protests of the men, Bobby grasped the steering wheel and broke it in two, laying the halves against the steering column. Then he lifted me out, laid me on the stretcher and ran to his truck. Seconds later, the ambulance screamed away toward Albuquerque. Second miracle.

"For some reason that day, I decided not to go to the dealership. I decided to take the day off and just hang around the house. Joyce had to go to the store, so I drove her over and when we were coming back to the house, we saw the accident—it was really bad—and when we drove by, I thought how much that car looked like yours. We were about a mile away when I realized that it had to be your

car!! I turned around and parked behind the bank so Joyce couldn't see because I knew it was bad. They were all standing around trying to figure out how to get you out—you'd been trapped inside a long time. I leaned in and said, "Rita Baby." You smiled and said, "Bobby Baby." You were in shock, talking and talking—oh! you looked terrible! Your hand—your hand was swinging around! It was so bad—it was so bad and looked so awful! You were dying—I knew you were dying and I couldn't let you die because I love you..."

The last time Bob Watson had seen me was five weeks before on that Sunday in church when he had stood beside Tom, listening as Tom vowed to love and honor and protect me. Now he and Joyce were speeding ahead of the ambulance to get Tom, knowing that time had already run out for the bride.

Inside the ambulance, the paramedic screamed to his buddy, "Faster! Faster! Go faster! I'm losing her!! I'm losing her!"

"We went as fast as we could go. My buddy was driving as fast as he could go--we never went so fast for anybody before. I never tried so hard in all my life to keep someone alive as I tried to keep you alive..."

Bobby stopped outside Tom's office, surprised to see him running down the steps shouting, "What's happened to Rita?! What's happened to Rita?!" He jumped into the truck and they raced to Presbyterian Hospital, arriving minutes after the ambulance. It was too late.

"The doctor turned from the bed—he had covered you with a sheet. He asked who I was. I said, 'I'm her husband and you can't let her die!' The doctor said, 'I'm sorry, it's too late.' I shouted at him again. When you heard my voice, you spoke. The doctor yanked the sheet back and checked your heartbeat and your eyes. Your stomach was rising like water in a bathtub. There was no heartbeat, no pulse, no respiration—your eyes were gone. He covered your face again and turned away. I grabbed him and shouted at him, 'You son-of-a-bitch, you can't let her die!' You raised *your head under the sheet and said, 'T.J., what are you doing here?'"*

The doctor snatched the sheet away and shouted out the door, "I want doctors!! I want nurses!! NOW!! NOW!! HURRY!! HURRY!" Bobby and Joyce watched as doctors and nurses rushed from every corner of the emergency room, some running ahead of the stretcher, opening doors down the corridor as others pushed the stretcher, running as fast as they could run down the hall into surgery. It was the beginning of the end, but the miracles never seemed to stop.

So the daylight hours of that beautiful December day crept slowly into darkness, a darkness that was just beginning. Far away on a frozen snow-covered hill in Montana, the telephone rang at the farm. Mother answered without an inkling of the terrible news the next minute would bring. Her own life, too, would be changed forever as she listened.

"Is this Mrs. Whitmer?"

"Yes, it is."

"Is Rita Whitmer your daughter?"

"Yes, she is."

"This is the State Police in New Mexico. She has been injured in an automobile accident and is not expected to live."

It seems like they shouldn't say things like that... Mothers deserve kinder words when their worlds are to be shattered. But what is, is. The officer told Mother the few details he could, expressed his regrets and hung up the phone. Everything in Montana changed, too.

Once again, we are reminded of what living is for. We are here to learn and to grow and we cannot grow if we do not share. Each day of living provides words and events and sights and sounds that become opportunities for us to practice making decisions about our lives, from moment to moment. If no challenging events happened in our lives, we would never be challenged to make a difference. If our hearts and souls never knew new emotions, we would never be challenged to accept new limits of our feelings. If there were no challenges, there would be no change. And without change, there is no growth.

So, in an instant, my mother was challenged with the most terrible event that any parent can face...the loss of a child. In another instant, she had called my brother, Clint, a hundred miles away, and told him of the accident. Quickly they arranged to rendezvous in the town nearest him which was enroute to Billings and the airport, another two hundred fifty miles away. In minutes she gathered clothes and was driving across the frozen snow-covered prairie where a desert world and unthinkable events waited. In their own race against time, she and Clint fought ice and snow and freezing cold for eight treacherous hours before reaching the airport, barely in time to make their flight. It was the first time my mother had flown.

MIDNIGHT

She was the first thing I saw, her smile loving and tender as she looked down at me. I was not surprised at all to find her there—it seemed almost that I expected her to be there. Speaking softly, she told me that she and Clinton had flown down. I thought to myself, "Mother flew for me." Oddly, the significance of her flight was not lost on me—she *flew* to see me?! Many long weeks would pass before I knew the truth of my condition.

I never asked where I was—I knew. The hospital room seemed familiar, yet unfamiliar of course because I had not been in one in years. The air seemed cold to breathe, my body heavy and empty at the same time. Great white bandages on my right arm seemed odd and clumsy like my body, bulky and overweight. No pain registered—I was calm inside, like something was finally over. The ending I knew was going to happen had finally happened.

Though I seemed to know the accident had happened, I asked Mother if I had wrecked my car. She said simply, "Yes." I told her I had "dreamed' about it and told her my version: I was driving in the left lane behind an old red pickup truck with sideboards. Suddenly the truck swerved into the right lane exposing a car stopped dead ahead of me. That was all I remembered of the dream.

Until I told my "dream" to Mother, no one else had surmised the truth. The police report claimed that I drove down the highway at 60 miles an hour or faster, with clear visibility for a mile, and drove straight into the rear end of the car stalled there. The only citation issued was to me, faulting me for the accident because no one else had heard about the old red pickup truck.

Lying in the warm bed, I knew somehow that my injuries were terrible, though I never asked anyone. No one volunteered details. It didn't seem to matter anyway. Most of all, I was safe from Tom now. He couldn't hurt me in my hospital room. Now I could rest.

The injury list was formidable, though, each problem addressed during nearly fifteen hours of surgery. Dr.

From Daylight To Dawn

Spingola and his team struggled to keep me alive, repairing and removing mangled organs, while Dr. Maron and his team labored over my hand.

Oddly, even the hospital seemed prepared for me! The new Swan-Gans machine, one of only two in the nation, waited to be used for the first time. Designed by doctors who believed a trauma victim had greater chances for survival during surgery if their own blood was re-routed back into their body, their invention prevented the trauma of foreign blood transfusions, pumping the body's own blood instead.

One machine was in New York, and the other was in Albuquerque at Presbyterian Hospital. I was the first trauma victim to be tested on it, and it would be the first saving grace at the hospital for me in the long battle still waiting so far ahead. Third miracle.

Operating rooms have no history. Life and tasks are present time—what do you do *now* to save the patient? Dr. Maron knew nothing of the girl beneath the green cover, nothing about her life riding the range in Montana, playing the piano, making her living as a secretary. He only knew that she was 24 years old and had very long bones! Carefully, delicately, he threaded his way through the intricate mass of broken bones and ligaments, reconnecting blood veins, fastening lifeless tissue and nerves and muscle. On and on through the hours, he worked, restoring the lifeless hand and fingers. He had no idea he was also restoring the lifeline of my soul…carving dreams from the treasure he was weaving for me in these darkest hours of my life.

Hours later when he left the operating room, he did not know if his efforts had been successful or if they were in vain. Would the girl behind him ever use her hand again? How much feeling would she have? How much dexterity? How much pain? Only time would tell…if she lived.

That question loomed for everyone. Bob and Joyce and Tom sat in the waiting room. Would she live? Mother and Clinton sat on a plane looking out over the frozen Rockies. Would she be alive when they landed? Throughout the

Angel Talk

long terrible day in the operating room, everyone knew the odds of my survival were holding at almost zero. Too much time had passed before they had gotten me to E.R. Hope was non-existent.

In Intensive Care with Mother beside me, breathing minute by minute was a victory, a dubious milestone for the doctors who watched and waited, waited for 72 hours to pass. 72 hours. The magic number. In a trauma case, it takes the body approximately seventy-two hours for the vital organs to "absorb and respond" to trauma. Now the doctors had no illusions of what would happen by the third day. They informed Mother and Clint of the bleak possibilities—not much hope—and thought what an odd fellow the husband was.

Bobby and Joyce had watched Tom sob and shake for hours in the E.R. waiting room. Now his show of grief and sorrow hardly seemed genuine, but to Mother and Clint, how could they know the truth? They knew little of the man he was...or wasn't.

But in my world, reality was simple. I was safe in the hospital bed. Tom couldn't get to me. Already, in a few hours, I had rearranged my priorities to fit the safe cocoon I was in. Mother and Clint would help protect me from Tom...simple. The doctors and nurses were protecting me—they wanted to save me, not hurt me—Tom was no longer a worry. The past was done. I was safe.

The first two days were easy and fast. I didn't feel bad, wasn't hurting anywhere. But sick people don't think straight, and seldom make good decisions. True to form, I ridiculously thought I would be there only for a short time, asking the nurses when I would be leaving! Little did anyone know what awaited all of us!

But on the third day, things seemed different. Mother did not come to see me in the morning as usual. When she finally arrived, she was somber and worried, explaining she had been shopping for clothes. Even as sick as I was, I thought how odd that she was shopping--she disliked shopping. Something was wrong. Soon Tom came to my room, distracted and ill at ease. He, too, evaded my questions. After he left, I asked the nurses, "What was the matter?" They, too, remained aloof and solemn, leaving my mother to reassure me that I should not worry, everything was going to be alright. Her calm, steady voice convinced me as she put her warm, loving hand on my brow. Then the fourth day came...

Without any preamble, Tom walked into my room followed by Mother and several doctors and nurses. Everyone seemed agitated and nervous as Tom leaned over me and announced dramatically, "I have to tell you something. The house burned and they didn't save anything." Unable to comprehend his words, I exclaimed, "What do you mean the house burned?!" Cold, without emotion, he flatly repeated, "The house burned and they didn't save anything."

I stared at him in disbelief! He wasn't joking. Truth crawled through my sick brain, suddenly too much to bear. I felt small and vulnerable and weak. It seemed the weight of the world fell on my heart and pushed me deeper, deeper through the pillows. In a flash, memories of the prairie fires, of homes burning, the trucks burning in the wheat field, our high school burning—all the black rubble still smoking the morning after, stark and final, swept through my mind. Memories of total destruction filled my overwhelming despair. Over and over I said, "My piano—my beautiful piano..." Then two nurses each gave me a shot and I fell into a spinning well of blackness. The fight to live began.

Mother had begged him not to tell me about the house. The doctors, too, absolutely opposed him telling me, fearful that another shock to my system would be disastrous, possibly fatal. Still, he insisted. Why, he had a right to say what he wanted—he was my husband—he was in control. So, he proclaimed the unbelievable truth and proved the doctors right.

In the following terrible weeks, no one knew for certain whether his terrible announcement was the final death blow to my broken body and spirit. The doctors and nurses surmised it was the catalyst, but no one placed blame because no one had hope that I would live.

A dying person exists in a different world unique to the living, a wispy reality of threads sweeping to and fro between endless expanses of present earth space and future death time. Each moment is a reality like gossamer fronds of seaweed clinging to the ocean floor against the ever-changing currents tugging constantly. Sometimes the currents carry earth reality away into oblivion where it changes and becomes something else forever. Man is committed inherently and subconsciously to fight the death currents with life currents. He must maintain life—save it—keep it—sustain it—extend it, a drive that has astounded and baffled humankind since history began.

That power to survive becomes not only greater but also more uncontrollable to the victim or the participant. Living becomes isolated into intense fragments of nanoseconds that are each a contributor to extending that life or threatening it.

So it was with all the days and nights that tumbled into each other after Tom's cruel pronouncement. My collapse was total. Breathing became everything; pain was nothing. Thinking became a struggle to capture the one factor that might assure me my battle to live was won. I wanted to live. And I knew I was fighting for my life, though I never heard anyone say I was dying. I never asked anyone and no one volunteered the information. My mother's face was calm but worried; my brother's face was smiling and confident.

But Tom? Tom was cold and angry, standing silent beside my bed, his face empty of emotion. I could feel his rage, what he didn't say. Through my minute by minute struggle to live, I knew things didn't turn out quite the way he thought they would when he married me. Countless times he had bragged, "I've got me a young one to push me around in my wheelchair!" Now, the tables were turned—who would be pushing whom?

His anger boiled at me when he visited. When he closed the door, fear overwhelmed me again. Not even with the nurses a few feet away could I feel safe. I was completely helpless, a victim not only to my injuries but also to him. As his anger increased, I thought in helplessness, would he try to hurt me here in the hospital?! Too tired to think of what he might do or what he thought, I struggled to think of something that would help me survive, keep me safe from him. I wanted to know I was winning my battle against death, but nobody said anything about winning.

It was a silent world. No one seemed to talk very much—maybe because they didn't think I could hear or that I could think. Maybe they thought that I didn't want to talk. Or, maybe it was because they didn't want to talk; maybe they didn't have anything to say to a dying person. Who knows what it's like to die, anyway, what it really *feels* like? Who sits around talking about dying while it's happening? Who sits next to a dying person and says, "What are you thinking? What are you feeling?" No one.

Sitting up was better than lying down. Lying down was better than sitting up. One pillow was better. No pillow was better. Two pillows were better. Please sit me up. Please lay me down. Without a single cross word nor hint of hesitation, the nurses did everything I asked, tenderly, kindly, as though whatever this dying girl wanted, she got. Then and there. Who knew which was her last breath? Why not do what she asks?

And for every minute I fought my private selfish war with death in my mind, the doctors and nurses fought it in my body with everything they could find—their experience, their medical books, friends, counterparts across the country and around the world. They called doctors they knew in other cities, who called doctors abroad, each to find if perhaps they knew something that could save the girl in ICU. They thought of everything that had never been tried and tried it. Anything that would ease my distress was done, including having the maintenance men build an extension on the bed so that my long frame would rest more easily.

Angel Talk

The men came to my room with their tools, their blue work shirts bright and different from everyone else's whites. Lying helpless and dying, I sensed their urgency as they hurried to attach the extension, looking sideways at me, trying not to make noise with their pipes and wrenches! Their faces reflected pity and sadness, but awe, too, for I must have looked a sight with all the tubes and wires connecting me to the machines. I wondered who they were and what they thought of their strange task for their long-legged patient! Their efforts were not in vain, for immediately I was able to rest. Later, as my condition changed and I was moved to other rooms in ICU, the maintenance men were summoned and moved my bed extension with me!

Every one of my many doctors worked tirelessly to save me, side by side with the nurses who also gave away their hearts and souls. They were as constant as the sun I never saw, though I drifted through the days oblivious of the dusk and dawn, feeling the work shift change with their changing touch and tender voices. Every night without fail, a kind, soft-spoken nurse named Katy started her shift by gently rubbing Alpha Keri lotion on every inch of my skin that escaped bandages. Though the doctors were afraid of moving me and creating blood clots, she soothed my skin carefully and seemed to love massaging my feet as much as I loved her to do it! In all the long, long weeks I lay in ICU, I never had a hint of a bedsore or lesion on my body.

But every day was only a new challenge to make it one more night. And every night was another question mark if I would make it one more day. Someone brought a tiny artificial Christmas tree with lights and they placed it on a high shelf so that I could see it blinking. It became not only a symbol of Christmas, but also of God's power and will, and I was shored by its happy company. Anything was worth trying to save me. As my prognosis spiraled downward, my mother sent for my sister, Patsy, in Ohio, where she was working on her Masters. Unwilling to deny any factor that might contribute to my recovery, she came. Yes, I needed all the positive energy I could find.

"When I walked into your hospital room, I was shocked! This was the dream you had written to me about! It was exactly as you had described it in your letters! You were lying in a bed and all the little lights were the lights on the monitors! And later, Mother and I went down to the gift shop. There on the shelf was the book, "I Heard The Owl Call My Name."

Now that the house had burned, my family took a room at the motel across the street from the hospital, taking turns holding vigil in the ICU waiting room. One night as Patsy waited, there was a flurry of activity and rushing of doctors and nurses in and out of ICU. She hurried to the door asking, "What is it? What's the matter with Rita?!" The doctor hardly slowed as he said, "Her blood won't clot! We're trying to get her blood to clot!" Instantly, Patsy's studies in nutrition rose in her mind and she exclaimed, "She needs Vitamin K! She lost her supply of Vitamin K when she lost her liver!" An hour later the crisis had passed; the problem was alleviated. Had they put Vitamin K in the i.v.? Who was to know and who cared? If Patsy's knowledge made a difference for a moment and gave me a few more hours to live, who cared? That was the reason she came—to make a difference—to increase the odds of my survival, and she did. Something worked and no one needed to take the bows.

So the weeks of December crept slowly by, slipping and sliding on the thin, cold treacherous ice of death, pushing and pulling life to and fro in a desperate battle for solid ground that was never there. Positive thinking is a formidable force in a conscious battle for survival. But in a weakened and threatened mind, that same power takes on its own energy, becoming a greater competitor through the struggle to succeed. As I grew weaker and weaker, I knew consciously that I was losing. But in my subconscious mind, I fought harder and harder to control the factors I could—and one of them was sleep.

Angel Talk

Sleep. Sleep meant that consciousness succumbed to that place in limbo where we no longer think, where I would, therefore, no longer be trying to solve my problem with death. If I slept, I would be out of control. Being awake, on the other hand, meant I was alive and thinking, still able to plan or figure out a way to win my private little war with the Grim Reaper. I needed a solution, a g-o-o-o-d solution, and if I were awake, I could find it.

So, I refused to sleep. I wasn't going to lose a moment of consciousness that might give me another way to stay alive another day. Sleeping would cost me the battle and I was determined to win.

Three long, tortured days and nights passed without sleep. The doctors rallied to combat my new worst enemy—myself—and failed with every effort to convince me to "rest in peace." Watching their patient lose ground daily, they finally told my family I absolutely had to sleep or I would not live. Now it seemed everyone was desperate for me to lose control! Mother talked; Clinton talked. Patsy came to my room and explained softly to me, as to a child, that I had to sleep, to rest, so that I would be stronger. She smoothed my fevered forehead, her long cool fingers moving to and fro like a poultice to my anguished soul. It seemed to take forever for her soft, crooning voice to ease the forebodings I saw in sleep, but at last I believed her. At last I let go and slipped into unconsciousness that eased the doctors as much as it did my broken body.

But peace was not to last for long. For every success, there seemed to be two more failures. Finally, the trauma was too much and had lasted too long. All the blood vessels collapsed along with my heart, kidneys and lungs. Over and over the doctors brought me back with defibrillators. They called in a renal specialist, Dr. Erickson, who ordered kidney dialysis. And, in order to accomplish dialysis, Dr. Spingola stood beside my bed and carefully explained what he had to do...

"We're going to take you down to surgery to put shunts in your arm for dialysis. I'm not going to be able to give you anesthesia because your heart has failed too many times—I'm afraid if we put you under, we won't be able to bring you out." His careful words were immediately lost somewhere in my feeble mind as they rolled me into the icy operating room. Then, a nurse positioned herself at my head, another at my feet, one at my bandaged right arm and another at my left arm. Dr. Spingola looked down, his beautiful brown Italian eyes calm and steady, and said, "Rita, you have to hold still now. You have to hold very still." Suddenly his words earlier made sense. The truth hit like a ton of bricks!

He was going to cut open my arm—put shunts in it—shunts so I could live! And I was going to feel every cut of the knife, every stitch of the needle!! He needed me to hold still so he could find the vein for the shunt!! That was it—hold still and live! Move and die. It was my choice...All that Montana deal-with-the-crisis character rose in me. I braced myself. He bent over my arm without another word and sliced an incision open near the left elbow.

It is amazing how hot a cold blade can be. Surely he was swift making the incision—surely it didn't take much time! But the probe—Lord God Almighty, the probe!!! It was the probe he inserted, that long, stainless steel probe in the incision that did it! He was fishing for an artery to position the shunt! I could feel it moving back and forth—or did it go up and down?! The pain was so terrible I bounced on the table uncontrollably; the nurses held me down. I looked to my left to see if I was doing what he asked—hold still! Was I doing my share? Was my arm still? It hurt so bad I couldn't be sure I wasn't moving... but it was still. Dr. Spingola fished.

But it was a useless effort—no good artery could be found. Muttering, he quickly took up a waiting needle. Was it quickly? He inserted the needle and began to close the incision, one stitch at a time. Eight stitches. Sixteen holes. One in, one out, on each side. Sixteen points, in, out, in, out, in, out...Sixteen screams in my mind that I couldn't scream because he had to do this to save me. I could take it! I could take it! He wanted me to live...he wanted me to live...

Angel Talk

On he worked, closing the incision, oblivious to what I was feeling or thinking. After all, being great includes being able to control your emotions. And he was one of the best. Quickly he finished and just as quickly, sliced my arm open again, this time at the wrist. Again he inserted the probe. Again he started fishing. Again pain exploded like cannons in my mind, my mind that was still filled with silent screams from the first incision!

How could anything hurt so badly! It was unbelievable!!! But Dr. Spingola kept fishing, silent and determined. The nurses held me down; the long probe climbed up, up, up inside the vein. But still the pathway to dialysis was elusive.

But it had to happen. Dr. Spingola *had* to find a vein. Again, he reached for the needle and suture and without a word, began closing the incision. Again the stitches--in, out, in, out--became silent screams. This time there were nine stitches...eighteen holes, nine on each side...in, out! Would they never end?!! Screams I couldn't scream were still silent because I had to take it...I had to...I had to help him help me live.

Dr. Spingola finished the sutures, still silent, still determined. He wasn't through yet. Again he sliced my arm for the third time, a small entry below the first incision that seemed to have happened a long time ago. But this time, the third time, it was too much. Yes, it was a small incision—I could feel it was small! You can't measure something you can't see and you can only suffer something you can feel. This time I had felt enough. I turned my face toward the nurses, their eyes sad over their masks, and I screamed, "____, Lor-r-rd!!"

Loud and long the sound stunned poor Dr. Spingola! So engrossed in his work, surely envisioning the artery he wanted so desperately to snare, my screams jerked him out of his concentration as though I were probing him! His beautiful brown eyes blazed angrily at me over his mask as he scolded, "You certainly are not a very good patient!" With only a thought of, "Let's trade places and see how you do!" I fainted away into painless darkness.

From Daylight To Dawn

When I woke, I was back in ICU, two shunts taped firmly to my arm. The third and fourth incisions worked! He had been busy long after I checked out!

Happily, Dr. Erickson and Dr. Spingola discovered that dialysis eased the stress of the failed kidneys as well as the shocked lung crisis, easing my breathing and the strain on my heart. Dr. Erickson ordered dialysis again—whatever it took to save his patient. But he also knew that too much time had passed; the new traumas, and old ones, had been too much. The constant battle to breathe, to live, was exhausting...my strength was gone. Though so many people were trying to save me and my family wanted me to live, it was not enough. There was nothing else I could think of to stay alive; there was nothing else I could do.

Mother leaned over me where I lay still in my bed, unaware that the blinking lights on my machines had faded from my sight; darkness was closing around me. I could no longer feel the bed, not even the sheets that were hot around me. My room became a black void above me, below me, beside me. I was suspended in a black square; the ceiling was slowly coming down, the walls slowly moving in as the darkness became deeper by the moment as though someone was closing the blinds in my brain, slowly, one by one.

Still, a flicker of wanting to live cried out, trying to control the fate I knew was imminent. Fighting the blackness closing in, I thought, "There's got to be something I can do! I've got to think of something! I've got to think of something!" I looked at Mother's face and whispered, "Mother."

She leaned closer and said softly, "What is it, dear?" "Mother, sing to me." "What do you want me to sing to you?" "Sing hymns to me."

She knew her daughter was dying before her very eyes and choked back a sob at my request. I waited for the hymn...nothing came. Her tears got in the way, shining in her eyes from a light that came from somewhere. I couldn't understand why she wasn't singing. She was my last hope to keep the blackness away and she wasn't. Mother wasn't singing. Determined to try one last time, I struggled to sing myself. But the whisper was lost--no breath came, no words came. I had no strength left to breathe...it was no use. In the next instant, the blackness narrowed out the distant light and my last glimpse of life as I knew it was my mother's tears, shining in the light as they flowed down her face.

She said later that she rushed to the nurses' station crying, "Rita's dying! Rita's dying! Call Dr. Spingola! Call Dr. Spingola!" The alarms on my monitors sounded. Three floors below, Dr. Spingola's pager went off. Running up three flights of stairs, he rushed into my room where the nurses struggled to keep me breathing. Grabbing a scalpel, he cut my throat, inserted the tracheotomy tube and joined in the fight to save me one more time. But they didn't know--I couldn't tell them--that this time, everything was different.

They were sewing emeralds in my throat. I was in a cold, concrete chamber, fastened to a table upright by my ankles and wrists, surrounded by white-coated Nazis. They were experimenting on me and seemed disinterested in how much pain they were causing me; they held me motionless as I fought to get away. The emeralds were large, magnificent stones of spectacular green brilliance and a surgeon sewed them slowly, in graduated size, into a necklace around my throat. I was above my body on the bed, looking down, watching three stones, four, appear beneath his white coat sleeve as he slowly sewed them into place. Surely they knew how much it hurt, but they didn't seem to be aware of anything except their objective. They were expressionless and deliberate, moving slowly and watching carefully as the designated surgeon sewed. Then I saw Dr. Spingola and the nurses rushing around my bed. I said, "It's okay now, Dr. Spingola. You don't have to worry about me anymore. I can breathe now and it doesn't hurt anymore." But they ignored me. They're not listening to me at all. I wonder why they don't see me up here...why can't they hear me? "Dr. Spingola, you don't have to work on me anymore. I can breathe now." There are so many of them around my bed...I wonder why they're not listening to me...

As dying people drift through the fragile strands holding them to life, like thin wires clasped to a wavering dirigible holding it to earth, waiting to lift away, their life awareness mingles with death awareness and the two realities become one. Together, though apart, they move in the same flowing stream, the light of human life ebbing into the growing light of death, drifting on the edge of change toward the end of the stream, an end which will be either a final darkening of the life light, or the breathtaking crescendo of the death light. Should, for whatever inexplicable reasons, the light of life flicker brightly again—to outshine the light of death!—life is restored. But the memory of the journey may linger, changing the traveler forever.

For many attendant mortals long cringing from the fact of death, as well as indisputable knowledge of such guaranteed and final endings, such memories may be clinically referred to as hallucinations. To the actual participant, however, they may become a real and lucid part of his future, obliterating normal living, never to be forgotten, never to be feared. Perhaps someday they may be understood.

The airplane waited on the tarmac, huge, beautiful and glowing white, with a long steep ramp leading to the open passenger door. There was silence everywhere. I stood at the top of the ramp inside the plane watching my body on a stretcher at the bottom of the ramp. I lay with only my face showing beneath a beautiful, brilliantly white cloth. Several incredibly handsome—beautiful!—young men with dark hair, dressed in gleaming white, wheeled the stretcher up the ramp, leaving my mother, my brother and my sister standing alone below, weeping silently. They stood, grief-stricken and helpless, watching the stretcher go up into the plane. Inside, the interior was upholstered in gorgeous, brilliant white satin, gathered in deep, soft folds everywhere along the length of the fuselage. The beautiful young men were somber but knowing of their task. They positioned the stretcher inside, parallel to the door. On my body, my eyes were closed; I lay dead. Out of my body, I floated in the doorway, looking down at the grieving faces of my beloved family. They did not see me and looked instead at the stretcher where I lay surrounded by the beautiful young men. The engines started. The door did not close. The plane waited on the tarmac.

There was to be no peace. Six hours later I regained consciousness to find both ankles and arms tied securely to the bed railing. I could not speak. An odd tug was at my throat, a new kind of pain. I went wild.

Now facing a new challenge, the nurses ran to the waiting room where my brother, Clint, sat vigil. I was awake and mad and they needed help! Moments later, he burst through the door of the motel room, shouting, "C'mon you guys! We've got a tiger on our hands!!" Once again I was my own worst enemy threatening to undo all the good they had all worked so long and so desperately to create.

For whatever reasons that surge through a sick and fevered mind, I was a raging maniac. Everything was wrong. I was out of control. Tied down like an animal. Trapped. Couldn't talk. And I took it out on every soul who ventured near.

Someone produced a little blackboard with the alphabet and once again, Patsy leaned over me, crooning softly and assuring me that everything would be alright. Holding the board, she explained that I could communicate by pointing out the letters; I didn't have to worry about not being able to talk.

"You pointed to the letters and spelled out, 'Where have I been?' I said, 'You've been right here and the doctors and nurses are taking care of you.' Then you spelled out, 'No. I've been everywhere.'"

I call it traveling...traveling somewhere far, far away in that elusive endless expanse of earth reality and death reality. For, at sometime in that long, long night of death and the tracheotomy, I traveled to places few mortals know of and saw things and learned things most mortals only wonder of. The girl that woke that cold December day was different from the one who had slipped away. The girl from yesterday was gone forever and only looked the same as the one who finally rested quietly in a bed in ICU.

Though my broken and battered body was far, far from safe, I already knew in just a night that my soul was walking down a different road. I was stepping to a different drummer, past feathers from Angels' wings everywhere.

Though my mind knew a different earthly reality, my human condition vacillated still between desperate nights of crisis that eased with the daylight, but were strained by my distress at being out of control and unable to talk or use my hands. Further, since having earned the dubious notoriety of being a fighter, they kept me tied, able to be released only when a family member was present! My compliance was guarded, but my awareness of time and happenings around me still accurate with reality.

Christmas was near. One day when Tom sat angrily by my bed, I wrote a crude note with my left hand telling him what gifts I wanted him to buy for my family. With no one else in the room, he exploded in shouts and curses, furious at my stupidity for not realizing we had no money. The house had burned, for God's sake!! How could he buy presents! On he raged. It was my fault the car wreck happened! It was my fault the house burned! It my fault he was in this mess!

Now completely helpless before him, I lay still watching him. All I wanted was to buy Christmas gifts for my family who were far from home. Instead, I realized the violence I had known for years was not back in the past... it was as close as he was. As long as he was near me, I was a target for his abuse. Even sick and helpless, I was stunned at his hideous behaviour. The old worries for my safety re-surfaced.

What would I do? I couldn't talk. My hands were tied. Sudden new fears overrode all the safety and security I had felt for weeks. The abuser was back, and he was going to do something to hurt me. I knew it. I knew it.

Angel Talk

This was the first of his many rages at me, lying helpless, unable to ring the nurses for help...unable to wipe away my tears. I did not know that the worse was yet to come, that my life would truly be in God's hands in the long weeks ahead and only He could save me.

Time passed slowly. The constant presence of my family dissolved my fears of Tom. No one knew of the brutality I had endured in the years since meeting him, but I never fathomed he would dare to bring such behaviour into the hospital. But I had also never been critically injured before either; I also had never fought for my life. But, lying helpless, I thought of him and how he must feel as his past repeated itself. Another young wife was dying in the hospital, just like his dead wife sixteen years before. Back then, she, too, had black hair and white skin and he had watched her die, too. Yes, what was it like for him to stand by and watch someone die?

But my mother and my doctors were no fools. All of them grew increasingly cautious watching Tom's strange behavior and inappropriate reactions toward his dying wife. He spent little time in the waiting room and less time in my room. No one asked where he went nor had expectations of him. After all, the house had burned and he obviously had other things to do than sit vigil over his young bride.

One night, though, my safety zone was destroyed. It was the moment I had feared, the one that promised me I would never be safe again. Without a greeting, Tom walked in my room carrying a pillow, closed the door tightly behind him and walked to my bed. Wordless, he lifted the pillow and slowly brought it down over my face. He hadn't changed at all--he was still as evil as ever, only this time, silent. He still wanted me dead, and this time he would make sure of it.

Now he brought the darkness over my face. And like before, I was too tired and too weary to care, to fight. Unable to speak, to free my hands, I lay still as the pillow came down, down, down, his face contorted with hatred over me. Suddenly a cheery voice exclaimed, "Oh,

From Daylight To Dawn

hello, Mr. Anderson! I didn't know you were here!" With incredible finesse, Tom fluffed the pillow saying, "I was checking on her!" and rushed from the room. Unable to speak of his actions, I lay helpless. No doubt about it, God would have to save me now...

All my fears remained silent, unspoken. I had no way to cry for help, no way to ring for a nurse. Terrified of the retaliation to my loved ones that Tom had threatened nearly two years before, I knew a message by the blackboard letters could not be clear enough. What could I say without speaking? So, every day brought a new worry that Tom and not my injuries would be my death machine. Daylight was a time to live, and nights were a time to die and God was my only Protector.

Breathing was a fight to make it to the dawn. Dawn became my marker in the window behind my bed. I prayed, "Lord, please if only I can make it to the dawn, I promise I'll do something with my music." It was all I had to barter my way to the next day as I watched for daylight to show in the window behind my bed. With my hand injured, and now my throat silent, the odds of "doing something with my music" were almost nil. Still, it was all I had left in the world—I could gamble, I could barter. I needed to live!

But not always did the night hold only desperation and dying; nights were made for lovers, as well! For late one night when all was quiet, a beautiful nurse came to check me. She was silent and attentive; I lay silent and still and she presumed I was asleep. Then she moved away and I heard whispers exchanged as the door closed. But the door closed them in, not out! He must have been handsome! For certain he was daring, for he caught her in a close embrace that she yielded to! And there in the shadows beneath the tiny flickering lights of my Christmas tree, they kissed and giggled like Santa's elves! Her blonde hair and their whites shone in the darkness as they teased each other in muffled kisses! I lay listening to them, barely seeing them, knowing they thought I was numb with impending death. I wondered how they could be so brazen, but maybe it was just the season! Maybe, too, though, it was just that death was too close around them, too much, and for just a moment they had to escape its touch, even if escape was on its doorstep!

Christmas neared and Tom tried one more time to end his bride's life. Late one night as Mother rested at the motel, he also presumed she was asleep and slipped out the door across the street to the hospital.

Mother said, "I had a terrible feeling when I saw him leave and I hurried into my shoes and followed him. I was right behind him! When I got to your room, you were asleep. He was standing over your bed with a pillow. I said, 'Tom! What are you doing with that pillow?!' He acted like he was fluffing it and raced out of the room. I knew then what he was up to."

Vigils became different then; rest was no one's friend. Mother took Dr. Erickson aside, carefully explaining she did not believe Tom had her daughter's health and best interests in mind and hoped that special care could be taken to "make certain Rita was safe." Already puzzled by the odd circumstances of his endangered patient and her strange older husband, he listened, wondering if her motherly concerns could actually be warranted. But he did not forget—and Tom did not forget either. Maybe there would be a next time.

Clint leaned over my bed holding out his hand where three silver pendants were draped. "Here. Take your pick. It's almost Christmas." Slowly my fingers reached for the cross inlaid with coral and turquoise. It said everything my lips couldn't, and it made me feel even safer and more hopeful; something for God was around me now.

Then, after two weeks of vigil, Clint had to go; he left me with the cross and returned to Montana. Now the safety net of his presence—man against man--was gone. What would I do now? How long, how long would I live against my worst enemy? I didn't wonder long.

On Christmas Eve, Tom brought his son, Thomas, to the hospital to see me. Still unable to speak with the trach, I lay silent, primed for an explosion. He was primed

From Daylight To Dawn

too, waiting until the nurses were gone to erupt into a tirade like the other one.

"It's your fault this happened! If you hadn't had the car wreck the house wouldn't have burned! Now I don't have anything! No money, no house! I can't work!! It's all your fault I'm in this mess!!" On and on, Tom cursed, his voice rising, louder and louder. Speechless and terrified at his attack, still unable to move nor speak, I lay helpless as he raged. Thomas tugged at his sleeve imploring, "Dad! Dad! Please don't say that! C'mon, stop!" His pleas were useless until the child dragged his father from the room just as the nurses came in to see why the monitors had changed. Thomas never visited again. Though Tom stayed away for days, my terror at his return never left—he would be back, I knew it. He would get me—he would try something again—he wouldn't stop until I was dead…I knew it.

But Mother stayed; Patsy stayed. Rex arrived on Christmas Day on special leave from the Army, more afraid than ever since there was still no hope that I would survive. Each bad day after another made the good days and recovery farther away. Nobody could say that time was on my side.

With my family near, I rested and fought harder, knowing that healing has no substitute for love. It will always be the greatest motivation, the deepest balm, the richest influence, the surest cure. And when all remedies have been ministered, all medicines have been procured, the gentle presence, the tender touch, the loving words of those who truly love will strengthen the tenacious threads of life that otherwise would have shredded. Whispered prayers of sincerity are heard long after the dull roars of deceit and even the faintest heart will gladden and restore itself with the exhilarating rejuvenation of love. My family's unwavering devotion expressed through their presence, letters and calls sustained me, rekindling the dying flickers of life that had been slowly smothered long, long before that terrible day on the highway.

Like a new generation of circus stars learning to walk a tightrope, I kept tumbling from the wire of death to be caught each time by the careful net of life the determined doctors and nurses and my family wove for me. But time was finally running out; my organs were too badly damaged; my body could not hold up under the stress. Dr. Erickson watched helplessly as my energy faded into another dream.

"I was no longer in pain and knew that I would not hurt nor be sick again. I stood at the top of a staircase leading down into the basement of an old warehouse building with high ceilings and fans turning slowly overhead on long, steel rods. It did not have the usual dust everywhere and was lighted, but the steps leading down into the cellar were dark; I was reluctantly compelled to go down. At the bottom of the stairs I turned left, walking past counters and shelves piled high with antique furniture, clothing and old toys. A beautiful worn painted hobby horse enchanted me—it seemed to have belonged to me before and now I wished again that it was mine. Feeling like a grown-up child, I wandered through the jumble toward the back of the giant room, feeling more and more apprehensive and afraid, wanting to leave. I approached an old barber's chair and stood looking at it, wanting to sit down in it; but I knew if I did, I would die."

Finally, the tenacious bubble of survival burst. Dr. Spingola and Dr. Erickson knew I could fight no longer. Desperate for anything to ease the burden on my lungs, Dr. Erickson ordered dialysis. It worked, but only for a short hour. Desperate, he ordered it again. Once more the pressure was eased on my lungs, once more for a scant period of time but not long enough to pull me from death that was hours away. Knowing the risk to my system—how many times can the human body sustain the repeated trauma of dialysis? But what did he have to lose? Once again he ordered the last dialysis, three in one day, and walked down the hall to the room of a Catholic nun to pray.

It had been enough. The third dialysis bought enough relief to my lungs to allow me to rally—the last daunting crisis was past. Slowly I began to show tiny signs of improvement. The nightly plunges toward death were replaced with steady gradual improvements in my vital signs and my strength. The pressure on my lungs diminished until finally, after days of uphill progress, the doctors told my family that I would live.

Angel Talk

DAWN

Different things, happy things began to happen. My lungs improved; breathing became easier. Some of the tubes were removed and the monitors became just that: quiet sentinels tracking my heartbeat instead of being harbingers of crisis. The restraints on my hands and feet were removed and, at last, the tracheotomy tube. Now just a bandage covered the hole in my throat, and I could talk by pressing on the bandage—in control again!! Time seemed to speed up; the darkness drifted away. Recovery was becoming a reality. Patsy returned to Ohio; Rex flew back to Fort Lewis; Mother stayed...thank God Mother stayed.

With some of the tubes gone and speech restored, they moved me to a room in ICU with fewer machines. Friends were allowed to visit briefly. I rejoiced to see them and the doctors reported to Mother that I was making very good progress. It would all change quickly, though, with another attempt on my life—one I nearly lost.

Tom came by to visit late one night after I had received my sedative. As always, the nurses were charmed to see him and left him alone to visit with me. Groggy and weary, I fell asleep quickly while he was there and did not wake for several hours. But as the soft morning light wakened me, I felt something wet on my chest and arms and looked down to see the sheet and blanket soaked in blood! In disbelief, I lifted my hair—blood dripped from the strands onto the cover! I was in trouble!

Instantly I thought of the boys in Viet Nam waking in their own blood in battle. But that weary feeling of fighting again overwhelmed me—now I was too tired to be afraid, too weary of the whole fight to live to be alarmed at why I was bleeding. All I wanted was to find out, get it taken care of—just fix it so I didn't have to worry about dying anymore...I just wanted to live and rest in peace and quiet. Peace. Peace.

Stunned at the amount of blood covering me, I rang frantically for the nurse! Raising my arms and shoulder,

I searched for the source of the blood. No gashes, no bruises showed. But my hair was wet with blood--it had to be up high. I lifted the gown by my collar bone and there, with every beat of my heart, blood spurted an inch from a broken needle in the i.v.! Just then a nurse walked in, stared at the bloody sight before her, screamed and ran out the door, slamming it behind her! Fighting back tears, I despaired, "When, Lord, when will it all be over?! Oh, Lord, please help me let it be over!!" Too sick and tired of being sick, I waited for the nurse to return.

Moments later, two nurses rushed in carrying fresh linens and locked the door without saying a word to me. Obviously guilty, they hurriedly replaced the needle, sat me up and half carried me to the end of the bed. There they left me, perched on the edge of the mattress as they yanked the bloody sheets and coverlets off the bed. Nearly unconscious from loss of blood, I swayed like a spineless dummy toward the floor. After all, it was the first time I had sat up alone in weeks. Grabbing at the table to save myself, I watched the nurses frantically roll up the blood-soaked foam mattress.

It was a sickening sight. Blood had soaked all the way through the four-inch thick foam to the other side. No wonder I couldn't sit up! How much blood had I lost?! Still the nurses were silent, grimly whipping fresh sheets onto the mattress. Disgusted and insulted at their behavior, I asked, "May I have some water, please? I would really like to clean my face." One nurse seemed to become aware of their blood-covered patient and left the room, returning with a cloth, basin of water and another gown. Placing them on the table beside me, she rushed to help her partner.

It was odd to see the water in the basin...I had not seen water nor felt it in weeks. The only moisture I had known were damp cloths the nurses used to bathe me. It was amazing to watch the cloth on the water as it drifted, curling around my bloody fingers in an instant, heavenly balm to the overwhelming grief in my heart. But the cold, bloody gown around me and my hair dripping blood brought a sudden despair of everything in my world! Who did this to me?! Why did this happen?! My heart was breaking in hopelessness—everything was futile, useless! I felt that I would die all over again.

The nurses were finishing the bed when I asked, "May I have a towel for my hair, please? I really would like to get it up." One of them pitched a towel across the room, ignoring my precarious swaying on the edge of the bed. Revolted by them, I grasped it feebly, wrapping it clumsily around my hair with one free hand—anything to get the blood away from my body. Still wordless, they gathered up the bloody testimony of their neglect and left the room. And then my mother walked in...

Mother, my beloved Mother, stumbled in shock at the ghastly sight of me, teetering on the edge of the bed. She rushed forward, crying, "What has happened?! What has happened?!" At her voice, her embrace, it was over. I couldn't be strong anymore. It was all too much. Then, for the first time since the beginning of all those terrible days and nights and all those weeks and weeks before that had seemed to last forever, I cried. I cried for all the hurt and pain from all the times I wouldn't let myself cry...for all the hopelessness, for the trying and failing of all the ugly months and years before, for the suffering I had brought on my family, my friends. For all the reasons I never said and never even knew, I cried as though I would never stop.

Mother held me close, rocking me until finally my sobs ceased. Then she gently helped me into the clean gown and wound the towel around my hair. I told her what happened. Then carefully holding me with all the love a grieving mother has, she guided me, shattered and shaking, down the side of the bed, helped me lie down and covered me. Seeing me quiet again, she left to call Dr. Erickson.

At Mother's anguished summons, he rushed to ICU to find the terrible situation a reality—how could such a thing happen?! Aghast at the irresponsibility of the nurses, Dr. Erickson saw that the offenders were

From Daylight To Dawn

summarily discharged and other reprimands delivered. Quickly, three blood transfusions were administered to replace the blood I had lost. Then without ado, they moved me immediately to another room outside the ICU doors, knowing my recovery was desperate all over again. Now, a new battle began to restore my fragile margin of health, set back now by weeks.

A nurse's aide arrived to wash my hair, filling a basin with gallons and gallons of water. Over and over she washed and rinsed until at last it was clean. Surprised at her task, she exclaimed, "Boy, you were right! Your hair really did have a lot of blood in it!" I thought, "They really must think sick people are stupid! Of course I knew there was a lot!"

Settled in the new room, a nurse came to say a bath had been prepared for me—my first! Bath and sleep!! The terrible day was finally over!! What greater comfort is there to a broken body and shattered heart than a wonderful warm bath?! My mother helped her wash away the bloody traces of the morning; then they wheeled me to my room, tucked me in. With a quick sedative, I fell asleep, knowing the terrible ordeal was over. But I was wrong...

Dragging up out of deep sleep, I felt someone shaking my arm, calling my name. Struggling to waken, trying to see, to understand where the voice was coming from, I saw a stranger beside my bed. The door was closed; a man peered into my face. Groggily, I asked, "Who are you?" He excitedly said he was from the insurance company for the woman I crashed into. I had to sign the paper he brought so they could sue me. Hurriedly he explained that the time limitation to sue me was almost gone. The hospital refused to let him in to see me before—I had to sign right then!

Weak and confused from the day's earlier events, I couldn't believe a person would do such a thing. I asked if he had a card. Agitated and nervous, he handed me one and I slid it under the sheet, ringing for the nurse. Repeating his demand for me to sign the paper, his voice rose in anger as I refused, still ringing desperately for the nurse. His demands became curses, louder and louder! Where in God's name was the nurse?! God help me get away from this madman! Where was the nurse?!! When will this ever end?! Still I refused the pen he thrust at me as his curses grew louder than ever. Lord God Almighty! What was he going to do?! This can't be real! It can't be happening! When will it end?! God! When will it end?!

She heard the cursing before she opened the door and saw him leaning over the bed, thrusting the paper at me. Stunned at his intrusion she demanded he leave immediately; to her shock, he refused! Now directing his tirade at both of us, the fool refused to leave! At last she screamed for help; nurses came running to our rescue followed by security guards. The intruder was hauled away leaving my nurses with one more attempt to calm down their anguished patient!

For the second traumatic time in a day, I lay assaulted and exhausted. And for the second time that day, Dr. Erickson was enraged to learn of another threat to his endangered patient! Using the business card I stowed under my sheet, he dispatched an irate letter to the company citing their responsibilities for any harm to me on hospital property. They would be held liable for any complications resulting from the intrusion. Hours later, the insurance company returned a letter foregoing any further interest in my case. Finally, and perhaps for certain now, the last ordeal was over.

At last Dr. Erickson and Dr. Spingola told my mother that the threat was past. Three days later, she came to say goodbye. Though comforted with the doctors' presence, her worries showed on her face. She feared Tom's behavior would get worse. After all, being sick, weak and defenseless seems to permit a level of cruelty by humans to other humans that is astonishing in its baseness. The victim is vulnerable to a point that few people understand until they have suffered such an offense. Mother was right. Tom wasted no time proving once again the extent of his evil thinking.

From Daylight To Dawn

The day after my mother was gone, he came to my room. As always, he was irritated and angry, not happy I was better, out of danger and that I would live. Strutting through the door, he closed it, walked to my bed and said, "It's been a long time—haven't had any in a long time—c'mon baby, just a quick one." Dumbfounded at his words, hopelessly incapable of repulsing him—why I could not even hold up my head, I said, "Don't you think this is no time for that?" Laughing cruelly, he stepped to the side of the bed, unzipped his trousers and pulled my body toward him...

Minutes later when he was gone, my tears flowed into the pillow. But there was only God to hear my whispers. "Oh, Lord, please help me...please help through this terrible, terrible time..." There was nothing else to say, nowhere to go. Now there was no one who could change the nightmare I was living. Not in 1975.

Nearly six weeks had passed since the accident before the doctors said I could leave the hospital. Leaving depended upon what Dr. Maron, architect of my hand, said about my hand and what Dr. Spingola said about my insides. Accompanied by a nurse, Dr. Maron came in smiling, his wing-tip shoes clicking. With a confident flair he tossed a cloth containing surgical tools on my bed. It was time to take the pin out of my hand. Without ado, he removed the bandage, attached a brazen bit—it could have been from my father's tool bench!—to the protruding pin. Slowly he wound the screw upward, out of the bone. He lifted it out, a nurse staunched the little burst of blood and he covered the opening with a bandaid. Then he leaned back and looked at his handiwork.

Carefully, tenderly, he touched my fingers up and down, searching for mobility and warmth, feeling them carefully as he contemplated his work from weeks before. Pleased, he said, "Touch your fingers." Thumb met fingers, quickly and easily. "Can you feel them?" Unaware of his worry of failure, I replied blithely, "Of course." Smiling now, he said, "Do it again." I complied. Then he bent over my hand, not touching it, looking at it with a beautiful, proud, rapturous look on his face. He breathed softly, "That...is...fan...tas...tic."

Realizing then what he had done, I looked at him, handsome and happy, gazing at my upturned hand. His face never changed as his eyes studied my hand, surely remembering again his own magnificent fingers finding their way through the torn jungle of tendons and veins and muscles he faced weeks before. It was my turn to be proud as he gazed at his miraculous feat. Feeling he was the same as his words, I thought, "No other words could have said it better!"

Then he roused from his reverie and announced happily, "You can go home now!" He did not know the girl lying before him had only terror waiting outside the hospital doors. She had weakness, fear and vulnerability as compatriots in her life. She had no clothes, no purse, no makeup, no job, no car, no house. And, she had a husband who wanted her dead. Nothing had changed while she was sick. She had no place to go except where her husband wanted. She could not intrude upon her friends for safety now. But, she did have God, and she was alive because He had left her behind. Now He would have to keep her alive and save her from the worst enemy a woman could ever have.

The day, the hour had come for me to leave the hospital. Tom waited in the chair, irritated and surly, for me to finish combing my hair at the mirror when a tiny nun in a navy blue habit stepped in the doorway; Tom rose at sight of her. Solemn-faced she asked me, "Are you Rita?" At my "Yes" she took my arm and said, "Well, my dear, sit down. There is something I have to tell you." Turning to Tom, she asked, "Who are you?" "I'm her husband," he replied. Satisfied, she responded sharply, "Well, you sit down, too. You need to hear this as well." And then we heard her story...

"My name is Sister Beriswell. I was a patient here on this floor last month and heard about you. Everyone knew about you. One night, Dr. Erickson came into my room and he was weeping. He said, 'Sister Beriswell, we have a

From Daylight To Dawn

little girl in Intensive Care and there is nothing we can do for her.' We knelt there in my room, and the other doctors and nurses came in and we prayed together for you. Then they had to leave to go on to their duties, but I stayed and prayed. I want you to know, my child, that never in my 42 years as a nun have I ever felt compelled to pray for anyone as I felt compelled to pray for you. I prayed for you through the night and into the morning. Then Dr. Erickson came into my room and he was smiling. He said, 'Sister Beriswell, she's going to make it!'

"I left the hospital weeks ago but I have stayed in touch with Dr. Erickson, asking about you. When he said you were going to be leaving today, I drove down from St. Michael's in Gonad to tell you this." Smiling slightly, she kissed me on the cheek. We embraced and with a tender smile and tears in her eyes, she whispered, "God bless you." Tom stood; she instructed coldly, "Take good care of her." Then she walked out the door. I never saw her again.

A few minutes later, Dr. Erickson and Dr. Spingola came in to say good-bye. Dr. Erickson, now the primary physician in charge of me, told Tom he wanted to see me in his office every Monday, Wednesday and Friday morning at 9:00—he was heeding my mother's warning!

Indeed, my doctors had won their battle but it had been a terrible one against terrible injuries and terrible odds. The list was daunting: splenectomy, tracheotomy; extended left hepatectomy; repair of lacerated right lobe of liver; repair of laceration of pancreas; operative cholangiogram; diagnostic peritoneal lavage; insertion of left radial artery; acute renal failure; right heart catheterization (Swan-Gans); traumatic shock lung; pulmonary edema, non-cardiac in origin; right wrist debridement and irrigation, open Steinmann pin fixation reduction, carpel tunnel release; fracture of right wrist.

Dr. Erickson smiled and said, "Well, Rita, go home, take your vitamins every day and thank God you're alive, because that's the only reason you are." He and Dr. Spingola shook my hand and walked me to the nurses' station where, to my surprise, dozens of the doctors, nurses, aides and maintenance people waited. All the employees who had helped me over those long, terrible weeks were waiting to say goodbye! Word had passed that I was leaving the hospital that day and they came in on their days off and from departments throughout the hospital to see me. No one smiled—this was no celebration for anyone. My survival was unbelievable, a gift they were honoring with their presence. It was not until months later that I learned the odds of my survival had stood at zero almost the entire time I was in the hospital.

Each person shook my hand solemnly. Many had never seen me stand and had no idea I was so tall. But now as I stood bravely before them, none of them imagined how weak I was, how exhausted I was to stand so long with their goodbyes. At last I walked with Dr. Erickson and Dr. Spingola to the elevator, thinking only that I had no business leaving. I should have stayed...I should have stayed...

Tom seated me in a chair at the outside entrance while he went for the car. The wind brushed my cheek, ruffling my hair for the first time in nearly two months. It was winter when I came in. Now it was nearly Spring. I wondered sadly what waited for me out there in the sunshine, in the future. I was going home. No, home was gone. Burned. I was going somewhere...to nothing but the beat of my heart. I knew it would not be easy—it would be ugly again, for sure. As long as Tom was in my life, it would be ugly. But God had given me miracles, many miracles, and I knew, too, that He and every Angel in Heaven would be beside me with every step and every breath I took for as long as I would ever live.

Two years later, I was in Taos, New Mexico, and met a lovely Spanish girl who introduced me to her sweetheart, a handsome State Police officer. As I approached him, his eyes bulged, his face changed colors from healthy brown to red, white, purple, yellow, back to white as I neared. Obviously stricken at sight of me, he muttered some excuse and fled the room. Thereafter if I saw him, he would never stay in my presence again. Bewildered by his reaction to me, I wondered why he refused to be around me. Years later at my mother's home in Montana, I was sorting old papers and found an envelope with photographs of the auto accident. On the back of a photo showing the State Police officer in charge at the accident scene, was written his name.

My friend's sweetheart was the officer in charge of my accident! He had written the accident report, knew there was no way I could live, had cited me as the quick cause of the accident—no need to waste time on this one—she was a dead one. He presumed I had died and forgot about the case. Later when he saw me walk across the room that day, I was an innocent ghost from his past, someone he had charged with a wrong-doing they did not deserve. And he could not face me. Indeed, there is justice in the world, and there is Divine Intervention.

Six years later, I was in Nashville and stopped at a unique warehouse shopping area filled with little nooks of arts and crafts. A clerk suggested I look at the antiques in the basement and pointed out the stairs to me. As I stood looking down into the darkness, the overwhelming memory of the hallucination years before in the hospital filled my mind! Instantly I knew it was no hallucination at all. It was true...it was the same basement and it was in front of me.

Petrified with fear, yet knowing I had to go, I slowly walked down the steps. The rows of shelves I knew would be there waited, piled high with toys. Heaps of antiques sat everywhere. In the rear of the room, the hobby horse stood, just like in the dream. Nearby, the barber shop chair waited. This time I wasn't afraid of dying, but the shock of seeing the place was overwhelming; I fled without looking back. A few months later, to my disbelief, the building was totally destroyed by fire. To this day, I have yet to understand the relation of that unbelievable hallucination to the antique store and my life!

For all of those who were with me during this tragic time, they were also uplifted by the Heavenly gifts that we shared during those long weeks. Remembering those miraculous events that allowed me to live is more special than I can say. Bobby took the day off...the car wheel missed the gas line...the hospital had the Swan-Gans machine waiting...my body survived dialysis three times in one day...my mother and the nurse walked in on Tom as he was attempting to murder me...Sister Beriswell, friends, people prayed for a girl they had never seen before. And, all those years before in high school and college, my obsession with feelings I had to "hurry up and live" and "I don't have time to waste" were true. My intuition was already telling me of the future, but I did not know my life would last only as long as other people would honor my life. Other people, friends and strangers, would be compelled to protect me and did not hesitate to pray for an innocent girl.

Throughout our lives, all of us witness the magnificent orchestra God conducts for us. He clarifies ways for us to become better contributors to life on this planet. His miracles follow us, leaving us to judge ourselves and our decisions in the future for the impact they make on our own and others' hearts and souls. And as we continue our life journey toward death, we come to realize that death is a solitary involvement between one's self and God, an experience no one else can share. It is ours to meet alone as our decisions have prepared us in this last experience we can ever have on Earth. Death marks in its brief passing the victories, the losses, the challenges, the milestones, the neglect, the love, the enlightenment of the events and times we were gifted with. We can say those events are simply time on Earth, a curious phenomenon in the course of living. Or we can say they are precious blessings through the divine glory of God and all His Angels!

From Daylight To Dawn

RECOVERY

Sweet dreams
Ricochet across the windows of my mind
Windows closed before
Now since the crash
Wide open to the earth
And people that I love.

Great and garish scars
Are heavy trails on tender skin
Sentenced fingers ache
To kiss the ivory once again
They do—more loving than before
Melodies throw wide the door
And music reaches almost to yesterday
Pain is but a light year away.
Thank God—and Barry Maron.

Memories
Of Christmas days and crumpled dreams
Tomorrow will sing of better things
Surely—for I have life again.
And all those days and nights
Of silent supplication
Welling in my heart
But silent at the surgeon's knife
Have no voice
Except the ears of God...
He hears.
But the darkness, Lord...
The darkness is so heavy—please—
If only I can make it to the dawn...

Angel Talk

Mother
Your hand is so cool
I'm not surprised at all
To find you here.

The hospital sheets
Are stiff and cold but grow so quickly warm
Mother, sing to me;
Sing hymns to me.

The darkness is everywhere.
Dr. Erickson is there.
I learn later of his prayers
And knew not that I needed them...

The days and nights
Tumble into Christmas.
My tiny tree blinks colors bright—
Rex brings me his Christmas greetings
I cannot speak to tell him my delight...

Patsy's voice is low and warm
And at long last
I fall into a labored sleep...
Thank you for the peace.

McClintlock smiles
And best me choose a pendant
My fingers reach a tiny cross
My tears are warm
My heart is calm
My thanks are rampant...

And after weeks I walk
Not well—
But jubilation is mine
For I have life again.

From Daylight To Dawn

Today
With every ray of sunshine and warm breeze
And every rose and smile
I see the world again and I am pleased.

My tomorrows lie serene
On the river banks of diamond dreams
And yesterday is gone.

I shall reach out and touch the world
And over all the miles I trod
Remember always that I, too,
Put out my hand
And touched the face of God.

May 17, 1975

Angel Talk

My Parents, Marilee and Boone Whitmer

From Daylight To Dawn

Dr. Dale Erickson

Dr. Lawrence Spingola

Dr. Barry Maron

Robert B. Watson

4

Calling Down the Rain, 1975

PSALM 72

6   He shall come down like rain upon the mown grass;
as showers that water the earth.

Angel Talk

It seemed that everything in Dallas was steaming. The muggy July air hung between the trees in stalemated pockets of moisture waiting for a breeze to blow it through their shimmering leaves. Even the skies were a hazy blue looking as though they were, themselves, waiting for a way to make the rain fall from their heavy heights.

But all of it was wonderful to me! Every ray of sunshine and every humid breath I breathed was an exhilarating moment! Slowly but surely I was recovering from the auto accident, knowing someday I would be an able-bodied human being again—not my old self, though, of course. Who could go through such trauma and be the same, never change, pretend it was "in the past"? No one. Besides, I didn't want to pretend it was in the past. It was mine—I felt it, suffered it, understood it and knew I was learning from it. All those weeks of dying made me the tallest, most grateful recovering girl in the Southwest and I was determined to make my life matter more than I ever had before.

A new priority, a greater responsibility filled my mind now, too. I had to get well so I could keep my promise to God. Yes, He let me live. Now I had "to do something with my music." Of course I had no idea what that would be, but someday I would know. Someday I would keep my promise to God who had left me on Earth.

The face in the mirror was pale—unbelievably pale. The reflection looking back was a stranger. Only my long black hair was familiar though now a tiny fringe of bangs topped my forehead. What a kindness the doctors had given me when they saved my hair! I wondered what they thought when they looked at the white-faced girl before them. Determined and undaunted, they struggled to bring me back and bent to their work as though everything they did would save her, make her whole again.

Now in front of the mirror, I was their dream come true—whole again! Patched up and missing a few parts, but feeble, pale, scarred and whole! Knee surgery a few months after the accident had been successful and I was finally able to set my crutches aside for that "just in case" time I needed them. The green eyes in the mirror were resigned and ready for my new priorities: getting well and rejoicing every day at living!

It helped, too, to be in a green world and not the brown one of the desert. Green was and is a comfort color to humans; it was new to me and I loved it! Trees swaying in the winds, countless shapes and sizes and colors of green leaves everywhere contrasted so from the narrow desert plants and brown sands of New Mexico. For just a while I didn't have to think about all that had happened, what used to be—the burned house, the loss. Yes, the total loss of everything I used to have. None of the ugliness would come back for a while, I knew. Tom wouldn't dare harm me now. Right now all I had to do was rest, visit with my elderly mother-in-law, Maggie, and be glad I was alive. Even the bugs crawling everywhere and the relentless humid heat were nothing. They and a thousand other things some considered nuisances never fazed my exuberance at living. I didn't know what my future was, but today I was the Queen of Living!

I had known miracles when I lay in the hospital dying. There could never be anything nor anyone who could ever make me deny, reject or pretend that my days would not be an exercise toward a special future. Nights in the dark hospital room had been lit with dancing, glittering stardust...Angels...Angels protecting me, covering me with Their loving presence as I struggled to live. Now life was truly a beautifully wrapped package, a cocoon for me to live inside, enjoy, and make as wonderful as I could for as long as I could. After all, I was going to live for as long as God was going to allow.

As is well understood, the deserts of New Mexico did not know rain often, so I had not seen nor felt it once during the months of recovery. For some inexplicable reason, I thought about it constantly, longing to feel it, asking everyone around me when it was going to rain as though the reality of it would restore my fragile bond to life. Who could understand why such a simple thing was so important? Why did simple rain matter? Maybe it was just that rain is water, water is life, life was mine again and maybe I wanted the connection. I didn't know and didn't care. I just wanted it to fall.

That wondrous day finally came! Finally the first summer rains poured from the hot blue skies and my happiness knew no bounds! Seeing it meant I was alive to see it! Hearing it was as if the Angels were talking through it and I was invited to listen! Clattering on the roof, it tumbled down in soft warm drops, a loving solace to my weary heart and soul, answering my prayers with every drop. The temptation to feel it was too great and I went outside on the driveway to paddle barefoot through the puddles. Worried for my health and, I am sure, my sanity, Maggie insisted I go inside. I ignored her, and reveled in the rain. Tom puttered in the camper parked on the drive and shouted at me to get in out of the rain. I ignored him, too—what harm did it make to splash a little in the puddles?! Right now every drop was mine and I was going to love every one!

Then something else happened...It stopped. It stopped. I never thought it would stop—but it did! After only a few brief minutes, it stopped! Gone! Finished, through, over with, done! Sure, rain in Dallas is different, but I just thought it would be like Montana where massive thunderheads gathered in the giant sky, thousands of feet over the horizon. Then fierce winds with thunder and lightning would drive the rain to the ground and it would fall for days. In New Mexico, cloudbursts were brief, heavy torrents that were quickly absorbed by the thirsty desert sands. But Dallas? Apparently summer showers fell quickly, stopped just as quickly, skies cleared and it was over. I was completely shocked when it disappeared into the summer air.

Now standing bereft in the drive with no more rain, my disappointment left me on the verge of tears; I felt as though my heart would break! I waited in vain for more raindrops. My new loss was too much—I wanted it again! Without a thought except for my own selfish wish, I lifted my face to the clearing skies, held my arms upward, and called out loud, "Oh, Lord, please, please let it rain again! Oh, please, just for a few minutes! I want to feel it again just for a few more minutes! Please, Lord!" I stood, silent and sad, arms uplifted, eyes closed, praying over and over with all my heart to God in Heaven that the rain would fall again on my parched and broken body and soul.

And...it came. It fell gently on my uplifted face. But it was different now...it felt different...This rain was like warm velvet...a gloriously warm, soft, soft, loving velvet rain! My heart pounded with joy! He had heard me!!! He was there with me!! Jubilant at my blessing, I looked up to see above my head perhaps a hundred feet, a little silver cloud sending its velvet rain straight down upon me!!! In a glance I saw the beautiful little cloud reached barely to the center of the street, not even to the houses on each side where I stood, and only just behind me covering Maggie's house! It was just big enough to make sure the raindrops fell on me! It was my own little silver cloud! Mine! My very own perfect, little silver cloud in Heaven with velvet raindrops that were falling only for me!!

Ecstatic, I laughed out loud, pirouetting in the puddles, proclaiming, "Oh, Lord! Thank you, thank you! Oh, thank you! Thank you!" What else could I say?!! What else was there to say? Tom heard the rain, my exclamations, and stepped to the door of the camper to see me in rapture, soaking up my glorious velvet rain! His mouth fell open and his eyes bulged in stupefaction. From his vantage point, he, too, could see across the street where the rain wasn't falling! He looked up, around, scanning the empty blue sky where only the little silver cloud lingered above me, soaking me with my rain.

Tom had heard it all--my pleas to God for rain and God's answer. And it was happening before his very eyes! Truth lay in the eyes of the beholder! Still laughing, I lifted my hand to the sky, snapped my fingers, and said, "How do you like that for a hot line?!" Still stunned, he turned back inside without a word.

My breathtaking silver cloud stayed only for a few minutes, just like I had asked, just for a few more minutes.

Then just as quickly as it had come, it was gone! What a happy girl stood on that driveway!! Glorying in my message from Heaven, my whole body buzzed with exhilaration and delight. I couldn't believe what had happened! Still at the same time, I wasn't surprised.

All my other miracles were as near as the purple scars on my skin, but this one was different...different perhaps because my plea was such a frivolous request—such a child thing. It was selfish, too, to wish for such a simple pleasure that mortals would think unimportant. Maybe it was different because Tom was there and heard me, saw the silver cloud, saw the rain. Maybe it was because God knew I needed it and He needed Tom to know of His Heavenly Power. Maybe it was because not feeling rain for so long had made it special beyond words. Whatever it was, I was speechless myself and happy beyond words! The truths before me were real and there could never be anything in the world that would ever diminish them in my heart.

True to the promises of God, reminding us that His glory never dies, that beautiful summer rain in Dallas did not end when night fell. God's powerful message and the ever-present comfort and protection of His Angels became continual, abiding sources of strength for me during the terrible years that lay ahead. Through all the impossible hopeless times when more unbelievable agonies seemed to go on forever, I relived those moments on that summer day when God had smiled down upon me. I was only more determined than ever to live and restore my life, my health, my broken dreams. I believed with unwavering conviction that God would never put me through all that terrible suffering and sadness, sustain me with miracles, to only cast me by the way today.

My miracles were a communication of love and faith and trust that I could keep, never forget. They were truths I could keep with me to share with others. Believing in God and sharing my faith became my responsibility to always believe in His love and power and glory—belief and trust that I knew firsthand could change others' lives as it had mine.

Now as I reflect upon those days, some sorrowful, some filled with unspeakable agony, I see them as a communication, a learning experience, a proving time from God and His Angels to me. They were important essential experiences from others to myself, from myself to others as a testimony to life, that wondrous Gift of God. And they are a truth and testimony that shall remain with me as long as I live. After all, we must remember that God is Love. Love is Life. Life is Commitment. Commitment is Responsibility. Responsibility is Communication. Communication is the Word. God is the Word.

5

Blessed are the Believers, 1976

PSALM 62

8   Trust in him at all times; ye people, pour out your heart before him; God is a refuge for us. Selah.

Blessed Are The Believers

It did not seem possible that in the short space of scarcely more than a year, my life had covered almost every imaginable challenge and heartache a soul could bear. Betrayal, abuse, marriage, auto accident, injuries, house burning, poverty...it seemed to never end. Only five weeks after my very reluctant marriage, everything I owned, everything that existed in my life up to that time—was gone. I had no car, no clothes, no job, no health, no house, no furniture—everything was gone.

Now sick, tormented anew by Tom, his cruelty and ruthless demands, I knew my life would never be normal, not even close to something good and decent, as long as he was in my life. Lack of money created even greater desperation. But the insurance company, suspicious of Tom's involvement in the house fire, put off paying for the loss. Finally, a year after the fire, the claims were paid and we could begin the futile attempt to put our lives in order.

It was not to be. Too much was too different, and much of it was me. In that short year, miracles had changed my whole being. Nothing was the same. Resuming life as I had known before was impossible, especially with the individual I was married to. Why pretend it could ever be the same? Since Tom's attacks in the hospital, fear of him shadowed every look, every word we exchanged. He thought of how vulnerable I was; I thought of how not to be vulnerable. His drunken tantrums and violent temper were always a moment away, arm in arm with beatings and abuse he would not hesitate to deliver. I ended the marriage.

It was over quickly—in three days. After waiving the thirty-day waiting period, I went before the judge. In one sentence, "Is this marriage irreconcilable?", all the caring, commitment, pain, suffering, desperation, disappointment, useless hope that had blackened my life with Tom was in the past. Thank God it was over that easily. No such long, dramatic fight for anything that was left. With only three suitcases to show for twenty-six years of living, I hurriedly made plans to leave the desert and all its memories behind. It would be easy. Little did I know how wrong I was.

Too weary, too exhausted from the endless struggles to even think, I wanted only to go home. I wanted to be with my mother and family who loved me. I wanted to see normal people in normal lives, people who cared for me without judgment or condemnation. Between God and all the Angels and my family's support, I knew I would be safe. I could restore my health, get a job somewhere and somehow make the rest of my life the positive experience I so desperately needed it to be. Now with the sudden divorce, I was free!

Going home would be a surprise for my family, especially since it was March. Who in their right mind anyway would want to fly to the foreboding plains of Montana in winter?! So I told only my sister, Mary Ann, of my flight arrival. She agreed to meet me at the airport—we would surprise everyone else afterward! It would be a surprise alright—one of the biggest we would ever know in our lives.

Freezing cold, snow and ice buried Montana. What a shock after the warm desert! But the sun shone brightly on my renewed spirits. Tom and the past were a thousand miles away and being safe in a new life was the only thing on my mind.

Mary Ann greeted me with equal enthusiasm. She exulted at being in town as we raced from shop to shop, cramming as many sights in our short day as we could. Finally, with early winter darkness upon us, we set out on our hundred-mile journey to Grass Range.

Mary Ann's pickup truck appeared to be the usual reliable vehicle necessary in rural Montana, but as the miles fell behind us, I began to seriously doubt its dependability. Without warning and to my horror, it plunged toward the road ditch, consigning us, I was sure, to certain death! Mary Ann yanked the steering wheel, dragging the truck back on the icy road, saying, "This darn thing! Butch said we're going to have to get it checked!" I thought, "Sure. Right. How 'bout turning around and doing it right now!" But, no clattering or clunking promised a mechanical problem. Eager to get home and believing we were in no imminent danger, Mary Ann "put the pedal to the metal." I breathed a fervent silent prayer to God to keep us safe as we roared down the narrow road across the dark, snow-covered prairie.

But my peace of mind and feelings of safety did not last long. Again and again with no warning, no sound, the truck would suddenly dive for the ditch. I was petrified, certain that after narrowly escaping the terrible evils of life with Tom, I had been freed only to die on the lonely, frozen wastelands of Montana surrounded by hungry coyotes and starving antelope. Already exhausted from the endless events of the preceding months and years, and now the emotional coup of a quick divorce, the new thought of imminent death in the crazy truck was more than I could bear.

"For God's sake, Mary Ann, what's the matter with this thing?! What's it doing this for?!" She replied regretfully, "Oh, yes, Butch said there must be something the matter with it. We'll have to get it checked."

Unfazed and with nothing else to do but continue our journey, she roared on, me breathless with terror and growing more devout by the moment as she bubbled and chattered about all the things we had not talked of in years. When at last we slid into the driveway, my relief and gratitude to God and all the Angels for finally delivering us safely was nothing short of paramount! Her husband, Butch, and their children were delighted to see us and we visited into the wee hours of the night. Yes, my new life was happening.

After relating details of our terrifying ride, Butch said we must take the truck to town next day to have it checked. Next morning we started out on the thirty-mile venture, now dubious of getting a repeat of the vehicle's prior plunges toward the ditch. True to our fears, we were not disappointed as the thing careened suddenly toward the icy ditches. Once again, my silent prayers filled heart, mind, soul, and every cell of my weary body. At last, we arrived at the repair shop, left the truck and dashed around town shopping, unaware we had already touched the tender fringe of death too many times...

Winter sunset fringed the sky with orange and yellow as we waited in the doorway of the repair shop, happy and chattering as sisters would. Shortly the owner approached, grim and unsmiling. Without ado he blurted, "Mrs. Parks, your husband has been trying to kill you!" His statement was flat, unemotional, shocking us both to silence. Everyone knew Butch adored his wife, was kind and considerate to people everywhere. Now we listened in stunned silence as he explained.

"When we put the truck up on the hoist, the right front wheel fell off. We didn't pull it off—it fell off!" Again he emphasized, "It fell off when we lifted it off the ground." We stared at him, as shocked as he and his men must have been when they hoisted the truck up!

Inexplicably, the day suddenly seemed bleaker, the wind colder, life different. Finished with our business, we drove somberly home. I could think of nothing except how glad I was that I had prayed all the way from Billings and all the way to the repair shop. Obviously we had needed every whisper...and Heaven had heard each one.

All the old terrors of the past years jumped into my mind. How quickly our lives are over! In a second—unplanned, unexpected—no time to save yourself! Again I had another event to thank God and the Angels for Their attention. Surely my Angels were getting tired—their wings were losing feathers fast! But the horror of the truck ride was not over yet...In a few more hours we would learn exactly how much we had really needed Heaven's help.

That evening following supper, the telephone rang with our brother, Clint, calling to chat with Butch and Mary Ann and "check up on everybody." He said to Mary Ann, "Well, I hadn't talked to you guys in a while and wanted to see what was going on." She replied, "Well, Reet's here and we've been having a wonderful visit. She's going to be here for awhile—she and Tom are divorced and she's come home to get her life squared away!" She waited at the stunned silence on the line. Finally, stammering and obviously upset, Clint gasped, "Rita's there? How long has she been there?" Surprised at his distress, Mary Ann recounted my situation until Clint hurriedly said goodbye and hung up the phone.

Several minutes later, the telephone rang again; it was Mother calling from across the state. She asked carefully, "Is Rita there? Clinton called and said she was there." Mary Ann repeated the news of my divorce; then she listened in stunned silence as Mother quietly told her the chilling details of an experience none of us will ever forget.

Two or three weeks before my divorce, Clint had awakened from a terrifying dream involving two of his sisters in a pickup truck. The truck had crashed and both sisters had died. Vivid in every detail and shocking in its clarity, the dream left him with such fear that he stayed at his bedside praying such a tragedy would not occur. Clint quickly considered the whereabouts of his six sisters. None of them lived near each other or where it was possible for two of them to be together. One lived in Washington State, one in Nevada, three in separate towns in Montana and I lived in New Mexico. We were all far apart and regular communications among the family indicated no plans for any of us to be together. Comforted by the reality of the sisters' locations, his fears were only slightly eased, but not for long.

The vivid nightmare remained such a disturbing horror that he called Mother and discussed it with her. They agreed that the portent of the dream and its clarity warranted greater consideration. They called Patsy in Washington and discussed the tragic dream with her. Equally upset as they related the details, she agreed that it was, indeed, a foreboding premonition. Though logistics obviously disallowed the probability of it coming true, the outcome was too dreadful, the dream too vivid, too disturbing as it lingered on their minds. It could not be disregarded. They had to do something. They agreed to set up a prayer chain with friends and relatives for all the family members. The prayers would continue for weeks... until Clint called that snowy winter night...

There lies among the family a sure conviction that had the dream and its dreadful portent simply been accepted as an obvious impossibility, two sisters would have died. I believe so, too. Had Clinton not respected the persistent horror of the dream, had he never called Mother to discuss it, had they never solicited Patsy's advice, had the prayer chain not existed, there would have been insufficient pleas to prevent the tragedy. For Mary Ann and me, even as we drove down the icy roads, my own prayers had been desperate and imploring, not casual references to an unwelcome situation one had to contend with. The plunges to the ditch were real! I *knew* we were in danger of dying!

Fortunately and obviously by the persistent nudging of God and all the Angels, such desperate clarity, details and tragic outcome of the dream forced the family to deal with the issue, impossible though it was. They reasoned that, just in knowing Clint had dreamed it, just for the tragic thoughts they suffered from it, only the power of prayer could diminish the sadness it produced.

Over the years of discussions and philosophizing about dreams and their interpretations, my family and I generally agreed dreams are incidents to learn from. They can be opportunities to change that which may be made known in the dream, or to prepare for that which is yet to come. Recalling those beliefs, there is not a glimmer of a doubt that the Angels followed Mary Ann and me as we drove home. They were with us again next day as we drove to the repair shop.

Today, we have all been left with a deeper, stronger trust in the trembling balance of truths in our lives. Such truths become decisions governed by time and leave us vulnerable and innocent participants in the mysterious progression of Fate and Heavenly decrees. Simply put, it was not our night to die. But without prayerful pleas from others, we would have.

Such events show us that as recipients of God's grandeur and gifts, we have a responsibility to make greater and never-ending efforts to nurture and develop our intuition. We must hone our senses, ponder our perceptions to allow that slender edge of advantage when we see, feel, hear and somehow know the odds are against us. In order to reach the unknown goals of our souls, we must acknowledge when our lives are challenged. We must believe that our faith and the power of God will allow our futures to be more than what we see before us.

6

Going To The Sun, 1976

PSALM 50

10 For every beast of the forest is mine, and the cattle upon a thousand hills.
11 I know all the fowls of the mountains; and the wild beasts of the field are mine.

Going To The Sun

My return to Montana magnified my prayers of thankfulness to God for delivering me safely home. Though far from well, I at least had hopes for a future of my own. It was to be a short respite from Tom, though. Three short weeks after the divorce, he appeared at Butch and Mary Ann's door, weeping and repentant, begging me to return to him. Or please, please at least go with him on a trip so we could talk—go to Glacier Park and talk. Watching dismayed at another performance of shameless blubbering, I thought, "Well, this isn't new. I've seen this before."

My value had suddenly been reinstated as a coveted wife, surely because he no longer had legal access to me. Though I had gone from a coveted "young one to push him in his wheelchair" to a sick, useless female he had repeatedly tried to kill, I was now the independent ex-wife, someone from whom he could not bear to be parted.

At sight of him, all his old dramatic displays of anger, remorse and cruelty leaped from my memories. This show of streaming tears could easily turn to rage in an instant. Without a doubt, I knew he had a knife on him somewhere, and a gun in his boot probably, too, both of which I knew he would not hesitate to use if things did not go his way. Though none of my family knew the danger they were in, I did…and that was enough. My sister's home and any person in it were safe only as long as Tom chose. Now today, my reactions to Tom's outpourings would determine how long anyone would stay safe. And I could not risk anyone's life for mine.

Terrified at the grave potential of violence, I quickly agreed to go to Glacier Park—anything to get him away from my family. Though too sick and weak to care about very much at all, I also had had no time to decide what to do with my broken health and shadowed future. Maybe the mountains would be a respite…get him away from my family, too. Glacier Park it was.

When one has been away from the mountains long, it becomes too easy to forget their mighty strength and power, too easy to become far removed from their reassuring comfort and security rising solid and forever high above. But returning was to love even more the quiet refuge of valleys and swaying emerald trees breathing with the blossoms of wild flowers and climbing scent of pine everywhere. Montana's mountains were so different from the prairies and the desert. Now they sent me an ancient invitation to restore myself in their serenity, reiterating my need of them.

Years had passed since I had been to Glacier Park. As their spectacular grandeur soared into sight, my heart yanked the same as the last time I had seen them! Nowhere in the world do mountains welcome strangers into their valleys and streams like the world of Glacier Park. Magnificent wild animals roam in passive disinterest of human beings, responding to the inherent aged summons in their splendid world as though knowing their safety is guaranteed within the boundaries of the park.

Yet still, while their ramblings follow peaceful trails for foraging, their exposure to visiting humans varies with their number. Their proximity to the highways and travelers changes every day. Only on occasion are they seen, and their presence can in no way be insured for the benefit of eager tourists and their ever-ready cameras.

As we drove into the park on the Going To The Sun Highway, I ignored Tom and his incessant talk of why I should return to him. Reveling in the breathtaking scenery and natural splendor, I was jubilant as we slowly drove down miles and miles of the famed highway. Every perfectly shaped pine tree, jutting crag of granite and scampering squirrel left me as excited as a child! Imagining the animals and birds hidden in the great forest, I impetuously decided, for whatever curious reason, that I wanted to see a moose.

Signs posted along the highway said, "Wildlife At Large", each one enhancing my hope of seeing the magnificent beast. Life was mine again and nothing would do except for me to glimpse that giant, elusive creature of Nature! He was out there somewhere, wandering through the forest, burying his head in the rivers, perhaps even pursued by relentless fans like a movie star. The thought of him was an inexplicable delight and I pronounced to Tom with confident finality that I wanted to see one.

I had seen a lot of wild animals in my travels—buffalo, deer, antelope, animals in zoos and countless smaller animals on the plains of Montana, but, I had never been in the natural environment of the moose. Today I just wanted to see one! I was determined! This was my day to put my happy eyes upon his reclusive hide, a zeal heightened by signs warning visitors to remain in their autos. "At large" narrowed the mystique, as well as territory, of the moose's wanderings and was exactly the way I wanted him to be—at large and in my sight!

My chattering and exclaiming about seeing my moose continued, accelerated by every sign we encountered. Tom grew more and more irritated at my ceaseless wildlife wish, surely because I exhibited more excitement over being in the park than seeing him and listening to his selfish concerns. By the time we reached the end of the highway, marked by a giant wall of frozen snow, his patience was done. As we turned around, I intuitively felt he was secretly glad we had ventured thus far without a sight of my elusive quarry. Still I chattered on, my hopes still bright as I confidently searched the thick forest beyond the roadside for a sight of my moose!

Much time, probably two to three hours, had passed since my first pronouncement to see a moose. As we left the cold and snow of the higher altitude, Tom finally had enough of my prattle. He took the offensive, outlining all the reasons why I would not, could not see a moose that day. They were logical reasons, probably quite accurate, believable, and acceptable—to anyone else but me. But, since I possessed an inflated opinion of what should be available to me, due mostly to my new love of life, and regardless of probability or impossibility, I remained adamant, all the more determined to see my moose.

Suddenly, he snapped, "You're not going to see a moose today! The only way you'll see a moose is for a miracle to happen!" I retorted, "Well, a miracle is just going to have to happen then, because I want to see a moose!" Not even I could believe my determination! And over a beast that wouldn't know a human from a camel and surely wouldn't have cared! A foreigner in the wilderness is a foreigner! On we drove, me privately wishing my invisible moose would suddenly materialize just to show my sour companion it was possible!

Then, as we rounded a curve in the road, we saw several cars ahead where people stood at the edge of the pavement, some setting up camera tripods while others held cameras in the ready. Tom stopped the car to ask what was going on. Someone excitedly replied, pointing toward the dark forest. "There's a moose in there!" They were the only words I needed to hear and the last thing Tom wanted to hear! Triumphant, I erupted in exultations of I-told-you-so's and insisted we pull over as well. Fuming, Tom drove out of sight from the bystanders and stopped, probably to remove me as far from my quarry as possible.

Suddenly at that moment, a baby moose dashed from the woods, stopped at the edge of the road with only the pavement between us, and looked at us, his baby ugliness endeared forever to my joyous eyes!! Tom sat speechless! I hissed in elated whispers! But I didn't have the camera! It was in the trunk!

Going To The Sun

Quickly I opened the glove compartment and pressed the button to open the trunk. Still that darling little baby moose stood still watching us! He was waiting for me! Why of course! He had to be! I prayed for him and now I got him!! How could it be otherwise?! Not the noise and movement of the trunk opening nor my hissing through the open window made him move. He just stood there, still and watching! I thought, "Lord, if he's this good, let's just take it as far as we can go!!"

Slowly, slowly, I opened the door, slowly, slowly stepped out, crooning softly to him as though he understood every word I said. Never taking my eyes off him, slowly, slowly, I edged to the back of the car, talking as I eased up the trunk lid, reached for my camera, raised it and snapped! At the new sound, he turned away and dashed into the forest! He was gone!

Excitement and determination are strange partners sometimes, and I rushed to the road where the bystanders stood. "Come on! Let's go find them!" Everyone looked at me, including Tom, in surprise—obviously they believed the road signs! Finally someone said, "We're not supposed to go into the forest--they'll chase you!" I said, "They won't do anything to you unless you do something to them—

come on!" But the cameramen stood silent and afraid, refusing to follow me. Still not satisfied with one glimpse of that baby, I left them behind saying, "Well, I'm going to find them and get some pictures!" As the forest folded around me, I heard them calling, "Come back! Come back! You'll be killed!" Moments later the woods silenced their fading voices and I was alone!

Thrilled at the sight of that baby and now the search for his mother—she couldn't be far off!—my heart pounded, almost vibrating off the trees as I walked deeper and deeper into the green haven. What happiness to have seen that little guy! God loved me! He gave me my baby moose! But I wanted more—a picture of him, maybe his mother, too! Suddenly I knew I just might succeed! My elation transported me unafraid through the darkening wilderness. I would find them!

The stillness was shocking. How profound being alone in a strange world! The pine trees became more stately than I ever thought a tree could be. Thick grass grew lush and green beneath the branches. No birds twittered—an invader was in their midst. Only dead silence surrounded me. I felt like Goldilocks, afraid and not afraid, marveling at the magic of the moment and that I should be given the opportunity to live such an incredible experience as this!

Not wandering right or left, I walked straight ahead through the forest as though I knew exactly where I was going! The farther I walked, the darker and more silent the woods became. Moving steadily, I prayed, "Don't be afraid, don't be afraid; this is what you wanted, this is what you asked for!" A tiny, lingering twinge of fear nudging at my better sense was quickly thrust away as I walked deeper and deeper into the wilderness. They couldn't be far!

And, suddenly, there he was! Just ahead of me in a small clearing on the other side of a giant log some five feet in diameter! He had seen me long before I saw him and now turned away, trotting to the edge of the clearing. And, just as I expected, there was his mother! Magnificent in her size and wildness, she stood between us with her head down, grazing on the luxuriant foliage opposite the giant fallen tree in front of me. She watched me, almost casually, her eyes never leaving me, but the threat of my presence seeming to emanate from her body. Whispering endearments to her, I moved closer and closer as she continued munching, watching her through the camera lens. The baby disappeared into the forest, dispatched by his mother with perhaps a flick of her ear.

Closer, closer I came, my loving words soft and steady. Closer...closer...she never moved. At last I was near enough for decent pictures and began clicking the camera.

Angel Talk

Even at the foreign sound, she still did not move but only continued chomping, still watching me carefully. The image in the camera window was incredibly close. I shook with excitement at actually seeing these wonderful creatures—my miracle was before my eyes!! With the giant fallen log only inches away, I stopped, still speaking softly to her—she was less than ten feet away!! Abruptly she lifted her head, chewing steadily, watching me with both giant brown eyes, her ears wide! She still wasn't afraid! I could have sprung to the treetops with happiness!!

Then, as though saying, okay, I've had enough of you, she turned her head away, watching me with only one beautiful, brown eye. Then she laid her ears back. It was time to go! Animals speak with their ears and hers were talking loudly! Now, instantly I began backing away. My endearments changed to thank you's, telling her I was leaving, thanking her for her time and cooperation as I backed farther and farther out of her world, removing the threat I was to her.

What a lady! What a queen! She never moved as though she knew she could charge in an instant and eliminate this intruder, this menace to her baby. As I moved backward, her fear seemed to diminish—she seemed to relax, as did

Going To The Sun

I! Knowing how foolish I was for embarking on such a trek, I also knew I had to put as much distance between us as possible before I turned my back on her. If I turned my back too soon, she could do anything—then I would be the hunted and she the hunter.

Still talking to her, I moved farther and farther away as she grew smaller and smaller until the tension between us seemed to disappear through the trees. Suddenly she was hidden by foliage. I was alone again, the danger to her and to me now gone. I turned away toward the road, overwhelmed with the utter silence and solitude. The forest seemed to swallow all movement, all sound, all life. She was gone. I was totally alone without her. For some inexplicable reason, I was overcome with sadness.

Now my walk through the tranquil, beautiful green world hammered home the reality of my accomplishment—no, my gift from God. The green world was like drinking from a heavenly fountain of serenity that would flow only until I heard a human voice and saw a human face. With a total sense of fulfillment and enchantment, I touched the soft green fronds around me with tenderness and longing, wishing I could hold them forever, stay forever, free of the fear and demands that stood waiting at the roadside. I could keep them a little longer, if I stopped. I walked more slowly, lingering in the silent forest as though it were a time tunnel of evolution—a healing time, a special restoration time that belonged only to me, just for me.

Though I made my steps short and tried to stop time, the magnificent green wall of forest finally parted to reveal the roadside observers waiting for a sign of the dreamseeker! Surely when I stepped into the clearing they would see that I was changed, different. But they couldn't know the wonder I had just seen, the gift I had received, the miracle I had asked for, or rather demanded, and received!

The bystanders began calling out as though surprised to see me alive, asking excitedly if I had seen them. Tom was silent. Maybe they knew from my face that I had known another part of God's special world. Maybe they could hear it in my voice when I spoke. Maybe they could feel the peacefulness I was filled with. Maybe my elation became a new smile and softer voice enriched by my new wilderness miracle.

At last we drove away from the group of tourists and my miracle place. Tom was thoughtful and silent, I was warm with happiness. But it wasn't over, for a few hundred yards down the road, two people walked toward their car as we approached. Dazzled like myself, they said, "There are two bull moose back there in the river!" Without hesitating this time, Tom parked the car and followed me into the forest one more time.

Even deeper into the wilderness than my baby moose and his mother had been, the river ran quiet and lovely through the wilderness. And there, past the beautiful trees two gigantic bull moose stood in the water! As we crept closer, peering through the trees, they never looked up! How wonderful they were, plunging their giant heads through the water foraging for food! Then with great splashing, they raised their massive racks into the light, chomping contentedly on the drenched greens hanging from their mouths. Hidden safely behind a tree, Tom watched with veiled excitement as, over and over, the two moose raised and lowered their heads, feeding in the river.

But for me, Adventurer of the Day, I could not be satisfied with the grainy, obscure picture that distance would ensure. I had to get closer for a good camera shot! Slowly, slowly I crept through the forest underbrush until the foliage cleared by the river. Awestruck by their magnificence, I got my pictures of the moose, giant and unaware of the intruder into their majestic world! Wanting more, I edged closer until suddenly the larger moose raised his giant head from the water, swung his antlers and looked me square in the eye! I nearly fainted! Though in water nearly to his shoulders, he could easily charge across the scant seventy-five yards between us in seconds! Before I could get to a tree, he would have gotten me!

Going To The Sun

I had enough! I was satisfied! This time, backing away from the river was a quick trip! The bull moose watched me until I was out of sight, out of mind in seconds! As the fragrant underbrush closed around us, we walked through the beautiful solitude to the car. Yes. Miracles do happen.

Going down the Going to the Sun Highway was much quieter than going up. Tom never spoke, nor did I. What was he thinking? I didn't care. Maybe he was finally getting the message that God really was in charge! Maybe he was thinking he needed to remember that God answers prayers and He was as close and as able to protect me as He was to drop moose in my path.

I smiled in satisfaction and gratitude for my wonderful gift from Heaven, understanding firsthand the incredible reality of the day. Both of us had learned something out of this world one more time. I had seen my weary heart be blessed with one more reason for hope in my future, and never allow my faith to falter.

God and His wilderness blessing changed the searching part of me that day, giving me memories of bliss that left me feeling like a child forever blessed with magic. He had also shown Tom the power of His love. I spoke my wish and God answered. Tom had heard the wish and he saw it come true. How could he ever forget that truth?

My unforgettable moments in the forest would never diminish, would forever shine in my heart, unforgettable in their detail. God let me rest my heart and soul on the shoulders of the mountains, just as I had hoped I could. They sent me away with their strength and serenity, but also with a special, special memory that would be a precious haven in the many storms that lay still ahead.

7

The Cow In The Corn, 1979

PSALM 34

4   *I sought the Lord, and he heard me, and delivered me from all my fears.*

Angel Talk

The giant harvest moon shone blood red on the horizon, ominous and unearthly, transformed by smoke from forest fires and prairie fires. Montana was burning from border to border. Scattered across the magnificent state, wildfires raged in the Rockies, out of the foothills south into Wyoming and westward into Idaho. Toward the east, lightning strikes sparked more fires that burned huge checkerboards on the wandering prairie, taunting precious wheat fields all the way to North Dakota.

As fires sheared the mountains of their splendor, casting them into decades of desperate recovery, farmers waited, too, to shear the fields, and instead, reap the bountiful harvest of their crops. Montana's natural wealth suffered a strange and tragic contrast of simultaneous gain and loss. The wonderful harvest was tainted by the smoky haze and perpetual smell of burning pine in the wind.

Such was the welcome awaiting me when I arrived from New Mexico, this time to help my twin, Wanda, and her husband, Milton, with harvest. Smoke from the distant fires was so thick it drifted through the buffalo berry bushes along the creek banks and hovered below the hillcrests. All the ranchers and farmers knew the danger of fire anytime, anywhere, and Wanda and Milton were prepared; fire extinguishers, shovels and gunny sacks were at hand. Even the children, Kristi, age 8, Jeannie, 6, and Ross, 5, knew the threat as we readied ourselves for the weeks ahead.

Yes, in only one glance at the fields around me, the entire harvesting event promised to be quite an adventure, one I had not joined in for years. But like so many times before, it would also turn out to be an adventure that would remind us of God's constant, reassuring and comforting presence, albeit in the craziest of situations!

Deep in the Missouri Breaks where the fields waited, shale hills patched with sagebrush, stiff grass and occasional cedar trees ranged rough and wild, changed little from the magnificent hunting grounds where roaming Sioux and Assiniboine Indians had lived for hundreds of years. Small wheat fields were carved out of reluctant prairie meadows and flats among the rugged hills and buttes. And, to the perpetual distaste of nearly every farmer and rancher, as well as cow and horse, rattlesnakes crawled with imperious disregard from beneath every rock and stone, every crack and every crevice. Constantly threatening regardless of time or place, their menacing hides could be expected beneath every truck and automobile on every homestead in the country. Of all sizes and only one shape, they were just beginning migration, slithering ahead of winter like ants before the fire. Not good. It was going to be an adventure, all right.

After my renewed introduction with fire and rattlesnakes, getting used to a few eccentric old trucks—and neighbors as well—was nothing. In almost no time, I was hauling wheat, double clutching the gears in the old Chevy truck as it groaned under the load of wheat, and praying triple prayers with every mile that we would make it up the hill to the granary and back safely to the field for another load.

But, it was a joy to be away from the city—no sirens, no people, no noise—only the earth and the sky. They ask me if the skies in Montana are really that big and I have to say, yes, they are even bigger than I remembered. During that harvest, I spent day after day beneath them, watching the clouds sweep and sway and prance and dance above, just like long ago when I had woven childhood dreams of where they went in their puffy shapes. I had been lucky, and grew up to live the dreams I dreamed. Now under those wonderful skies again, I chattered to Kristi and Jeannie and Ross about my own childhood as we rode up and down the dusty roads hauling wheat.

They went with me often, content to run in the stubble fields and chase each other on the sunny prairie while we waited for their father to cut another hopper of wheat. They were darling little companions and endeared me with their polite tolerance, awareness and respect for how I cherished them and strived to keep them safe. Always on the lookout for rattlesnakes, I drilled them in running exercises—dashing and stopping to improve their response time in escaping a threatening rattler. They did not protest, no doubt because they were just as anxious to run faster from one as I was anxious to make sure they could!

So we sat on the hills watching the prairie and skies, captivated by everything around us. To our happy surprise one beautiful morning, we were gifted with the sudden arrival of giant B-52's flying low toward us! They appeared on the horizon—literally out of the blue!—silent and giant, their sound barrier booming through the summer stillness ahead of them! What a sight to behold!

For decades, the isolated badlands of Montana's Missouri Breaks has provided a prime imaginary bombing target for pilots from the air base in North Dakota. Every summer they flew their practice bombing runs above the silent lonely hills. Now, as the great wheat fields streamed golden below them, they flew over us day after day, gigantic, magnificent and powerful, marking their bearings and jettisoning their phantom bombs.

We stood below waiting, a tall woman and three tiny children alone in the wilds, until suddenly they appeared beyond the hills. Transfixed, we watched as they came closer, dropped low, lower, lower until they were so close above us we could see their helmeted faces through the cockpit window!!! What a sight! What a thrill!! They took our breath away!! Transfixed by their magnificence, immense size, and the power and safety they brought, we shouted and waved, "Here they come!! Here they come!!" as they swept above us! Over and over they came out of the sun, flew past us over the horizon to make their turn and come in again, dropping so low they were only a few hundred feet off the ground!

The sight of them was spectacular! Here we were, children and a woman they would never know, never see face to face on the ground, but we were united forever on those rugged hills as we waved at them and believed they waved back! They were sentinels to the skies and

The Cow In The Corn

the country we loved and we rejoiced at the gift of their visits!

To our sadness, we were crushed when Milton finished combining the fields nearby and we moved to another field miles away. We were not to be disappointed long, however, for it seemed almost that our pilots missed us as much as we missed them! Hardly an hour after arriving at the new field, our gigantic friends appeared on the horizon and flew straight over our heads again! They found us!!

Waving and jumping for joy, we knew they surely changed targets and altered bearings just for our benefit! They had to have! Of course they wanted to see us! We knew it!! Our delight surely reached them as they skimmed slowly and magnificently over our heads, disappearing into the skies to return again and again! Yes, they were ours and ours alone on those wonderful, wonderful days!

It was after one of our B-52's historical visits that we had another visitor—a messenger telling us that Mrs. Moos called to say the Rosseland cow was in her corn and would we please get her out. This offense was no slight farm infraction and called for immediate action. We informed Milton when he stopped to dump the hopper; he agreed we had to get the cow out of the corn. We climbed into Old Blue and set out to capture the beast and take her home.

Old Blue was a beat-up old blue pickup truck with doors that flew open at a bounce and a screwdriver for an ignition key. Though a marginally dependable remnant of an earlier machine age, Milton kept it running and used it for roughneck farm work. Now Old Blue was part of our new adventure as we headed in the direction of the cow and the corn.

Her name was Tiger—no other name could have fitted her better. Striped like a tiger, her brindle hide was brown and tan and she was a renegade from her horns to her tail. I had already learned firsthand of her treachery, for, while helping my twin with milking another docile beast, Tiger had sneaked up soundlessly behind me in the barnyard, intending to trample me unawares. Some deep

Angel Talk

intuition had made me look around where, to my horror, I saw her charging without a sound, eyes mean and horns ready! Shocked at her evilness, I shouted at her, waving my hand. With eye contact, she halted, head still down and waited until my back was turned. Moments later I sensed her coming for me again! And again! She was determined and mean together!

Each time she charged, I turned in time to shoo her off, scolding my twin for keeping such a dreadful beast around to harm the children. Tiger was lucky she had an owner other than me. I would have hauled her to the sale yard with streamers and balloons tied to the trailer and ribbons in her horns! Now as we drove toward the corn field, I wondered with great trepidation what this latest stunt with Tiger would bring. What a sweet surprise awaited us!

I was not the only one who suffered her insults. Tiger's frequent escapades into other farmers' fields had already established her notoriety and her exploits were well known in the community. This day proved to be no exception. Not only was she already miles from home, but she had wrought considerable damage to Mrs. Moos' corn. When she saw us in Old Blue, she knew immediately she was the hunted and determined not to go where we were determined to put her.

It is well known among farmers and ranchers that there are few cows, finding themselves liberated and happy far from their corrals, who cooperate with their humans, especially in a corn field. Tiger immediately began proving the point. With me and the children in pursuit, she fled the cornfield, galloping in the opposite direction from her own barnyard. Like a juvenile, she curled her tail over her back, leaped over ditches and sprang with gazelle-like bounds even farther across the endless prairie. She had no intention of returning to her own personal barn.

On and on we chased her, farther and farther from home. She was as wild as the toros in the Mexican mountains! It was useless to try to get close enough to rope her; soon, with no hope of capturing her, we resigned ourselves to following her in Old Blue, hoping to get around her and get her at least started in the direction home. She was a crafty old bitty, though, and wise to the ways of humans. Effortlessly she eluded our attempts to get around her or turn her with skill and daring that even we learned from.

Time passed with no success—she was in control and refused to think of home. More and more quickly I was approaching the realm of profanity, heightened with an intense desire to see her reduced to hamburger. Finally after nearly two hours of hopeless pursuit, it became apparent that she was remaining in control and we were losing the Happy Trails game.

Our time was running out. Soon we would have to empty the truck Milton had been filling during our absence; we could no longer yield to this creature's miserable behavior. Our priority lay first in getting the wheat hauled to the granary and Tiger was jeopardizing our success to the max. I rearranged my priorities and announced, "Well, children, we no longer have any more time to chase this stupid cow all over the country, so we had better put in a requisition to God and all the Angels for some help."

Kristi asked, "What's a requisition?" I explained carefully that when I decided I needed help from God, I called it "putting in a requisition," like some people in businesses who ask for things on paper. Now I said we could ask God and all the Angels in silent prayer or out loud for help getting Tiger home. They understood, and as I said out loud my fervent prayers for assistance, they clasped their hands, closed their eyes and prayed as we drove helplessly down the road behind the fleeing raider.

If a cow could laugh, I'm sure Tiger howled with glee all the way down the fence. With her ears flapping and her tail high in the wind, she trotted defiantly, farther and farther away from home. We were miles from home, but with our requisition in to Heaven, we were ready for change, even help from neighbors. Anything to change the stalemate was welcome as we followed her at a cautious

Angel Talk

distance, bored, desperate and helpless with her crazy behavior.

We didn't have to wait long! Only a few minutes after our supplications to Heaven, I suddenly realized that her tail was no longer in the air! Then she paused, actually stopped to look around! She viewed her surroundings as though waking from a sleep! I said, "Look! Look, children! She's stopping!" We watched in amazement as she gazed at us with lanquid eyes, not mean and evil. Then to our shock, she casually did an about face as though she had intended to all along, and slowly, leisurely she started back down the fence line toward home!

Only moments earlier, she had galloped down the same fence line in bold defiance! Now we were dumbfounded as she walked purposefully, *as though being led* in the direction of home! I stopped Old Blue, too shocked to risk moving. Not trusting her new conduct for a minute, we watched breathlessly as she strolled past us as though we were a hunk of sagebrush. Suddenly she was apparently supremely content to be heading toward her barnyard!

Not wavering one step from her direction, without a single hesitation nor tarrying, she walked steadily along the fence line in the direction of home, miles away! We were breathless, elated, grateful! Our prayers were answered!! Why else would she be heading home?! We knew the truth! Yet, still fearful of aggravating her or somehow raising her ire that would start a renewed wild plunge in another direction, we cruised far behind her in Old Blue, muttering our thanks to God and the Angels and praying she wouldn't stop!

The children were as happy as I! Inspired by her astonishing change in behavior, her unbelievable motivation and docile behavior, we neared home and decided to take the situation to the limit! With curves in the road ahead, corners yet to turn, plus Mrs. Moos' tempting cornfield waiting over the hill, we feared she would hightail it again when we had to get closer and steer her exactly where she needed to go. I said, "Well, children, God and the Angels have done so well so far,

The Cow In The Corn

let's put in another requisition that she go where we need her to go—straight down the road, turn right, up the hill, turn left, up the hill into the yard, straight ahead to the corner of the house, turn left, through the gate and into the barnyard where she belongs!"

It was a ludicrous statement—a useless hope. Anyone dealing with cows anywhere would have said such a statement was totally stupid, unheard of and a waste of breath! Not only were we still almost a half mile from the house, Tiger still had many obvious avenues of escape, not counting Mrs. Moos' corn, now in sight, waving temptingly again along the entire fence row! But we had nothing to lose as we agonized at the potential rerun of Tiger's wanderlust and hunger. Unanimously we decided all the more enthusiastically to commit our dilemma to God and all the Angels!

We said our prayers out loud...and all of Heaven did not disappoint us! Tiger continued her stroll, oblivious to the sweet tassels of corn brushing near her nostrils; she casually made the first right turn down the road as though she were being led by a halter! We couldn't believe it and screamed and bounced up and down inside Old Blue until we thought surely she would hear us! Pounding the steering wheel, I exclaimed, "My God, children, she's going to do it! Kristi! Run quick! Run through the pasture and open the gate by the house so she can get in! She's doing it!! She's doing it!!"

Kristi leaped from Old Blue and raced through the cactus and sagebrush to get the gate open as Tiger unconcernedly continued her afternoon stroll. And stroll she did! Down the road and up the hill! Then, like she was invited, she turned left, walked straight down the driveway as though it were a daily event, turned left at the corner of the yard and went straight through the gate where Kristi waited. She was in!! In the barnyard! Home again after her flight hours before!! Kristi locked the gate; we double-checked the fence to insure her captivity and raced jubilant and rejoicing back to the field just in time to drive the loaded truck to the granary!!

We told our story and loved it! We told our story and believed it! It was an undeniable truth of the power of prayer and the power of a Heaven filled with Sweet Angels and a sympathetic God!!

All the world knows that the Lord helps those who help themselves, and we had, indeed, tried to help ourselves! But, too, we had exhausted all of our means of controlling this situation to a successful end. We were desperate, deservedly so. We appealed to God and all the Angels because the moment decreed there was no other way to success. There also had been no passing farmers, no vehicles; no one had seen the four helpless humans in Old Blue pursuing Tiger. No doubt about it, our rescue had been at the hands of Angels for all those dusty miles!

So, the children got their first introduction to miracles before their eyes and we were all left with a new devotion to our Heavenly Rescuers. We knew They were there if we needed help again because, after all, how could we ever forget our summer stroll with Tiger down a dusty Montana road!

8

Once Upon A Lifetime, 1980

PSALM 19

8   *The statutes of the LORD are right, rejoicing the heart; the commandment of the LORD is pure, enlightening the eyes.*

Angel Talk

Taos, its mountains and everything its ancient adobe walls sheltered was a solace to my heart and soul. When its desert sun lifted lazily over the mountains and glowed down upon the little village, its golden energy restored me just as it had the Indian and Spanish natives for centuries. They said there was magic in the mountains of Taos—in the light, in the air, in the sky.

Something special lingered in the smoky mists drifting along the river through the cedars and pines. It touched the heart and soul of nearly everyone who came there, and those who left carried with them an unforgettable peace and serenity that could be replenished only by returning again. Artists, writers and tourists alike flocked to bask in the lingering power of its antiquity. Giant old cottonwood trees swayed over little adobe houses, all braced inside with magnificent vigas and latillas, adorned with rugs and pottery and remnants of age-old Spanish and Indian customs. Inexplicable and without definition, Taos' ethereal essence stole my heart and let me rest. I drifted in the comfort and safety of her sage-covered mesas and pinon smoke and searched for my reason for being.

Although nearly two years had passed since the auto accident, still I remained a shadow of myself—not fully recovered from the injuries, without money, and worse, unsure of my strength to resume work. Wary of commitment, physically weak and unstable in decision-making that would allow me to accept responsibility for my life, I struggled through my daunting recovery.

To my regret, Tom remained his old self, unchanged after my injuries and struggle to survive. Always the abuser, he was selfish and determined to keep me his victim. Now raging at himself for agreeing to the quickie divorce, he refused to accept that the "young one" had gotten away. Always the typical abuser--narcissistic and driven by ego--he stalked me from state to state. Furious that I still evaded him, he hired a psychic, and a hunter until they found me. Pushed to my fragile limits, sick, poverty-stricken and powerless, I returned with him to Taos.

Once Upon A Lifetime

Life with Tom was no reconciliation. It was only a repeat of what had been before: violence and abuse, and every moment a useless effort at a decent life. Confrontation after confrontation erupted, day after day. Weary and despairing of why I had survived at all, I sought comfort in the constant unfathomable support and guidance of God and His Angels, uplifted by the miracles They had delivered to me already.

Though at present, the truths of my fragile health and situation with Tom were unavoidable, I knew my safety and my future lay not in what was at the moment, but rather in what had already been in my past. My miracles were undeniable truths, unavoidable strengths. Like countless others, I was a child of God, blessed with life. Obviously, something waited yet for me to learn, endure, change, influence. But I knew when the time was right, I would know it. Then I would move on and live my life, whatever it was to be, without my tormentor.

I had promises to keep to God "to do something with my music". And to keep the promise, I had to be well—I had to live. In order to live, I had to get well—and I couldn't get well if I was on the run. So, I endured life in Taos and tried to get well.

God had never disappointed me, but one cold clear winter day after another vicious tirade, I lay hopeless and drained, thinking of my useless life. My belief that someday I would be well was paling. Was someone out there who would really care for me? Was there a kind, considerate man in my future instead of the sick, brutal human controlling me? What waited in my future? How ever could I know?

Watching night fade away, my tears fell in sad reflection as a spectacular sunset swept its beauty over the snow-dusted desert. Whispered prayers for strength and understanding comforted me until at last I drifted to sleep. The gentle protection of God and all His Angels was around me. I knew They could not forget me...

Suddenly, out of a sound sleep, I jerked awake. I sat straight up in bed, completely aware of my surroundings,

Angel Talk

shaking with the clarity and vividness of a dream. Though dawn was hours away yet, I stumbled through the darkness to the living room, my heart pounding as though surely the walls would tumble down! Quickly I threw a log on the fire, rousing flames from the dying embers and curled up on the couch. Scenes from the dream were vivid, every detail burning bright in my mind like the piñon log in the fireplace. I watched the flickering flames and let my aching heart drift away into the dream again...

At the foot of a long flight of stairs against a white stucco wall, I stood with a young Spanish girl who fidgeted in giddy, uncontained excitement. Her lovely, long dark hair was tied with a bow and she wore a simple, very special, white dress. Obviously dressed for an important occasion, she waited in breathless excitement to escort me up the stairs where apparently the special event was to occur. Beside me waited a small, elderly lady with short graying hair, also attired in a beautiful, special dress. The woman was not a relative, but seemed very dear to me, and was kindly and solicitous as a mother would be. I noted unconcernedly that my own dress was not as special as theirs, though it was tea-length and of soft, white material. The lovely Spanish girl then led us up the stairs, still beside herself with excited anticipation at the surprise awaiting me.

As we reached the top of the stairs, a wide veranda spread before us. On the left, a long, elaborately decorated table held a huge wedding cake and other beautiful food. I realized this was my wedding reception—I had just gotten married. The table was placed in front of a wall of windows where hundreds of elegantly attired people—ladies in lovely dresses and men in suits and ties—stood waiting for me. At sight of me, they cheered jubilantly, raising champagne glasses in a toast! Overwhelmed that so many people were so happy for me, I greeted them and turned away to the right.

The veranda overlooked green pastures, or rather as a balcony of a golf country club overlooked green fairways;

large, square white pillars supported the roof. I walked to a tall, thin man who stood alone leaning against a pillar. Stopping in front of him, I looked up at him, which meant he was taller than I; he looked down at me. Soft, loose sandy-coloured curls framed his face. He wore a dark suit, boots, a white shirt open at the neck, which surprised me because the other men on the veranda wore suits with ties. As he looked down at me with the clearest, blue, blue, eyes I had ever seen, I thought, "My God, how he loves me." I woke.

Nothing in Taos was ever the same again after the dream. Before, only desperate confrontations and cruel realities faced me. Now, bleak reality was replaced with a beautiful, beautiful dream. Real or not, possible or impossible, it restored my hope in something good, something decent, something worth living for. It diminished the heavy burden of my life until I finally had the courage to leave Tom and Taos behind in search of the life I believed I was supposed to find.

It was not easy, though, when courage and determination were tried to their limits and my health and stamina faltered. I feared I would never be strong enough to face a future alone. It was later in another city that I found myself standing on a curb thinking of the uselessness of trying. As the bus approached I thought how easy it would be to end the running and the suffering and step in front of it. Suddenly, the stranger's face from my dream flashed before me with those stunning blue eyes and the look of astonishing love. His face held me and I was lost in the memory of the dream and him. Later, after rousing from my reverie, I found myself blocks away, the bus long gone, and no thought in my mind of ending my life. I walked on, thinking only of his face and wondering whether he was just a dream or was he really out there somewhere...

Fortunately, those moments of desperation were few, but each produced the same ending. Each time, in an instant, his face appeared between me and death, sweeping me past the boundaries of sad reality into a dream world that softened my despair. Each time, I returned to reality wondering if he was only my imagination, if he were just a dream or was he really out there somewhere.

Never again was I alone without him. He became a part of my survival—not an image I lived and dreamed of every waking moment, but a warm gentle reminder that sometimes we are blessed with a wonderful gift that belongs only to us and no one else.

Years slowly passed by. I recovered my strength, my courage and determination and finally returned to Albuquerque to rebuild my life. There, my health improved sufficiently that I felt ready to finally work again. Unsure of my injured hand, and fearful I couldn't handle the stress of an office, I considered the worst challenge possible: being a waitress. That would be the proof! If I could handle that, I could handle anything! It worked!

Within a year, I was more my old self than I had been in years. My scars had healed to white strands on my body; my tiny apartment was safe, secure and beautiful. I was strong, thin, happy, and even said funny things once in a while. Then, one day as I prepared for work, I would be reminded again that sometimes we are blessed with a wonderful gift that belongs only to us and no one else.

My eyes seemed bigger that day—greener and more sparkling than ever before; my long curls seemed more lustrous; my makeup smoothed on more glamorously than I ever remembered. Feeling especially exuberant and happy, I looked curiously forward to my luncheon shift at the dining room, regretful only that putting my hair up would spoil my curls!

In the dining room, Vittorio Beltracchi, the maitre'd, informed me I would work the lounge buffet to cover for an absent waitress. I was delighted--my wish to keep my curls down had come true! So, with Marge working the bar, we prepared for customers, happy at the promise of an easy shift.

It *was* easy—our lunch crowd amounted to only a few people and we smiled at our good luck. Early in the afternoon, two gentlemen came in, seated themselves at the bar, bantering good naturedly with Marge. I went on with my work among the tables. When a shadow filled the door, I looked up, and there, with sunlight streaming behind him, a tall, handsome cowboy stood in the doorway. I recognized him in an instant!

My knees buckled as I reached for the bar to keep from falling, my heart crying, "My God, there he is!" He wasn't just a dream!! He really was out there somewhere and he was standing in the door! I had found my reason for being.

Not even glancing my way, totally unaware of the shock he gave me, he walked past me to the bar. I clung to the counter to keep from falling and fell instantly in love with the stranger from my dream!

As he stepped toward me, I knew he was my dream without a doubt! He was tall, thin, had sandy-coloured curls beneath the brim of his hat, his white shirt was open at the neck—he wasn't marrying me, but he was real! His leather jacket was apricot-coloured with ostrich leather yokes, matching his boots. He wore starched jeans, was taller than I, and he had no idea what he did to me! I was so glad my curls were so great! In an instant he had reduced me to a quivering mass of jelly and I had fallen like a fool in an old-fashioned movie!

He seated himself at the bar beside the two men and ordered a drink, not saying anything as the men, whom he appeared to know, laughed with Marge. Shortly however, Marge was summoned away, leaving me to tend the bar. Still weak-kneed but thrilled, oh, so thrilled to be closer to him, I gazed into the blue, blue eyes I had wondered about for three years and fell deeper in love!

Definitely not a communicator, he seemed oblivious of my presence, ignoring my efforts to engage him in conversation while I poured his cronies' beer. Too happy to be crushed at his disinterest, I bantered with his buddies, rising to the occasion with rare form!

When Marge returned, I retreated to the tables, safer from my soaring heart and potential foolishness, but sadder at not being so close to him. He stood, walked over to me and looked down, just as he did in the dream. Without ceremony, he asked, "Are you married?" My poor heart leaped—he spoke—he spoke to me! I was so happy I wanted to laugh in pure bliss! With my heart losing time, I did laugh and say, "No I'm not." He asked, "Are you living with someone?" I said, "No, I'm not." He asked, "Are you in love?"

In one second I forgot the guy I was seeing next day and fell out of love like a falling star leaving Heaven. "No, I'm not." In the same matter-of-fact tone, he asked again, "Are you interested in any of the preceding?" I said, "I'll try anything once!" We laughed together and he walked out the door.

My feet couldn't feel the floor! But, suddenly the lounge was filled with people from a convention and Marge and I rushed to serve the crowd. Anxious and happy at the same time, I watched the door waiting for him to reappear— and he did! Seating himself at a table, he soberly ordered a drink, still oblivious to me, my curls and the stars in my eyes! My efforts to get him to talk—I loved to hear his voice!—failed miserably and I finally left him to get back to business.

Throughout our shift, he came in and out, still not talking. There was no time to do anything but serve him, forget about dreams. When he left and never returned, I set his blue eyes aside and concentrated on work. Finally, our shift was over; Marge and I agreed to meet at a nearby hotel lounge to relax and visit about our day. Now changed into boots and Levi's, I was seated at a table when she walked in—with him and his buddy!

My heart crashed; Marge had scored and I was out in the cold. To my rapture, though, we spent the evening dancing and laughing as though we had known each other for years. Such happiness I had never known. I cared nothing for what the next hour, day, year held—all I cared about was that my eyes could see his blue, blue sparkling ones, my ears could hear his wonderful laugh, and I knew my heart would never be the same again.

Once Upon A Lifetime

As weary as I was from the busy afternoon, the night slipped by in a euphoria I had never known. Over and over, the years of wondering went through my head. He wasn't just a dream, he really was out there somewhere... and now he was with me!! When the place closed down, we exchanged telephone numbers and parted, for I had much to do the next day before leaving with my now-former boyfriend.

At mid-morning the next day, the telephone rang. The voice I would have recognized in a hurricane said, "Miss Whitmer?" I said, "Oh, hello, Jerry!" Surprised, he said, "You recognized my voice!" Thinking how odd it was for him to say that, I asked myself, "How could I ever forget?!

His call was to invite me to lunch, which I accepted in a heartbeat. At the restaurant, we visited again as though knowing each other for decades. Talking was easy, interesting and covered countless subjects over the precious hours. He lived in another town and told me of his life, a Marine in Viet Nam, a broken marriage, his daughter. I told him of my life, a little about my broken marriage, my promise to God to do something with my music in Nashville. The hours flew by. Too soon, it was time to say good-bye. As we parted, I shook his hand and told him how much I loved our visit. He looked at me with the strangest look, as though, 'Is this all?' Just good-bye? Nearly three years would pass before I saw him again.

But time was never on our side. Neither was my past, his past, conflict, my fears, instability, promises to keep, and worst of all...Tom. Tom got in the way. Tom...stalking me, calling me, showing up at my job, terrifying me with threats of the returning past. Deep in my heart I always knew if he ever found out that I cared for someone as I did my darling from the dream, he would have raged. He would have harmed him, or even killed him.

Though our separate lives were at crossroads and fraught with many changes, Jerry and I were able to spend only brief times together, times that were obviously never meant to be more. He was the combination of all

Angel Talk

the virtues and criteria I imagined in a man. We shared similar thoughts, likes and dislikes, and for every moment I spent with him, I only loved him more. Though many years have passed since our parting, missing him has never gone away, never diminished, never faded into a memory. And as he said once, "There are too many years and too many people in between."

Of everything that has happened to me in my life, he was the greatest gift I have ever known. Nothing has made me happier than my dream of him coming true. Seeing him, knowing him, loving him, praying for his safety, his happiness, believing in his life, his hopes, his dreams. He was the love of my life, and will always be.

But he was my dream—I wasn't his. He was an answer to my prayers, the reason I never died. He was the reason I was able to get away forever from Tom, to start my life again, to keep my promises to God and do something with my music. He made me want to live again. He was everything in real life that I perceived him to be from the dream. He was the catalyst I needed to keep me living, believing in life, until I was strong enough to be alone. When he became a truth from that imaginary dream world, he was truly meant for me, but only for a little while.

There is a time and place for all things, and some things are never meant to be. He was meant to be a gift that would support me, uplift me, give me courage enough to leave behind the worst and reach for the best. And, I learned to love—with totally unconditional love, when such a possibility was destroyed.

Because our relationship never became us, together, I have been left with a perpetual sorrow for never taking the rare opportunity that might have allowed us to be together. I never said the words that the moment was waiting for, never let him know the best of me. But I also remind myself that if we were supposed to have been together, something would have allowed us to be.

So it was that knowing him not only saved me, but also taught me about life, and once again, about Divine

Intervention. We, as searchers and believers, must recognize the power and truth of a moment, whether it is a glance, a word, an action, a dream. We must see that moment for what it is, have the courage to respond, change what needs to be changed if we can, and then let be what must be. We must live with the honesty and consequences of our decisions, whether they may command a success or a heartbreak. For, regardless of the circumstances and the outcome, we remain puppets on the strings of Heaven, living and interpreting our lives as they have already been written by God and all the Angels.

9

The Navajo Angel, 1980

PSALM 57

2   *I will cry unto God most high; unto God that performeth all things for me.*

The Navajo Angel

On most winter mornings in New Mexico, glittering frost greeted the sun as it warmed the mountains and mesas, no differently that it had for centuries. And for centuries, the peaceful Navajo Indian tribes gathered beneath the shining purple mountains to share their ancient songs and pounding drums with the desert winds. Those long ago years had also led undaunted Spaniards through torturous New Mexico lava beds toward the Rio Grande Valley. The adventurers were in search of gold in the name of God and king, but found solemn Navajo weavers wearing magnificent turquoise and silver ornaments and jewelry instead of gold. The armor-covered intruders soon vanquished the Navajo, brought them before the altar of Christianity and changed their lives until at last they learned to live in unique harmony with another intruder, the white man.

So it was that during my years in New Mexico I was part of these three cultures, flourishing together, each contributing their crafts and colorful customs to the Southwest. Awed by the calm, serene lifestyle of the Navajo, I treasured the rare opportunities to associate with them, respecting their world and wishing I could know them better. But one sunny day my wish would be realized to a dimension few people know, changing my feelings to unparalleled, never-ending awe when a solitary Navajo Angel brought a breathtaking piece of Heaven to the door.

Saturday morning was the much planned moving day for my friends, Phil and Michelle. I arrived to help them, hopeful and confident it would be a short day; they hoped we would have them settled in their new mountain home by sunset. Sunset in the mountains—a wonderful goal and a dream come true with their new home waiting! But when their other helpers failed to arrive, we realized that hope was fading fast--we were on our own.

We were three people alone to pack, load and haul belongings from the three-bedroom home. Nonetheless, we tackled the project with great anticipation, emptying closets and hauling boxes and furniture to the waiting truck. The house was big, the job a huge one for three people, but the day was warm and bright as we worked toward their sunset dream of being in the mountains by day's end.

All day we worked, pausing from time to time to call for reinforcements from family and friends—all of whom were not available. We were it; no one was coming to help.

Finally, as the afternoon began to wane, we were nearly done; the house was completely empty, back yard bare of furniture, the last potted plant and scrap of wood loaded, and only three items remained to be loaded. Each of us made a final inspection of the house and back yard to ensure nothing was left behind. The three things waited by the truck to be loaded: the piano, the freezer and the great pine dresser. And, all three needed a whole lot more muscle than two tired women and one exhausted man could muster!

Sunset wasn't far off as I asked Phil and Michelle once again if there was anyone—anyone at all anywhere—who could help load the last three things. Friends, brothers, neighbors? Was anyone out there? There was no one...it was no use.

We stood on the front step, staring at the monsters waiting on the sidewalk. Resigned to my last recourse, I said confidently, "Well, we're just going to have to put in a requisition to God and all the Angels for some help. We can't do it by ourselves and They'll just have to help us out here." I breathed a prayer to the desert skies, walked across the lawn to the sidewalk and looked up and down the street, waiting for someone to come to our rescue.

At that moment, an old pickup truck with wooden sideboards slowly turned the corner at the end of the block and moved toward me. Laughing at the sight of the first passerby in seemingly hours, I proclaimed triumphantly, "Well, here he comes! Here's our helper!" As the truck approached slowly, the driver looked right and left as though searching for someone as he crept toward us. Not willing to pass up a live rescuer, I stepped into the street

The Navajo Angel

toward him, doing a time-out sign with my hands. The driver pulled the truck to the curb and stopped.

Laughing, I walked to his open window and said, "Oh! I'm so glad to see you! We've been waiting for you! We have only three things left to load—could you help us, please?! I would appreciate it so much!"

He never flinched, never said a word. He was a Navajo Indian, perhaps fifty years old with kind luminous dark eyes glowing from exquisite soft, smooth, shining skin. His long black hair was knotted and tied in traditional Navajo fashion and a band encircled his head above his eyes. Though simply dressed, he was a classic, somber, shiny Navajo gentleman.

Next to him sat a little girl about six years old and next to her, a woman, apparently his wife, also dressed in Navajo clothing. When I smiled at her, she returned a resigned look as though, "Here we go again...", then looked away as though bored with one more halt on their way home. Without a word, the man stepped from the truck and followed me across the street where Phil and Michelle stood dumbfounded in the yard. I introduced them; they enthusiastically shook his hand. The Navajo man did not speak. Scars showed on his arm as though from a terrible war wound and I worried to myself that the lifting may be too much for him.

As Phil thanked him for stopping to help, the Navajo man surveyed the scene. Then he walked straight through the gate at the side of the house into the back yard and returned carrying a giant wooden plank some four inches thick and eight feet long. Without a word, he placed it against the truck bed, turned to the piano and in moments had loaded it on the two-wheeled dollie and into the truck! We were speechless at the ease he displayed with the task!

Still silent and ignoring Phil, he quickly moved the dresser into the truck. Now realizing this job was really no job after all and would be over in minutes, Michelle grabbed a paper sack, filled it with frozen food from the freezer and rushed across the street to the woman waiting

Angel Talk

in the truck. By the time she returned, our Navajo friend was finishing the loading.

Moments later he was saying, "Is there anything else I can help you with?" Stunned and thankful nearly beyond words, we assured him that was all we needed, shook his hand again and thanked him over and over! Somberly he said, to Michelle, "Enjoy the mountains." Then he walked with me across the street to his truck. I closed the door, thanked him again and thanked God in my mind for delivering us!

As I turned to cross the street toward the house, they drove slowly away. Pleased that we would make our goal—the mountains by sunset, I stepped to the sidewalk and turned to wave good-bye. But they had vanished!!

Shocked that they driven so quickly to the corner and out of sight, I said to Phil and Michelle, "Where did they go?! How could they get there so fast?!" We stared at the empty street—where *had* they gone? They didn't have time to get to the stop sign, but they were gone! They had disappeared into thin air before our very eyes...they had simply vanished!!

Rousing from our stupefaction, Phil said quietly, "I wonder where he got that plank...?" I said in wonderment, "I don't know where he got that plank...I checked the backyard and there was nothing left in it. There was no plank." Phil echoed, "I checked it, too..." Then Michelle said softly, "He said, 'Enjoy the mountains.' We never told him we were moving to the mountains..."

We stood in dumbfounded silent rapture, blessed as glorious rays of the afternoon sun began fading into a spectacular rosy sunset. We knew we had seen a piece of Heaven. We had spoken to a Navajo Angel. We had watched him miraculously load those giant pieces of furniture!! He had come in minutes after my prayer was committed to the Heavens! He had answered without delay, without fanfare, without pretense. Our beautiful Navajo Angel had simply taken his earthly form, rounded the corner with his bored wife, aided humans in distress for a few minutes and then disappeared!

The Navajo Angel

The three people who started moving boxes at the house that morning were very different from the three that drove away from the place where their Navajo Angel had walked. Phil said later, "You know, I really never helped him—he just kind of lifted everything by himself like it didn't weigh anything!" And Michelle chuckled, "Yah, like they're really going to need that food!"

So, we marveled at his gift to us, his shining presence and wondered who he was, what part of Heaven he came from, why he came back to help us. Had he helped someone else while he was here on Earth this time?!

We have never been able to forget him! To remember him is to laugh with joy and love the memory of him, our Instant Responder and his Heavenly power! He was real for a few minutes and then he was only a memory!! But he left us with the reminder that Heaven is only a breath away from us here on Earth. It takes nothing to walk the bridge between our worlds--nothing to share the best of humanity with the best of Heaven. It only takes a belief and a prayer. Our Navajo Angel will forever be our reminder of that loving bond between all that is Earth and the wonderful all-knowing love and power of God and all His Angels who listen to every human's plea for help!

10

Promises To Keep, 1980

PSALM 9

4   For thou hast maintained my right and my cause; thou satest in the throne judging right.

Promises To Keep

It was time to keep my promises to God. In the five years since the accident, I had met enough challenges, passed enough milestones, restored my health enough to know it was time to go to Nashville and see what I could do with my music.

Through all those years of getting well and understanding the changes that had taken place within me—body, heart, soul and mind--my promise to God had stayed with me, a new responsibility I had to my new life. At last, I decided I was ready. The time had come to put plans in motion to leave Albuquerque and keep my promise.

Nashville was where the action was, a major music city, not as huge and intimidating as Los Angeles or New York. Rising along the banks of the Cumberland River, it was a rich blend of cosmopolitan/country living in lush green woods surrounded by sparkling springs, all dominated by the production of music. From the Grand Ole Opry to Christian hymns, Nashville delighted millions of visitors every year. Many of the world's greatest musicians found their way there, and, though I considered myself only "talented", Nashville seemed the place to go to keep my promise.

"Seeing what I could do with my music" also meant that I had to learn "what" I could do—sing, play, write? Had my tracheotomy ruined my voice? Would my hand allow me to play the piano as well as I had before? Had my mind improved enough to handle big city living? Was it sharp enough to write lyrics that mattered? I had to find out and there was only one way to do it...go there.

So, I laid the groundwork to leave, surprising even myself at how brazen and eager I was to change my life so drastically. Walking cold turkey into a strange town with no friends, no family there caused new criticism and judgments from many who knew me. Was I crazy?! What made me think I was going to succeed?! Surely they wondered just how much damage the car wreck had really done. But the plan hammered at my resolve. I could do it—I had to do it! My promise overshadowed the doubts and fears that had churned in my mind for years. I decided I had enough courage to create the time, make it happen. Regardless of potential conflicts, no matter how great or small the reward, I was ready. Nothing mattered more than just doing it.

It had happened in one quick minute on a cool May evening, after a year of asking myself when I was going to Nashville. My friends, too, had asked when was I going. I always said I didn't know when it would be, but I would know when the time was right. And one May day I made my decision.

Abruptly and without hesitating, I called my friend and demanded, "Michelle, come get me! We have to have a cup of coffee." Alarmed at my odd request, she came over immediately and we drove east of Albuquerque to an old truck stop at the top of Tijeras Canyon. Inside, I announced my plans as the waitress poured our coffee.

"I'm going to Nashville and I'm going to be there by September first. I'm going to write the Chamber of Commerce and get street maps and bus routes and I'm going to the library and do my research. I'm going to subscribe to the newspaper so I'll know where the shopping centers are and what real estate and apartments are like. I'm going to have at least a thousand dollars and I'm going to rent an apartment on the bus line because I won't have a car, and I have to be able to get to work. I'll get a temporary job as a secretary and they'll hire me permanently so I'll be set with health insurance. My apartment has to be on the second floor because I'm a chicken about being on the ground floor; it can't cost more than $220 a month. It has to have gas heat because that's cheaper than electricity; it has to have French windows and hardwood floors, and, the windows have to face the east so that I'll get sunrises and the morning sun every morning! And it has to be on the end so that when I get my piano, I'll only be bothering two people—one below me and one to the side. It has to be near a bus stop and a shopping center because I'll have to carry my groceries and I refuse to carry them far!"

Promises To Keep

Michelle listened in astonishment at this outpouring, applauding the finality of my decision and determination to go! The waitress topped off our coffee as we laughed about my plans, my independent soul, then more soberly about my commitment to God. Suddenly, I stopped in mid-speech as the waitress walked away. "Michelle, check out the t-shirt that waitress is wearing!"

As she passed by again, Michelle saw, too, what I had been looking at. There on her yellow t-shirt was a small logo: a rainbow over a city skyline with the word, "Nashville" stamped beneath it. The plan was a winner! Long before we walked into that truckstop, we were believers of the plan, but this little reminder of God's will nearly bounced us out of the booth! We laughed and clinked our coffee cups at the wonderful omen of my adventure!

Summer passed quickly into August toward the departure day. I bought a one-way ticket on the Greyhound bus, not wanting to make the transition from Albuquerque to Nashville in the brief hours of an airplane flight. First, I would go to Nevada to see my sister, Betsy; from there to Washington state to see my sister, Patsy; from there to Montana to see my Mother and family, and from there, south to Kentucky, my mother's old family home.

Every minute detail was covered—money, luggage, Nashville information—done! All my worldly possessions were packed in six small boxes my friends would ship later. It was disturbing to see thirty years of living wrapped in six little boxes...Life had not been easy trying to survive, and like people everywhere, possessions were a measure of success.

Losing my possessions in the fire did little to inspire owning things again. I got by with the bare necessities—a pragmatic, cold view of losing and one that would stay with me. Still with my pending adventure, the six little boxes stirred a longing in me to have a place to call home in Nashville—to add "things" to my surroundings, establish a sense of balance and belonging to my life that I had not had in so long. Yes, maybe I could make it happen there...

Angel Talk

From Albuquerque to Nevada to Washington I watched America go by and dreamed the American dream! At Patsy's home in Ellensburg, Washington, a friend of hers said, "Oh, you're going to Nashville? You'll have to look up my old high school band teacher. He's doing something in music down there and you'll have to get in touch with him and tell him I said hello. I'll call my mother and get his address so you can find him!"

Promptly the next day, she returned with the name and address of her teacher and I dutifully stowed it away with the promise that I would give him her greetings. A week later I left for Montana—had to stay on schedule—Nashville by September first! My little sister, Barbara, on summer break from college, agreed to ride with me as far as Kentucky to visit our great-aunts, after which she would go east to visit friends. What a cross-country trip it would be!!

Seeing the world from a Greyhound window in 1980 wasn't bad at all!! The weather was comfortable, non-threatening—no storms or tornadoes; scenery was great. What a wonderful country we have in our United States!! Barbara and I talked, ate crazy food and laughed all the way to Kentucky! Right on schedule, Mother's cousin, Carolyn, picked us up at the bus depot. Later at the Old Kentucky Home in Mount Sterling, we regaled her and Aunt Sarah with stories of Montana and our travels! They in turn showed us the house—pre-Revolutionary War vintage, filled with priceless relics and furniture from America's first days to the present!! What a thrill to see such magnificent parts of our country's early life!

But the schedule had to be kept! After a sleepless night in an old feather bed, visited by the old ghost of the Confederate General who rambled at will through the dark rooms, I woke on September first with stars in my eyes. Pink clouds of hope radiated in the sunrise with my promises to God! As I boarded the Greyhound bus and saw the first freeway signs saying "Nashville", my heart leaped! My dream was coming true!!!

Promises To Keep

Hours later in Bowling Green, a young naval recruit boarded the bus and sat with me. We talked for hours until he slipped into sleep. No sleep for me—I didn't want to miss the glow of a single street light!!! But time was clicking by—I measured miles and speed, worried I would miss my goal of Nashville by September first!! At the first sign reading "Nashville City Limits", I checked my watch. We rolled into the downtown terminal at ten minutes to midnight...I made my goal with ten minutes to spare!

Knowing my story and my dream, the recruit asked what was I going to do now that we were in town. I replied, "Well, when my brother asked that, I told him, 'I guess I'll have a cup of coffee.' So, now that I'm here, I guess I'll go have a cup of coffee." He laughed, we said our good-byes and I walked to the café for coffee!!

A half hour later as I left the restaurant, he was still waiting for his hotel limousine. Quickly noting that a hotel limousine meant a decent hotel, and may save precious dollars in cab fare, I said, "I need a room tonight, too--mind if I catch a ride when he comes for you?" He brightened at the prospect of not being a stranger in a strange town and said, "Sure! Sure! No problem!" At that moment, the limo pulled up, leaving no time to retrieve my bags from the counter. But since my carry-on contained the essentials I would need, my first night in Nashville ended with every plan coming to fruition. As I fell into safe, satisfied sleep, I knew what it felt like to be living a dream.

My budget allowed three nights of hotel expense while searching for an apartment—three nights. I had to find an apartment in the neighborhood that fitted the criteria I had chimed off to Michelle months earlier! Next day, armed with my Chamber of Commerce maps and bus routes, I went downstairs for breakfast and planned my first day in Nashville.

In the lobby, a beautiful, white-haired woman glittering with diamonds sat at a table distributing tour brochures to hotel guests. She offered me some and asked my purpose in Nashville. Explaining briefly my intent to "do something with my music," she said her son was in the

Angel Talk

music business and wished me success and happiness in all my endeavors! Gladdened at such a welcome to the city where dreams lived and died, I felt more than lucky to meet such a lovely, gracious woman. Then, with a proud smile, she gently said her son was Tommy Overstreet! What a way to start a day in my dream place!! Buoyed by meeting her, I walked to the bus stop feeling so glad I had the courage to keep my promises to God!

An hour later I was heading downtown, calm, matter-of-fact, business on my mind. First thing on the agenda was depositing the fifteen one-hundred-dollar bills in my Levi pockets. My city information contained an invitation from a major bank downtown; perhaps someone there could advise a suitable area to live in. But, the bus stopped and a cowboy wearing lizard boots stepped on. I still wore my boa constrictor boots from the trip—my other shoes were still at the bus depot. At sight of my boots, he sat down in front of me. Several blocks later, he turned and said, "You must not be from Nashville." I said, "No, I'm not. You must not be either, or you wouldn't be riding this bus and looking like me."

He smiled and we introduced ourselves, visiting animatedly until the bus reached downtown. Voss, now from Houston, had just returned to see his family. Today he was "bumming" around, getting used to the city again. Hearing my intent to find an apartment, he volunteered to show me the sights—and that he did!

All day long, we rode buses across the city. Voss showed me where I should live, where I shouldn't. We explored Centennial Park, the Parthenon, the river front, downtown—all the places he had known so long ago and that I would come to know soon. At lunch in the revolving restaurant of the Hyatt, we continued our visit until at last the day was done. Voss walked me to the bus to return to my hotel. We promised to stay in touch, and said goodbye. What a day! What a wonderful, wonderful day, from start to finish! Once again, I could only be thankful for such a happy, exciting strange introduction to a world I had only thought about for so many years!

Promises To Keep

Day Two found me with a bank account and a pretty good idea that I wanted to live in Green Hills—it fit all my criteria. Surely I would find a place in one of the many Victorian style homes...I had to—it was perfect! With one more day left on my budget plan, I slept soundly at the hotel and began my third day in Nashville, revived and determined to follow every lead, grasp every opportunity to reach my goals!

Belmont Boulevard in Green Hills was my bus ride that day, premier place of residency. Beautiful, old two-story brick houses lined the streets surrounded with magnificent trees. Serene, green and tranquil, Belmont was a solace to my heart after life in the desert and reminders of the past. I had to live there.

Many of the homes had been converted to small apartments to accommodate college students. But at each place I inquired, the apartment had just been rented or would not be available for a considerable time. Finally, tired and hot from the daylong search, I stopped at a big house where a man stood atop a ladder, painting the dormer windows. With nothing to lose, I greeted him, asking if he knew of any apartments for rent. He suggested I ask the old man, Vassar Mitchell, who lived in the house. He would return at 4:00 and would probably know of some place. Relieved to have at least one positive tip, I caught the bus to a restaurant, ate without a care and rested until 4:00.

Sure enough, back at the house, the old man sat swinging in his porch swing. I introduced myself and explained that the painter had suggested I inquire about an apartment in the neighborhood. The old man invited me to sit down and for the next two hours, he told me of his life. Since his wife's recent death, he now lived alone at the age of 84 with his seventeen year-old granddaughter, Denise. Retired from Bell Telephone, his time was shared between his junk yard on Second Avenue and his home where he was getting used to a teenager in the house.

Curious about someone so far from home, Mr. Mitchell asked me blunt, probing questions about my life, my character, my family. The more he heard, the more pleased and surprised he appeared at my courage to embark on such an adventure! God?! Keeping promises to God?! Yes, I explained, life and living mattered enough again to never stop trying until I had kept my promise.

Finally it was time to go. Mr. Mitchell and I had spent a wonderful afternoon on the porch sharing stories of our lives so different, so far apart. Just as I was leaving, Denise arrived, pausing only for an introduction before disappearing into the house. Then with true Southern hospitality, Mr. Mitchell offered, "If you can't find a place to live, give us a call; we'll be happy to have you stay here with us." For the third time in as many days, I was overwhelmed and humbled with the kindness and consideration extended to me by complete strangers. Thanking him over and over, I ran to catch the bus back to the hotel. One day left.

This was it--the third day, and this dog could hunt. Today was my day to find my perfect apartment! One inquiry at a real estate office led to another person who suggested another place and another person. Finally, after hours of walking, riding the bus to person after person, I found myself at an apartment complex on Harding Place. Modern, clean, comfortable, within the price range I needed, there was one vacancy. And, just like every person I had known since coming to Nashville, the manager was as gracious as she was lovely.

The apartment wouldn't be ready for two weeks pending a complete renovation, but it met two of my criteria—a shopping center a block away and a nearby bus stop. I paid the deposit and a month's rent, without seeing the place, and returned to my hotel. I did it! I had a place to live in three days! What a feeling of success!! But I didn't have hotel expense for two weeks. Then I remembered Mr. Mitchell's kind offer...

Opportunities that present themselves are interesting—when they knock, we can either open the door and accept them, or, we can keep the door closed.

Promises To Keep

There was no thinking twice for me—not when the past was two thousand miles away, I had major work to do with music and my future was shining like the Northern Lights! I called Mr. Mitchell.

He remembered me immediately! As I explained my situation, he repeated his offer to stay at their house. Determined to pay my way, I asked if I could rent a room for two weeks. Without hesitating, he said, "Call me back at 7:00 tonight and I'll ask my granddaughter."

What a kind, kind thing to say! What a town, what wonderful people! What had I walked into?!! A strange feeling of security swept over me as I rested, thinking about the three whirling days I had spent in this beautiful, historic Southern city and what was yet to come.

Promptly at 7:00, I rang Mr. Mitchell's home. Denise answered. I said, "Hello, Denise, this is Rita." Then with the same gracious, kind response I had received from all the other people I had encountered in town, she spoke words I shall never forget as long as I live.

After a moment's hesitation, her gentle voice was firm, "If you'd like to come stay with us, well then you're welcome." I was stunned at such a strong, mature response from a young girl. Thanking her profusely, I said I would come over on the bus that evening if it would be alright. She replied as though I had been a neighbor for years saying they would be waiting for me and looked forward to having me stay with them. I was overwhelmed.

Welcome me, they did. We spent two weeks visiting in the big old house, sightseeing, enjoying restaurants, getting used to a stranger from the West and a city in the East! According to plan, I quickly signed up with a temporary agency for jobs as a secretary. The past, my injuries, my fears seemed never to have existed. Denise and I became as big sister and little sister and Mr. Mitchell the grandfather I had not had since childhood. For the three of us, from three generations, three separate worlds, our time together was a rare, special sharing that all of us treasured each in our own way.

Angel Talk

Two weeks passed quickly. I was working every day and soon it was time to move into my apartment. The manager escorted me to the apartment and unlocked the door. In a glance, I remembered my conversation with Michelle and looked at a dream come true...

Soft and warm, the morning sun streamed through two giant French windows above the lovely green woods surrounding the complex. I stood in silent shock as the manager explained the new brown carpet covered hardwood floors; that since it was on the corner on the second floor, I would have only two apartments adjoining me—one to the left and one below. In case I didn't know, the bus stopped right at the bottom of the stairs and the shopping center was two blocks away. Oh, yes, the apartment had gas heat which was much cheaper than electricity, and she hoped I would be happy living with them, and welcome to Nashville!!

Totally stunned, I thanked her quietly, closed the door behind her, my heart pounding as though I would faint. I had not known such happiness since my last miracle! Yes, rent was $215 a month, I was safe and yes...I would enjoy living with them...

Nashville's spectacular introduction did not stop there. Two weeks later, true to my promise to Patsy's friend back in Washington, I wrote her former band teacher a note, extending my greetings from her and her family. He called me immediately, happy and pleased to hear from someone back home, and invited me to a recording session at a major studio on Music Row. There, in the dazzling world of music and everything I had gone to Nashville to find, I met Bonnie Raitt and her musicians, people whose names I had seen on record labels all my life! The band teacher from North Dakota "who did something with music in Nashville" was, in fact, one of the most successful producers in town!

So, it was that I began my efforts "to do something with my music!" Over and over, Nashville let me feel the loving touch of Angel wings and the whisper of God. With never-ending goodness and kindness all around me,

I was reminded that our most precious gifts of Divine Intervention can come from unexpected sources. At the most unexpected times, God's guidance lends us support through distress and difficult times we cannot always anticipate nor be prepared for! But, the dreamer in us can still pray for help, for gifts, for dreams. We can still hope. But, we cannot always know our prayers will be answered, that our dreams will come true. And when they are answered, when they do come true, we can only thank God that we have them, for that is the only reason that we do.

11

The Blizzard, 1983

PSALM 91

15 He shall call upon me and I will answer him. I will be with him in trouble. I will deliver him and honour him.

The Blizzard

Winter still held Montana close even though May brought clear skies and warmer days. The promise of spring was real, anxiously awaited by ranchers and farmers and, in fact, by every one of God's creatures and critters on that weary prairie. Every gladdened heart listened to the spirited warbling of meadowlarks and robins as they bravely challenged the last days of winter. Tender sprigs of green began shoving themselves out from under the cold snowy darkness of winter as plans for spring work began.

My abrupt return to Montana after Mother's sudden illness was a harsh yank back into Western reality. Wisdom comes at the price of the past in that country and everyone watched the changing skies for signs of weather or a rogue storm that could easily threaten their herds. Baby calves and lambs were arriving daily and their little lives were vulnerable like no other time. Weather can change too quickly, so the ranchers watched and waited in a world that was safe one hour and lethal the next.

Though driving for United Parcel at night allowed me to care for Mother during the day, my feelings about spring storms were like everyone else's. My nightly shuttle run covered 300 miles of empty prairie in northeastern Montana and North Dakota. Though spring was knocking on our doors, checking the sky for a "road report" was still the first thing you did when you woke up; weather talk was the first discussion after a "howdy" to someone. Maybe that big spring blizzard was coming and maybe it wasn't, but everyone knew if it did, it was usually a killer.

My UPS route began at six o'clock in the evening from the service center outside Wolf Point to Glendive's service center a hundred miles away, then on to Williston, North Dakota and back to Wolf Point. Highway conditions were usually good though the sixty miles to Circle was on the original road built in the 1920's. Narrow and dangerous, the shoulder was overgrown with grass, obliterating the white line most of the way. The road from Circle to Glendive over the Yellowstone/Missouri River Divide was improved but guaranteed to be treacherous in rain or snow. The next fifty miles of barren, unpopulated ranch and farming country stretched from Glendive to Sidney where I always stopped at the all-night gas station for a cup of coffee before heading out to Williston.

Night driving was an obstacle course, albeit entertaining, with wildlife as herds of deer appeared along the roadside, browsing or crossing the highway to another favorite feeding ground. Too often they stopped in the middle of the road, eyes glowing red in the headlights as they stood paralyzed by the glare. I came to know their favorite haunts and gullies, slowing in anticipation to avoid hitting them. Nearly every night, too, the cold midnight skies were filled with stars splashing from the Milky Way in magnificent displays. Sometimes I stopped my truck by the road and got out to gaze at the glorious sight above me. Searching for the constellations, I called them by name, gasping in awe when one of their stars would tumble earthward to spark a wish from my heart!

So the weeks passed, nights becoming less and less friendly as more and more deer lay beside the road. Fewer eyes would shine in the night...the animals were paying the price for grazing by the highway. Little did I know that the price they paid would be nearly the same as the one waiting for me in the dark freezing clouds forming westward over the Rocky Mountains. That rogue storm was coming.

On May 9th, the weathermen from Washington to Minnesota put out the word. A gigantic storm was on its way bringing three feet of sopping wet snow, zero visibility, thirty to fifty mile winds with wind chills below zero and impassable road conditions. Word spread; the world braced. Ranchers hustled to gather their herds to shelter—it would be desperate for all those new babies, and it would be a death sentence for any fool on the roads.

All day long we watched the storm's path on television, knowing it would be in eastern Montana by nightfall.

The Blizzard

Reports rolled in of heavy, water-laden snow disabling everything in its path, of snowdrifts up to five feet high, impassable highways and falling wind chills as the storm moved east across Idaho into Montana. Everyone was prepared to sit it out, everyone except the UPS service center manager in Wolf Point. His remote little corner of the world was business as usual, regardless of what Mother Nature was doing. No call came to Dan Witherspoon and me from our manager that our shuttle runs would be held. Expecting, like everybody else in the world, that we should hole up for the night, we reported to the service center, confident our manager would never send us out into the deadly storm. We could not have been more wrong.

"Load your trucks. You're driving tonight." Brusque, in command, he ordered us on our runs. With no discussion of the blizzard, its imminent dangers and the very real possibility of not making it through, we headed out. Dan drove straight north to Glasgow into the teeth of the storm and I drove south...straight into the waiting arms of God, all the Angels and my father.

It didn't take long for regret to set in. Fifteen miles from the service center, I knew I was in trouble. Why hadn't I said no, I won't go? Visibility was barely a hundred yards, wet snow was sticking to the windshield, the highway was covered in two inches of freezing slush and the windows were growing colder to the touch. Witherspoon and I, in opposite directions, were alone in a white tomb with no two-way radios, no cb's, and no one else on the roads. It took little to know my survival would be entirely up to driving skill, quality of decisions and however closely Heaven was watching. There was nothing moving in northeastern Montana except two brown UPS trucks and two fools in them.

Speed was out of the question. The sixty miles to Circle were two grueling hours of a slipping, sliding battle with the wet, freezing snow as it grew deeper by the minute, whipped in a menacing frenzy by the wind. When I finally staggered into the gas station, the guys reported terrible conditions northward nearer the Canadian border. Considering their report, I believed I was south of the major part of the storm and figured I would have time to make it to Glendive before it worsened. I was wrong.

On the Divide eighteen miles out of town, the world turned into a white hell of almost zero visibility. Now covered with six inches of frozen ice and snow, the highway was nearly obliterated by the driving snow, so heavy on the windshield the wipers would barely move. There was no place to stop, no one to meet on the road. The world was empty and cold and battered as I fought my way to Glendive.

Two hours later, I unlocked the service center door, unloaded my packages, loaded two packages bound for Williston, and sat down to rest. Trying to decide if I should go on to Sidney, I still thought I could get out of the storm. Maybe I was still south of it—maybe I wasn't in the worst of it. When another exhausted driver pulled in from his route in town, I asked him how it was. He said, "It's hell and it's not gettin' any better." When I asked if he thought I should keep going, he shot me a surly look, said, "It's up to you," and walked out. His night was over.

UPS company policy at that time did not make telephone numbers of managers, service center staff and buildings available to drivers. When they pulled out on their routes, their only contacts were the customers they were delivering to and the people they met along the way. Now it was ten o'clock at night. Immobilized by the storm, the world was locked away. I had no way to contact my own manager nor anyone in Glendive for road conditions or even advice. I could sleep on the floor in the garage or I could keep going.

But the stigma of being a female driver weighed heavy on my mind. Would they say, I "didn't get it done"? Would the manager and the other drivers challenge, chide, ridicule my decision to hole up and wait out the storm? Would they react like the driver I had just seen? Being a good employee and "getting the packages delivered" was a priority simply because my manager told us to drive.

The Blizzard

Regardless of his intelligence—or lack of it—I knew how to do that. I rationalized the odds: It was cold with the wind, but maybe still the storm was farther north and I could ride the edge of it. If visibility held, I could make it to Sidney—it wasn't that far. I decided to go for it. With my two little packages stowed behind me, I pulled out of the service center and headed toward Sidney.

As the street lights of Glendive disappeared in my rear view mirror, visibility narrowed in waves of driving snow, coming and going in the darkness. Telephone poles helped guide the way down the road, now buried in nearly a foot of snow. In no time I wondered aloud why I left the service center. But also, how long would it take to go fifty miles? I could make it. I could.

Once again, regret nudged at my mind as hours later, familiar lights of the Sidney gas station flashed in between waves of blowing snow. Exhausted, ready to forget anything brown with a UPS label on it, I struggled inside through snowdrifts for a weather report and cup of coffee. Shocked at sight of me, the surprised clerk, exclaimed, "What are *you* doing here?!" Even *she* knew I had no business being out in the storm—impassable roads, wind chill falling—the night had all the ingredients for death. Now, with my determination and foolish decisions added to the pot, the brew was boiling against me.

There was no doubt about it—I was in the thick of the storm. I wasn't south of it at all. But, with no one to call, no service center for refuge, no place to go except a motel room, my reasons for going on overrode staying. Still hoping the weather was improving, I bought some candy bars and pulled out of town. My decision was the worst one I could have made. I was wrong...dead wrong...

Once beyond the glow of streetlights the world became a foreign place of white—a white world of two feet of snow, lit by my headlights that were only a vague glow shining inches into the darkness. Visibility was zero. Nothing existed beyond the inside dash of the truck...no world except white and windshield wipers. No guard rails, no telephone poles, no hillsides, no farmyard lights, no fences, nothing. There was nothing except white on the other side of the windshield. I didn't know if I was on the road, going over a hill, heading for the ditch or at the bottom of one.

What a fool! I could have found a motel, slept in my truck—anything would have been better than the white nothing around me now that screamed of the terrible decision I had made! Only the dashboard of the truck and lights on the dials were real. There was no hope that something else would be coming into view for a long, long time—if I lived that long. Being a committed UPS employee "getting the packages delivered" became a gross human error in a race with the snow and cold and isolation…and waiting death. If I lost, I would pay with my life. God only knew how I could win.

Desperation limits one's personal interests very quickly. The threatening whiteness beyond the windshield meant only one thing: How was I going to survive? My soul whispered, "Oh, Lord, what am I going to do? Oh, Lord, what would Daddy do? What would Daddy say? Daddy would say, 'Keep going. Don't stop. Keep going. Don't stop.'" Though he had passed away eleven years earlier, his words snuggled into my mind. "Keep going…if you run out of gas, you'll freeze to death." Now it was true—I was alone, looking at death, hearing his words in my mind, over and over and over.

That brown UPS truck pushed snow with the bumper. The temperature had dropped below zero; the wipers no longer cleared the windshield. My routine became stopping, struggling through the snow to scrape the wet snow off the headlights and windshield, climbing into the truck, shaking with cold and fear, putting the truck in gear and starting forward. Forward. There was no other direction. I never knew if I was on the edge of a canyon ready to plunge to a frozen tomb, or if I was on the road. But I did know I was a fool for wanting to "get the job done."

My routine—scraping the windshield, clearing the headlights, fighting the cold—grew harder and harder.

The Blizzard

Growing weaker and weaker from stress, cold and exhaustion, I prayed, "God help me, God help me...Daddy would say 'Keep going, don't stop; keep going, don't stop.'" I fought my battle, thinking of my father, his words, his strength, his courage. By now, hours had passed since I started out in the storm, and now I was tired, too tired. Tired means mistakes...and then it happened...

There is a moment that puts a human in another plane, another world, another level of believing, another time that changes your life forever. That moment happens when sometimes humans get lucky, get blessed, get something. They receive a gift that changes their lives, saves their lives, makes them a different person, a better person, all in an instant. It happened in that UPS truck when suddenly the smell of "Old Spice" filled the cab...It was unmistakable! And with it I felt the presence of my father. He wore Old Spice, and now he was with me in the truck! I knew it! He was with me! Just as he had come to help protect me years before with the ex-husband, now he was with me on this terrible night to help me to safety... And he did!

Daddy stayed with me in the truck all night. I never should have lived through those hours. The snow, the cold, the canyons should have claimed the fool in the brown UPS truck. I should have lost my way through the blizzard—I should have gone off into a canyon. They wouldn't have found me until Spring. But the Angels were around my truck outside and my father was with me inside. His Old Spice filled the cab, his hands rested on the steering wheel keeping the truck steady on the invisible road, away from the ditches, the canyons. Feeling his presence gave me strength to scrape the ice off the windshield, off the lights. I fought the snow, the cold—I kept going...don't stop, keep going...

When at last the eerie glow of Williston's street lights shone through the darkness, they led the way toward the service center. The town slept, buried in snowdrifts five and six feet deep. My faithful truck pushed snow up to the headlights as I fought my way to the center. Now blocked with drifts as high as I was, the entrance door finally yielded after shoving snow aside with my boots. I staggered inside, opened the garage door and pulled the truck inside. Then with the warmth swirling around me, I collapsed to the floor in a near faint.

Safe. I was safe! My watch showed 4:30...in the morning. I had spent nearly eleven hours in the blizzard, fighting that old demon death with every mile. Spying a pair of coveralls hanging on the wall, I laid them beside my truck and in an instant, was asleep.

Though seemingly only minutes had passed, I woke with a start, jumping to my feet when the door opened across the room. A man walked slowly toward me, saying, "I sure hope you're going to tell me you're Rita Whitmer." I said, "Yes, I am." He heaved a great sigh and pronounced, "Boy, am I ever glad to see you! We've been looking for you all night!"

Long hours before, as the storm increased in ferocity, my brother, Boone, had called my service manager to make certain I was safe. When the man said he had sent me and Dan Witherspoon out on our runs, my brother demanded that he find out where I was. Ice and snow and no communication became a formidable foe for UPS as they began searching. The Wolf Point manager, Glendive manager, highway department people and the Williston manager tracked me from place to place, ultimately hoping I made it to Williston. When he saw me by the truck, it marked the end of a night no one would be forgetting soon. After reporting I was safe, the service manager battled the snow again as he took me to a motel where I slept until noon. But the terrible ordeal wasn't over yet.

By the time I woke, Williston was already plowing out from under the drifts. A dazzling blue sky and sunshine glittered in the 34 degree temperature. The snow was on the move, this time melting. Anxious to get back to Wolf Point, I drove empty the hundred miles on wet highway, arriving at my service center at five o'clock. Happy to be home safely, I reported to my manager who, without acknowledging my near deadly ordeal, said just as curtly

The Blizzard

as he had twenty-four hours before, "Go get something to eat. You need to go back to Williston in an hour." Stunned at his order, I replied, "Go back to Williston?! I just came from there! It's going to be black ice when I start back and there won't be any packages to bring back anyway! Nothing has made it in from the East!" Furious, he replied, "I said you have to go back. Be ready in an hour!"

That order became a life marker for me. He was my boss; I was his employee. I was a female driver, a Whitmer in northeastern Montana and he was making a point that he could control me, make my life miserable, jeopardize it and do whatever he wanted with it. Whatever his problem was, I was the object of his anger. My refusal to do his instruction would only blacken my record, my reputation and my family's lives forever. I wasn't going to live in Wolf Point long, but my family was, and I wasn't going to be the reason they had a miserable life there because of one mad man.

Those one hundred more terrible, treacherous miles on black ice to Williston gave me time to think about my life, the value of my life, my future priorities. I thought of the company I would choose to keep thereafter, the places I would choose to work again, what kind of person I wanted other people to remember me as.

And when I picked up those two packages waiting for me in Williston, I drove one hundred more miles, on worse, more terrible, more treacherous roads all over again. On that trip, I promised myself never again would I stake my life for anything of inconsequential value like those two packages. Never again would I accept the instruction of any living person over my own better judgment in any situation, life-threatening or not. Never again would I tolerate a bullying, over-bearing egotistical human being, not for any reason whatsoever. I resigned my position a short time later following another personal attack from this human, certainly not a man.

So it was that the blizzard became a turning point in my life. It was a time of immature decision-making for the benefit of others that had threatened my life, but had also clarified it. And, I knew again, beyond any doubt, that our loved ones, though gone, are with us still. Though they may be in the Heavenly realm, they are with us, hearing our prayers, our pleas. They are able to help us, to intervene in our lives here on Earth.

The blizzard became the experience that reminded me again how our lives have specific purposes. There is a time when our lives are done and we are to die. But in the time we are here on Earth, we are to learn, we are to establish goals and we are to accomplish them. We are to become enlightened human beings so that our lives can, indeed, be the will of everything that has already been written in Heaven.

12

The Birthday Party, 1984

PSALM 85

12 Yea, the LORD shall give that which is good; and our land shall yield her increase.

Angel Talk

Ten years had passed since I had lived again. Ten long years of full moons and brilliant sunshine, unending tears and rapturous joy. Time had stood still in a broken haunted body, and time had swept through the past and its sadness with the dizzying whirlwinds of a recovered spirit and restored soul. And those same years since the auto accident had diminished the losses of life and heightened its benefits that bloomed like courageous determined flowers on the fringes of my life.

The tenth anniversary of the accident came with the staggering realization that I had actually lived longer than I ever dreamed I would! As those ten years passed, I had felt my body and mind healing, my strength improving. But the emotional battering left me fractured, insecure, and unable to see myself as a complete, healthy person again. Still, as the December 10th milestone approached, it also marked the wonderful reality that I had, indeed, done what I said I would. I was, truly, together again!

On the anniversary day, I took leave from work to see Dr. Erickson and Dr. Spingola—just to see them, to thank them one more time for their attention and caring that long decade ago. From there, I returned to the intensive care unit of the hospital and asked if any nurses on duty would have worked in I.C.U. ten years earlier. Surprisingly, there were two of them there that day. I was able to visit with them, expressing my never-ending gratitude for their compassionate care during those long, long weeks so long ago.

After a few reminders of the date and circumstances, the first nurse, a tall, lovely lady, remembered amazing details about me, my family and the hospitalization. Talking almost excitedly, she said over and over how good it was to see me looking so wonderful, and, too, that it was so seldom they ever knew what became of the patients they cared for. Then she paused and said wistfully, "But I didn't realize you were so tall." How could she have known? I had been horizontal for weeks!!

As she remembered more and more, she became quiet and reflective, looking at me soberly. I realized later she

The Birthday Party

was thinking how ill I had been—that she never dreamed the person she had cared for would ever look the way I did that day. We embraced and when she left the room, her eyes glistened with tears.

It was the same with the second nurse, a tiny, bubbly little thing whose voice seemed so familiar, but I was unable to place her. She, too, remembered incredible things about me. Laughing merrily, she said, "I thought you were going to fall over on top of me!!" Then I remembered!! She was the one who took me for my first walk and I had been unable to stand!! We laughed and laughed, for everything she had thought that day was exactly what I had thought, too!!

She hugged me, too, and I left them with their gratitude singing in my happy ears. Happy that I had found them again, I rejoiced over and over that I had made the years count the way I had. I was so glad they could see for themselves the result of their devoted compassion and caring.

But passing milestones of progress or accomplishments sometimes need more than simple words of acknowledgement. As my 35th birthday neared, it seemed a real celebration was in order to note the significance of those ten remarkable years. I decided to have the second birthday party of my life.

Once decided upon, the party quickly became not only a celebration of living ten extra years, but also of my twin's birthday, and Christmas besides. I wanted it to be special, and dived into preparations with the excitement of a child waiting for Santa.

Invitations were engraved and sent out to dozens of friends and relatives all over the country. Many I knew would not come, but I wanted them to know I was celebrating life! The party room at my apartment complex was reserved. My friend, Gretchen, agreed to play the fiddle with me on the piano. And, last but not least, I began baking a wide assortment of my favorite holiday treats to serve my guests. After a lifetime of cooking from "scratch," I happily immersed myself in baking with the richest, most genuine ingredients, barring no expense. Food for my guests became a labor of love. And, as only God and the Angels can guarantee, the birthday party was also to be one more memorable day in my life!

While shopping for my party of nearly a hundred guests, expenses quickly mounted far beyond a paltry sum. Furthermore, in the spirit and tradition of the season, I also found special Christmas mementos to add to my collection. But I refused to buy them, though, in order to buy birthday supplies. On one shopping trip, I considered buying my favorite perfume, L'Aire d'Temp. Again, I thought twice and refused in favor of the party. Indeed, my priorities lay in providing the most pleasant evening possible for my guests--buying things for myself was impossible.

So, I touched the careful design on a lovely Christmas coffee mug, and said, "No, Whitmer. You have to buy walnuts." And, when choosing the Christmas wreath for my door, I set aside the little wooden fiddle to adorn it, saying, "No, Whitmer. You have to rent the piano." It was the same with the Lenox china Christmas tree ornament, and the Italian Amaretto liqueur for the fruit cakes...all my wishes I set aside without a hesitation so that I could buy something special for my party and my guests.

As the weeks passed in the hustle and bustle of Christmas, I remained caught up in the wonderful preparations. Finally, everything was done, the day had come. My dear friend, Sue, came to help prepare the serving trays; the food was beautiful, the room was beautiful. December 21st was the last party before the holidays--the hour was nigh.

My guests arrived dressed in beautiful holiday attire, "Christmas Chic" as I requested on the invitations. Soon they were visiting, asking who the caterer was, and enjoying themselves just as I had hoped. Many arrived carrying beautifully wrapped packages--I wondered what they could be. As the gorgeous room filled with my friends mingling in happy holiday spirit, my joy was complete!

The Birthday Party

Later, as guests arrived, a glance across the room showed the buffet piled with even more lovely packages, some identically wrapped! Surprised, I asked someone what the packages were for. Shocked, they turned to me and said bluntly, "Rita, it's a birthday party!" Of course! How foolish could anyone be! It had been so many years since I had been to a birthday party, I had forgotten guests took gifts! After all, what could anyone expect?! Born in the Montana winter, celebrating a December birthday was always impossible with brutal cold and towering snow drifts! Now embarrassed that I had not stated "no gifts" on the invitations, I thanked my guests and made music with Gretchen more happily than before!

My twin was the hit of the night even though she was in Montana! Everyone looked for her and was sorry she could not be there. Instead they teased me over a phantom--did I really have a twin?! We laughed at my childhood stories, ate food and celebrated as guests met friends they had not seen in years! What a small world we had there in that beautiful party room!

It was a happy, happy night! All evening long I thought how glad I was that I had lived, how fortunate I was to know so many wonderful people. Then, as that shortest day of the year drew to its end, my friends said their good-byes and stepped out into the frosty desert cold. Sue and Paula and Roman stayed to help straighten the room; we returned everything that remained to my apartment. Feeling warm and loved, I hugged them good-bye and closed the door on the celebration of my life!

Happy and tired, I lit a candle in the darkness and sat down, watching the flame burn steadily with the same warmth I felt inside. It was then that I saw the beautifully wrapped gifts on the table—I had forgotten all about them!! Now they waited like another silent hug from each of their bearers, making me warm all over again. Careful not to tear the lovely ribbons and wrapping, I slowly opened the packages. But this time, I cried, too…

My boss and his wife, John and Priscilla, had given my twin and me each a fine Lenox china Christmas tree ornament...Rusty and Cindy from work brought a large bottle of Italian Amaretto... Michelle decorated her gift with the same expensive little wooden fiddle I had set back...Richard and June gave me the complete collection of L 'Aire d'Temp perfume...another friend had given me a beautiful Christmas coffee mug...The packages went on and on...

Seeing was almost not believing. There on my day at the most special time of year I gazed again at the things I had denied myself for my friends' benefit. They came back to me as birthday gifts! No one knew I had wanted those things. No one had asked me what I wanted for my birthday. Each gift was chosen spontaneously by my friends, unaware of its significance to me. Now by the grace of God and all the Angels, they were with me again!

As the candle flickered softly in the darkness, I sat with quiet tears, marveling one more time at the goodness of God and the Angels. How incredibly inexplicable is the power of that great spirit. What kindness and benevolence to have viewed such simple sacrifices and then turn my own gift of giving into a gift of receiving!

The magnitude of truths before me humbled me to my knees. My thankfulness reached not only toward the bearers of those precious gifts before me, but further to the heavens, where I knew, one more time, the loving embrace of God had found me. While the magic day of my birthday reached closer to the dawn and Christmas, I was reminded again that God and all His Angels would always be there for me, everywhere, forever.

13

Angel Fire, 1985

PSALM 23

4   Yea, though I walk through the valley of the shadow of death, I will fear no evil; for thou art with me; thy rod and thy staff they comfort me.
5   Thou preparest a table before me in the presence of mine enemies; thou anointest my head with oil; my cup runneth over.

Angel Talk

That eternally uplifting season, Spring, had drifted into New Mexico on the sweet scent of flower blossoms and twitters of swooping birds floating above the mesas. From horizon to horizon, the desert turned a hundred shades of green rivaling the spectacular blue of the skies. Giant cottonwood trees spread their cool canopies above the Rio Grande, tracing its wanderings from the Rockies toward the distant tides of the Gulf of Mexico.

There where the sparkling streams left the mountains to become the Rio Grande, I longed to be also, safe in a resting place away from stress and demands of the city. Though traveling had shown me splendors of the deserts, prairies and oceans, still no part of the world could compete with my love for the mountains. Returning to them, if for even a brief time, became a thought that brightened and blossomed in my mind like Spring everywhere around.

I considered it a Godsend then, when Rusty and Cindy invited me to join them with other friends at a condo north of Taos at Angel Fire. Angel Fire! Even its name made me smile with happy expectation! Taos and its unique world had been one of my favorite places in the world since living there years before. Even though Tom was part of my life then, I remembered the beautiful canyon leading to the mountain pass above Angel Fire and thought how good it would be to spend a weekend in its peace and serenity.

Anticipation of the weekend was a warm comfort as I left Albuquerque that Saturday morning for Angel Fire. As the grand steppes of mesa swept past me toward Santa Fe, the mountains changed from the tall Sandias to the graceful peaks of the Sangre De Cristos. Driving on toward Taos, a calm I had not known for a long, long time filled me as miles of scenic grandeur gradually put my heart and soul at ease.

Quickly the miles to Taos slipped away and the village snuggled below the mountains. First stop was the Holiday Inn for a cup of coffee. The Holiday Inn, the jewelry shop from where I had fled years before. What would it be like? Could I handle being there again? Sure. Of course. The past was behind me. I had my own life. Tom was a million miles away, a thing of the past. Now as the familiar old coffee shop waited, I was even hopeful I might see someone I used to know.

Sure enough, Marcella was still waiting tables and many of the customers recognized me! We greeted each other happily, visiting about people who had come and gone, sharing memories of the old days. But pleasant memories also brought back the terrible times, even though I had healed in Taos and found an inner peace that let me leave Tom forever. Now sitting in the booth, the old memories scrambled out of their hiding places and confronted me again with their misery. Determined to work through them, I continued visiting with the customers, sharing their happy chatter until they drifted away to their own tables.

At last sitting alone, I pondered the moment, pleased that I had stopped by. Then suddenly out of nowhere and without warning, a terrible feeling of danger, a menacing anxiety swept over me. From head to toe, a feeling so foreboding enveloped me that I leaped to my feet, thinking, "My God, I've got to get out of here! I can't stay here! I don't know what's the matter but I've got to get out of here! I can't stay another minute!"

Snatching my purse, I threw a dollar bill on the table for Marcella and rushed out the door, tossing another bill to the cashier as I passed. Calling out that I had to go, I ran for the door! She was no more astonished at me than I was at myself as I rushed to my car, leaped in and sped away down the highway!

Driving as though the devil himself were after me, I left the inn behind in the dust! Don't stop! Don't look back!! Get away!! Get away! Faster! Faster! Of course I had nothing to run from, nothing to be afraid of, but still the black terror filled my entire being. As block after block of the old village faded behind me, the terror was gradually replaced with calm. Oddly, the farther I drove away from the inn the more the heart-stopping fear diminished. Finally at Taos Canyon on the road to Angel Fire, it was gone.

Confused and shaken at being literally terrified to the depths of my soul, I decided the fright was nothing—just an odd quirk that people get sometimes in new or different places. I focused on the weekend ahead as the familiar trees and homes appeared and disappeared by the canyon road. Gradually the fright left my mind as I drove into Angel Fire.

The weekend was exactly what we all hoped and needed it to be. Embraced in splendid scenery and solitude, the men golfed the weekend away while we women shopped and visited. Too soon it was time to return to Albuquerque. But the brief time of tranquility was better than no time at all in such a heavenly place. We returned to work, rested and restored, promising ourselves to do it again someday.

Happy serene thoughts of the weekend camaraderie lingered; the terrible fright at the inn disappeared. It was not until a year and a half later that I learned the weekend had been, in fact, one more tender embrace from God and all the Angels...

When the phone rang at my desk, the last voice I was expecting, and certainly did not need, was Tom's. Tom, that evil person who had caused my greatest sorrows, my deepest sadness was on the phone. When would I ever be free of him? When would he be gone forever from my life? After years away from him, I had no interest whatsoever in his life or what he did. No, I did not care about his life and did not want to hear his voice.

Great effort had been necessary to move past the scars of his influence; now he was calling as though he had some significance in my life. His voice brought it all back as, smooth and charming, he asked if we could have dinner since he was in town. Ever cautious, I considered his call a test, just an opportunity to practice dealing with the memories. Determined to override my fears, I agreed to meet him.

After a cool greeting and brief inquiries about former friends and family, he got straight to the point: "I hear you went to Angel Fire."

Refusing to show my surprise, I thought, "Here it is. Be cool. Keep yourself together." Calmly, I countered, "What about Angel Fire?" He replied triumphantly, "Marcella said I didn't miss you by five minutes."

Struggling to control my face, my heart plummeted. I never said a word. Dear Lord in Heaven!! How could it be?! I couldn't believe his words!!! He was there that day! Somewhere near!! My shocked mind flew back to Taos, the Holiday Inn coffee shop—I knew what he was going to say before he said it. Remembering my frantic flight out the door, I scarcely heard his words as he explained.

"I spent the night there and got up that morning. I couldn't decide if I wanted to go straight down for breakfast right away or wait. I finally decided to shower and get dressed for the day, and when I came down the stairs, Marcella said you hadn't been gone five minutes."

I knew my face showed nothing as my mind raced back to the terror at the inn. What is there to say? He wasn't going to know of my flight! He didn't deserve to know a thing about it. It did not matter that he should know those same Heavenly Engineers were still taking care of my cautious, fragile heart and soul. What did he know about fear? About terror from an abuser and hurt and anguish and a broken heart? What did he care about the hell he caused an innocent girl who didn't deserve any of it? What would he understand about God and all the Angels still watching out for the times and places and people—evil people like him—that could damage my life, or change it? What did he care about the course of my future, a life I didn't want shattered by someone like him?

I didn't tell him what had happened that day in Taos. I didn't mention that God and the Angels were still watching over me. It didn't matter to tell him—it only mattered that I knew what had happened and why it had. The only people who needed to benefit from that incredible warning were myself and those who knew me, those who would understand such a Divine Intervention. But, I was the only person who could ever save that memory and place it where it belonged in the already overflowing treasure chest of other miracles.

So, that is where it is today...in a treasure chest of special, wonderful moments from special days set aside from all the other thousands I have lived, survived, loved. It is special beyond comprehension to many, but to me, it is one more magnificent loving embrace from the Angels and a kindly pat on the head from God!

14

The Investor Angel, 1985

PSALM 107

43 Whoso is wise, and will observe these things, even they shall understand the lovingkindness of the Lord.

Angel Talk

1986 was a good year. I had a lot to be thankful for: good job, great friends and the New Mexico sun was good to my aching bones. I even had a little extra money to begin buying a bit of furniture and start living like a normal, single young woman in the prime of her life. Extra money was a security I was not used to—Frugal McDoogle and Cautious Consumer were my other names. Blowing my precious dollars would get me nowhere! Still in that perilous life situation I had known for so long, I was a long way from wealthy and thriving versus wise and surviving. I clung to my hard-earned dollars with selfish determination until a richer day came along!! Someday it would!

Consequently, the idea of shopping for clothes was a rare prospect, one that completely surprised me when I woke one Saturday with only that in mind! I decided today was the day to spend some money! Today I would buy something special—something worth keeping—keeping for a long time. What a goal! But I had no idea I would get something special, that I was in the market for *someone* special, too. A rare, unforgettable individual would find ME—and make me richer than I ever believed!!!

Sale signs in the Oshkosh Sporting Goods store beckoned—a good place to start. As usual in every strange place I ever entered, I paused at the doorway, searched for the exits "just in case", and casually glanced around the store to see who was present. Years of being stalked by the ex-husband had taught me well. Always be aware of who and what was near, how to get away if you needed to. Furthermore, in case of fire, everyone needs to know where the exits are—who can tell when emergencies will arise?

Noting I was the only customer, I strolled to the racks and began parting the hangars, enjoying the colors and styles in search of my something special. Suddenly a voice behind me said, "Do you invest in stocks?" Startled, I turned, surprised that my usual red alert awareness had missed someone walking up to me unawares and so *close!*

The Investor Angel

There beside me stood a short, balding, round-faced, pudgy little man, peering at me through old-timey round spectacles. He looked just like a green-eyeshade accountant from the 1930's, sporting baggy grayish trousers and an odd baggy-sleeved white shirt. A bow tie was fastened at his collar as he waited politely for my reply. Startled, I was relieved to see he appeared not only sort of *old*, but also quite harmless and quaint. At his words, I wondered how a little old man like he was could be interested in investments? How odd--a funny little old man asking if I invested in stocks...

Parting hangars, I answered slowly, "No...I don't." The little man never moved, apparently not satisfied at my reply. Now earnestly, he said, "Well, if you ever get any extra money, you need to invest it in Abbott Laboratories." Surprised at the persistence and almost urgency in his voice, I looked at him and said, "Abbott Laboratories?" In earnest, again he responded, "Yes. Abbott Laboratories. You should invest in Abbott Laboratories."

Still he stood without moving, his little round face as serious as though he were in church. Looking pitifully out of place surrounded by scanty little sporting clothing everywhere, I almost felt badly for him! Surely as a store sales clerk, he probably didn't get a chance to talk about investments much.

Feeling like I needed to placate him somehow, make him feel not so anxious, I said kindly, "Okay. If I ever get any extra money, I'll invest it in Abbott Laboratories." Immediately, his demeanor changed! Obvious relief spread over his face with my words! He said simply, "Okay," and turned away. I, too, looked down at the rack again, then glanced up. He was gone!!

How quickly he had vanished, I thought!! Glancing over the racks, I saw that he was indeed gone. Nowhere to be seen! He had vanished! Where did he go? He could not have moved to the mall doorway in the one second that I looked down and then up! There was not time for him to walk that fast! There was no possible way he could have left the store!

Angel Talk

Now curious at his disappearance, I approached the cashier at the checkout stand. From her elevated vantage point in the store center, she could see everyone in the store at all times. I knew she would know where the little man had gone. I asked, "Excuse me. Can you tell me where that little man went?" She said, "I don't know what little man you're talking about." "You know—the little man who works here—the one in the bow tie who was just helping me." Looking as though I were half-crazed, she replied, "There isn't anyone else who works here. I'm the only one working here. I don't know any little man you're talking about."

She wasn't the only one thinking I was nuts! I was thinking it, too!! Suddenly I was no longer interested in shopping—not even for something special!! I had had enough of special for the day!! One nutty experience in one store was enough for me!

As I drove home, my little round man kept rolling through my mind—how could I forget him?! He was real! He stood before me and we talked. We talked out loud. We exchanged words, dialogue, real communication as in real-life human verbal exchange. He was not any figment of my imagination and he told me about Abbott Laboratories, a real pharmaceutical company. I could not understand, though, why the cashier had not seen him. He had been beside me for a couple of minutes. Perhaps she was looking at papers and never looked up; perhaps her back was turned. Obviously, she did not see who I had seen.

He stayed on my mind...my something special. How did he disappear into thin air?! When I told a friend about him, she agreed to do some research for me in economics class—they were studying stocks and investments and had to do a practice investment for class. Abbott would be her project.

Over the weeks, she reported that my Abbott stocks were climbing steadily in a tremendous surge of profits! And they climbed and they climbed and they climbed. Her investment was the most successful of the class and

The Investor Angel

my Abbott stocks the most solid moneymakers in the class! Both of us wished we had the money in real life to really invest in Abbott!!

Many weeks passed by before I realized one day that my little bow-tied visitor in the store must have been an Angel—an Investor Angel!! What else could he be? He appeared out of nowhere, stood beside me, talked to me, shared his information, and when he finally got me to say I'd invest in his Abbott stocks, he heaved a sigh of relief! He had done his earthly duty!! Tipped off one needy American girl and he split—gonzo!!

Deciding he was an Angel finally settled my mind. Unfortunately, the needy American girl did not heed his words as she continued to scrape together pitiful monies that went elsewhere rather than into Abbott stock!! It would be fifteen more years after the economics projects before I followed Abbott stock again. Fifteen long years after the little man's visit before I thought of Abbott again.

One evening my brother, Rex, called and related his recent successful ventures in the stock market and other investments. Later in the conversation I told him about my little bow-tied Angel. He listened, astonished, agreeing that the little guy was, surely, an Angel! Later, he did his own research on my faithful Abbott and found that at the time of the visit from my Investor Angel, Abbott stock was just beginning a climb that has remained steady to this day!! Had I done what that little special fellow told me—if I had thrown any tiny extra money of ANY kind into Abbott, I would have been worth a small fortune today!!

Since that remarkable experience, I have looked back at the days that are different, days that are special from all the others, like that day. That was one day that could have set me up forever in a successful, thriving world had I heeded his advice!!

All of us have days like that—a day special enough that, if we pay attention, if we assign importance where it is due, then we can become something else that God intends us to be! I should have rearranged my financial priorities after realizing he was a gift from Heaven!! I would have had more money to help others who needed my bounty. I would have traveled a different road than the one I did. Would it have been a better one? Would I have been happier? Would I have made the positive difference I think I would have? We will never know.

Today, I can only assign some kind of tolerant acceptance to this story. For had I become wealthy, I would have missed the spectacular and miraculous times I have known in the years since I saw him! But we cannot re-live our lives. We cannot go back. But we can re-think some moments and know that if something special occurs again, then for certain we can gamble, we can bet on ourselves, we can re-arrange our priorities and believe in another perhaps happier or more successful ending. We can remember the soft, simple words of a little man in a bow tie and think, indeed, he was truly a gift from God. And it really is okay to tell the world about him! After all, something special just may yet come to someone else because of him!!

15

The Wheelchair, 1986

PSALM 55

4   My heart is sore pained within me; and the terrors of death are fallen upon me.
5   Fearfulness and trembling are come upon me, and horror hath overwhelmed me.

Angel Talk

Though the Canadian geese had left the north country far behind, their honking trails in the New Mexico skies brought vivid memories of Montana to my mind. Instead of basking in long droopy afternoons of sunshine, Albuquerque was suddenly buried in chilly evenings that came too early. Sweet piñon smoke that drifted away too soon on the wind was bringing winter without ado.

Long darkening afternoons were almost a welcome change, for winter held the promise of at least one or two quick snowstorms in its season. When the giant snowflakes fell on the desert, it seemed as though God was whispering that we need a change. Sometimes we need to be reminded that anything, even a sudden switch of the weather, can change everything—what we think, how we act, what lies ahead. Weather reminds us that nothing stays the same and we never know from moment to moment what the next moment will bring.

So it was when one of those cold gray afternoons slipped over the mesa. After another normal day at work, no more demanding than usual, I surprised myself by lingering in my office after everyone had gone. Dallying, tidying files, reviewing pending business, the minutes turned to a half hour. Aware of my delay, I wondered why inconsequential tasks suddenly seemed important. Finally scolding myself for staying so late, I leisurely locked my office door and strolled down the empty corridor.

The placards of semiconductor information on the wall seemed of interest, though they had been there for years. Nevertheless, I studied them as though never seeing them before, chatted with passing employees and generally enjoyed this unusual leisure time. Knowing I was really dragging myself to the lobby, I said, "Whitmer, what's the matter with you?! Get out of this place!" Still I remained unhurried, tarrying at the guards' desk until finally meandering down the hill to my car.

Before entering the freeway on my usual route home, I impulsively decided to turn the opposite direction over the much longer road leading north to Tramway Boulevard. Driving slowly, I wondered again whatever possessed me

The Wheelchair

to go so far out of my way. But the fading sunset across the mesa and buildings on the route interested me; I continued on my way.

Darkness was falling quickly, but the evening suited my mood...no hurry. I had all the time in the world. As I neared a shopping center, I thought, "Gee, there must be something I can buy tonight!" Buy something?! I was really out of character! Still, I parked and sat watching the traffic, thinking what a fool I was to be shopping when I could be home. I was aware, too, of an odd feeling of change, of needing to make decisions for whatever reason. Gathering my purse, I thought, "Well, you better change your shoes." Still in dress heels, I sat there in the fading light, deciding yes, no, yes, no. At last I changed to flats and went inside.

Time was on my side as I wandered up and down the aisles thinking, "What in the world is the matter with you, Whitmer? Go home!" Why getting home was such an issue I didn't know and here I was in the store making another decision. Feeling more foolish, I lingered, bought some toothpaste and finally wandered out of the store.

By now darkness had brought the lights of the city on. I drove slowly, stopping at a red light at Menaul and Moon, reflecting on the last couple hours. But decision-making didn't leave me. Again I considered, should I turn left to my apartment complex or go through the light to turn off the thoroughfare and then home. Just as the light turned to green, I decided to go straight. Moments later, I turned onto Lester Drive toward the senior center and met someone who would change my life forever.

In the moment I turned onto Lester, my headlights shone on a woman in a wheelchair wheeling along the curb down the right side of the street. Instantly fearful, I thought, "My goodness, it's really late for someone to be taking a granny for a walk!" Next instant I realized she was alone, moving rapidly down the hill! Already she was past me, pushing unconcernedly down the hill toward the busy street. She was wheeling straight into the traffic! She was going to die!

Angel Talk

Terror-stricken, I jerked my car to the curb, snapped off the ignition and jumped out, running after the wheelchair. Darkness closed around me in a gloom that seemed a portent of the tragedy happening feet away. Would I reach her?! Could I reach her?! She was going fast—incredibly fast—already so far away from me! My heart jerked in fear that she would reach the street before I could stop her! I was running for her life and forever changed my own...

Faster! Faster!! Run faster! Nothing mattered except catching her! Already the light had turned green at the intersection a block away! Three lanes of oncoming car lights suddenly became a rushing blur toward us as she rolled faster and faster unheeded down the hill! How could I reach her?! How could I stop her?! A terrified sob grabbed at my throat as the world stopped—stopped as though life had been turned off and I moved in slow motion. No sounds, no smells, no senses, no motion entered my consciousness. I saw only the granny ahead, rolling through the dark blackness that had only splashes of car headlights and pinpoints of lights from houses across the boulevard.

My brain became a computer, aware of a million, billion things happening around me. Yet, everything was eerily still, silent. My senses concentrated their miraculous power into an acute awareness, isolating every minute detail in the still, suspended world I was running in. My terror became muffled grief in an all-seeing glance as I realized I might not reach her!! I thrust my arms higher, prayed to God to help me—that I could get more air in my lungs, push my arms higher, stretch my legs farther! Still the world was silent—stillness everywhere! Even my desperate breaths gulping air were smothered in silence! Motion, time, air meant nothing—only catching her mattered! Seconds seemed long, desperate minutes trapping my mind with an intensity that measured everything I could see and feel in micrometers, nanoseconds.

Still the granny shoved the chair forward, faster, with strength that amazed me. Grieving I could not match her speed, I prayed, thinking, measuring, breathing, sobbing,

The Wheelchair

God let me reach her! I stretched my arms higher toward the Heavens, up and back in desperate rhythm—God help me breathe! God help me run!! Choking back soundless sobs, thinking desperately they would take too much energy—energy I needed to make my legs run faster, I ran down the hill, chasing away death.

Nearby buildings disappeared in the darkness of desperation—all I knew was silence, the granny rolling faster down the hill...and death waiting at the bottom. My brain measured the speed of the granny, the speed of the cars, the air I was pumping into my lungs, the energy to my legs, the length of my strides to reach the granny. Awareness reached a height almost beyond human. In the same second, my heart was breaking as another part, the human in me, seemed to die at the almost sure reality of not reaching her.

Time was up. No more time to try—stop her now—do or die now. She was feet—only feet!—from the street, the traffic. Choking back a sob, I lunged for the handles of the wheelchair just as, to my horror, she thrust the wheels forward. The handles lurched out of my grasp! One second, one instant was left!! Without breaking stride, with everything in my heart, body and soul, I threw myself forward. Reaching, reaching, my fingers touched the handles, grabbed. My feet slid, stopping her...stopping at last.

Feeling resistance, the granny thrust downward on the wheels trying harder to go forward! Cars whizzed by only inches away!!! Still she pushed forward. Stunned at her power, I skidded, quickly turning the wheelchair away from the street toward the hill. She was safe.

Suspended time, motion, sound became real again. Every cell within me, every inch of my skin was buzzing. Cold air stung my face; cars rushed past; lights blazed invading the vacuum I just stepped from. Looking at her, the rushing of the passing cars seemed far, far away. The granny looked up at me in an odd silence. Realizing she was truly safe, I was suddenly warm and comforted, my pounding heart happy.

Angel Talk

I heard myself saying gently, "Where are you going?" What a foolish thing to say! Her eyes were a blank response, no recognition, no comprehension, no reaction. Then she replied in garbled meaningless gibberish that no person could understand. What did she know? What did she say? I only knew she had no clue of what she had done.

The granny was clad in a velour jogging suit, tied in the wheelchair with slippers on her feet, and totally unaware of the danger she had been in.

With my heart pounding, I gently pushed her wheelchair toward the senior center at the top of the hill. Again with astonishing strength she propelled herself uphill, dismissing my presence without a glance. Moments later we entered the lobby and I let her move away from me, watching as she disappeared down the hallway.

Two matrons seated at the desk looked up as I walked in with her. Approaching them, I said, "I want you to know that she made it almost all the way to Menaul." Their startled faces proved their ignorance of the granny's escape. My voice was flat, without emotion. One woman screamed and dashed down the hall after the granny; the other woman drooped in her chair, her face horrified at my words.

Suddenly feeling incredibly sad and relieved at once, yet longing to hear some kind of response, some expression of responsibility, I repeated, "I want you to know she made it almost all the way to Menaul." The woman stared at me incredulously, unable to reply. I turned sadly away toward the door.

Suddenly, it was all too much. Tears flooded my eyes—my legs shook at the realization of how close this pitiful, helpless, unknowing human had come to a terrible death. Stepping outside into the cold darkness, a helpless feeling of sadness plunged into the depths of my soul. Why was I so sad? Why was I not elated that I had caught her? Was it because the people responsible for her had not done their duty? Was it because of the terrible, unthinkable horror that would have occurred if I had missed? Darkness

The Wheelchair

enveloped me, sharpening my senses to the cold winter air, piñon smoke, the tall pine trees standing sentinel before the glistening city lights. But only sadness and silence stood with me on the step. And then I saw the lights, the only lights on the street...

Truth hit me like a bolt of lightning. The headlights of my car streamed like silver beacons of enlightenment. I was supposed to be there for the granny!! There was no one else to do it!! Only me!! No other cars drove on the street. No other cars turned onto the street. No other people walked from the office buildings. No other residents stepped from their apartments. There was no one—not one person on the street to see the granny, to stop her, save her. Only me. In the entire long, grueling seconds of my duel with the granny's imminent death, no one else in the world joined us on the street.

The reality of what had happened stunned me. Only three other times in my life had I felt that rare, absolutely true reason why I lived, why I survived the auto accident. Tonight was another. I breathed a prayer to God for letting me live, to be there, to be His tool, an instrument of His will on that dark winter night.

Now I knew why I had been making strange decisions since leaving work. The granny was the reason. She was the reason I delayed at the office, took the long way home, tarried at the store, changed shoes, went straight at the light on Menaul and Moon. All the way home, that long, long way home, those decisions I wondered about were not mine at all. At the gentle persistence of God and the Angels, I was running out the clock, measuring the moments until time put the granny in motion, until she made her great escape and was on the street wheeling toward her death. But she also had a rendezvous with me as I unknowingly made all the right decisions to see her, to stop her, to save her.

Time. In that brief moment of time, running alone to reach her, alone in the millennia of moments that seemed eternity, there was only one person in the world allocated to be on the street to save her. There was no one else.

Angel Talk

Sobbing in my car, shaking in the darkness with relief for averting the terrible tragedy, I prayed in gratitude, comprehending the humble guidance, kindness and magnificence of God and His Angels for helping me. As the memory disappeared so quickly into history, I recalled how critical every decision had been. Changing one decision would have changed the outcome of the whole tragic episode. Stopping for coffee instead of stopping at the store, and worse, if I had not changed my shoes, would have cost the granny her life. I could not have run as fast, run as hard, run as surely if I had not changed my shoes. That one simple little factor would have slowed me, prevented me from reaching her. The terrible consequence was too much for me to bear, to even think.

Yes, all the decisions I contemplated and made would have been for nothing had I made one single decision differently. If I had been less tuned into that steady intuitive part of me whispering back at me, I would have failed. That heavenly network of reality, magnificent realm of space, time and action slammed into my soul, and I was glad, so very glad, that I had lived.

Home was a half block away. As I lay exhausted, happy and sad for the granny, I wondered if she had sons or daughters who would be as glad as I that she had lived. I wondered what her name was. I wondered why she couldn't speak. I wondered what she knew and what I would never know. My awe at the power of God and all the Angels overwhelmed me as I prayed in deeper gratitude being able to keep her safe for one more day. I prayed with thanksgiving that my decisions had been the right decisions, and mostly that I had the strength to run fast enough to reach her.

There were only a handful of people I told of this terrifying event. A year later, when telling my brother, Rex, he listened awestruck. Finally, he softly said, "You have to take it one step further. You weren't there to save the granny—she was already lost. You were there to save the drivers of the cars that would have struck her. They

The Wheelchair

were the ones who would never have recovered from such a terrible accident."

Suddenly, I realized he was right. The whole sad story took on another dimension with the knowledge that there is always another level of involvement in life. We may or may not know or understand it, regardless of how closely we think we are tuned in. Life can change in an instant, never be the same again, just like the weather. There is always one more difference we may make in someone's life, whether we accept the responsibility, or not.

This tragic episode, though it had a happy ending, reminded me of another one that did not have a happy ending. He was a handsome, young officer who, while fishing with his father and small son, drifted into falling water from an overhead conduit. The boat capsized throwing them all into the frigid lake. He was able to swim with his son to the safety of fishermen in another boat. Then without hesitating, he started back through the freezing water to drag his father to the safety of another boat. With the boat too small to carry his weight as well, and though flagged from exhaustion, he began to swim for the distant shore. Bystanders stood watching, caught in the drama of this heroic rescue, watching as he neared the inlet where they stood.

But to the horror of bystanders, his feet became entangled in fishing lines a scant fifteen feet from the bank—fifteen feet from safety. Now too exhausted to call for help, too tired, too weary, he floundered desperately in the shallows. But not a single onlooker dived in to save him. No one came to his rescue. To their shame, not a single person threw him a rope, a line, an oar. No one did a thing...nothing. They simply stood on the bank and watched him drown...watching as the last desperate bubbles disappeared across the water.

Today his memory rests behind the glass of a picture frame, a beautiful, strong young man devoted to saving people's lives without a hesitation, without a flicker of a thought. All that is left is his widow's grief, his son, a medal for heroism awarded posthumously, and a few years of memories immortalized on yellowed newspaper clippings. None of those people on shore that tragic day tried to make a difference in the last moments of his life. No one made an effort to help him, not even after watching the courage in his brave heart unfold before them. Not even the fragile bond of humanity between strangers was enough to break the chains of fear—fear for their own lives—fear that stayed their actions and condemned their own courage forever.

In a tragic unanticipated moment, they were faced with a decision—to help a fellow human in danger, or to let him die. Not one of them could bring themselves to make that decision, to give him their time, their effort—a nominal effort with so many so near to help rescue him. Even if the bravest did not know how to swim, they still could have thrashed around and dragged him to safety in seconds. But they didn't. They were without courage to make a decision, and so he died.

Though many years have passed since stopping the granny, I remember the night as though it were only yesterday...all the thoughts, feelings, efforts of those terrible moments. And, I can only imagine the feelings of that magnificent officer swimming across the lake, probably like every other time before when he tried to save someone's life. Perhaps he had thoughts similar to mine as he swam through the icy water. But I know there is nothing I have ever tried so hard to do as reach that granny.

I used every ounce of energy and strength within me, blotted out every factor that would have stolen a fraction of energy, and breathed prayers all in the same instant to try to reach her. I was spared the unforgettable feeling of never reaching her, but that wonderful officer was not spared the unforgettable feeling of never reaching shore.

Many times I have prayed for courage, for strength to endure difficult times in my life, times that rose in an instant, or changed in a moment. But, none of the blessings I have known will ever be greater than the blessings God and the Angels have surely bestowed upon the soul of that young officer since the end of his own last day.

16

The Camper, 1987

PSALM 97

3   A fire goeth before him, and burneth up his enemies round about.

The Camper

As humans have known for ages, time has a way of changing heartache to happiness, despair to contentment, darkness to light. We have always known that dawn brings opportunities to ponder happiness, sorrows, sources of discontent. We also know that by the time enough sunsets spread their rainbows into the night, time will have brought clarity and enlightenment, understanding and hope, and our lives are generally directed toward the true goals of our hearts and souls. So time has shown us that time is the pathway to change that allows us to learn, to share, to grow—to become the best that we are to be in our lives.

For me, years passed with time being kind to me, healing my heart, my body, my mind. After all, I was alive—a functional, independent, contributing person, able to work and make decisions as I restored my life. Recovery led to phenomenal health and hope for good things in the future. I felt I could face the worst, including sudden reminders of those terrible years with the ex-husband.

At last, really and truly in control of my life, I determined to make changes that would ensure my well being and guarantee calm and safety—I found a new apartment. Safe on the second floor away from intruders or unwelcome situations, it even had a parking area below my window where I could see my car parked. All my ducks were in a nice row, work was good, writing was getting better. Perhaps I would even write that hit song someday.

It didn't take long to appreciate the new groove. Life was good. Friends and building good memories became the norm. When my brother, Rex, flew down from Seattle for his birthday, I had a happy hour party for him with dozens of friends from work. As we sang "Happy Birthday", Rex gazed down at his birthday cake glowing in the darkness. I thought what an honor it was to have lived so that I could see such a scene—a room full of my friends singing joyously that a special person in my life had made it one more turn around the sun.

Also since the accident, safety on the road was a real issue for me. It was easy to understand then, why my car was a four-door 1974 Ford LTD, a "tank" that, as I said, "provided as much steel as I could find between me and the next guy." My car was a safety zone that had saved me many times from bad drivers and I considered it a safety zone as important as my apartment.

Fortuitously, at the new apartment complex, one parking space behind our building was wider than the others, obviously poorly measured when the lot was striped. No one in my building had a car as big as mine, and I soon realized the big parking space was always empty when I came home. It was almost as though people were leaving it for my great big old car, something appreciated doubly as I could see the space from my second floor bedroom window. Over the months, I came to accept the space almost "as mine".

So days, weeks, months drifted by. No darkness shoved its way past the light, no intrusions into my happiness existed, until one night after work. As I drove to the parking lot toward my space, I was shocked to find it occupied...not by a car or a pickup truck. It was occupied by a camper...a Travel Queen camper.

The camper screamed at me, a black reminder of the past...it was a duplicate of the one owned by the ex-husband. That other Travel Queen camper had escaped the flames when the house burned; we lived in it while we shoveled ashes off the house slab. And it was where the ex-husband had brutalized me and I had been too sick to fight.

Sight of the thing sitting on its supports sickened me. Without a truck under it, it was obviously going to be there for awhile. Struggling to keep away tears, I thought, how could it be?! Why did such a thing have to be parked there, in my space?! Why did it have to be a *Travel Queen*! Why couldn't it have been some other little old camper shell thing without a thousand cruel memories to blast at me?! I sped away and parked on the other side of the building.

Of course any resident had a right to park where they wished. Whoever owned the camper certainly was not bothering anyone. It was out of sight, behind the building; plenty of spaces remained for other vehicles. But no one knew what it did to me. How could they know?! Only a few friends knew of the terror and horror of those years. What good could it do to talk about it? How could anyone benefit from hearing such things? Now, certainly no living soul would think that a camper parked behind an apartment building would matter to anyone except the owner. Who cares about a camper sitting in a parking space behind a building?

But the camper made the past real again in one glance. The scars are called "post traumatic stress disorder," and the smallest, most inconsequential thing can trigger memories of a trauma. A word, a glance, sound, smell, an image in a movie, a look from someone, the shape of a building--anything can bring it back. The victim relives it again without escape until reason presides over fear.

With the presence of the camper below my window, my safety net disappeared. Every day I dreaded leaving work because I had to drive into the parking lot where the camper and memories were waiting. If I glanced beyond the bedroom curtain, those sorrows shadowed happiness that I needed so desperately. So I parked far away, avoided that side of the building, kept my eyes averted when I walked down the sidewalk toward my door. Anything helped, but the camper and the past were so *near*!! And it hurt so badly...

Many would have said, "Get over it! It's no big deal! It's just a camper!" But no one knows the ramifications of abuse unless they have been through it. Few people understand that the victim may be trapped, unable to end the trauma until time and something good fill the space. Time. Time allows victims to create opportunities and experiences of happy memories, smiles, pleasant words to displace the trauma. Good times, pretty sights, joy, laughter, accomplishments will thankfully and ultimately free the victim.

So, when a victim watches a sunset disappear into the night, and says, "I had three hundred minutes of something good today," or, "What a great weekend we had!" they are, in truth, replacing the horrible memories with beauty and happiness that will bury the trauma until it no longer controls and destroys them. Time is the magic that allows the wonder of life.

But I couldn't get past the camper. I couldn't forget it was there, feet away from my world. Days passed. Weeks passed. My rare glances to check on it always confirmed its presence. I considered moving to another complex just to get away from the thing. Finally one night, my fear would change when apparently even the Angels got tired of listening to me moan over the intruder.

Mother called one evening and, several minutes into the conversation, an odd light flashed through my apartment, repeating almost like a strobing light. I said, "Just a moment, please, Mother; something is happening outside—I have to see what's going on." I opened the front door; nothing. But in the bedroom the moving light grew brighter. I pulled aside the curtain and looked down to see fire trucks, lights flashing, and firemen preparing to douse flames roaring from the camper.

No word could describe my feelings! In an instant, warm relief flooded through me—my nightmare was over!! I stared in disbelief at the scene below. Tears started. Had God and all the Angels rescued me again?! Then I told Mother what was happening. I told her the whole story, now about light instead of darkness.

Mother listened, I am sure remembering when she and Clinton had rushed to be with me, the nights they stayed at the house before it burned. Her words were wise, reassuring, agreeing that surely, one more time, God and all the Angels had taken mercy on my beleaguered soul and had intervened. Who was I to be so lucky?! What did They have in store for my life that They would be such great guardians of my heart and soul?! Then, too, how could I ever be anything except Their servant in acknowledgement of such blessings?!

By the time I told Mother good-bye, the camper below my window was a smoldering mass of charred metal and ashes. Looking again through the flashing lights of the fire engines, I thought how it resembled those terrible years—black, ominous, ugly. How, in brief moments, can a huge obstacle be reduced to nothing—nothing with no power, no possibility of creating harm or sadness? I thought how the black memories of the camper were destroyed by the light of fire, partnered with the lights of the rescuing firemen and their fire trucks.

The symbolism of past and present was gigantic in my mind: the sunrise of my restored life receding into the darkness of the past, only to be recaptured by the light of the all-changing, permanent power of the flames. Not lost on me, also, was the fact that Tom had burned the house, willing to create despair for the sole sake of money. Now, this camper, this terrible intruder in my life, was destroyed by the same force he used to destroy his property and mine for his own selfish benefit.

After the night of the fire, the constant awareness of this kind blessing stayed with me. No doubt about it, the passage of time carried again the light of love. Time changed reality so something good and better could displace the negative. Those few brief minutes of flames impacted my prayers ever more, pleading from my tiny human point of view that I might always be an instrument of God's will.

As humans we live within the parameters of our humanity, just as the camper changed my parameters and how I functioned. But as enlightened humans, we seek greater involvement within the parameters of Heaven. Understanding the gift of time, we are able to appreciate our lives on Earth, learning and growing and sharing. But hopefully we become enlightened and grateful by the staggering power and grace of God, His abiding love, light and protection. They are the greatest gifts a mortal could receive, but understanding these gifts and being worthy of them is the greatest responsibility a mortal could ever bear.

17

The Mexican Serape, 1989

PSALM 17

4   *Concerning the works of men, by the word of thy lips
I have kept me from the paths of the destroyer.*

The Mexican Serape

It was cotton, woven thick in bright red and white and blue stripes. The colors were right—America's—and I loved it from the moment my brother, Clint, handed it to me saying, "Here, this is for you. You might need it sometime."

He had just returned from Acapulco, Mexico where the sparkling blue waters had yielded the elusive, much-coveted marlin—a trophy every Montana fisherman wished for when the sub-zero winter winds howled outside the door! Most residents of the northlands would have made a run for the border if cattle and sheep and just surviving were not a priority. Now they vicariously enjoyed Clint's big score—the fish, the sunshine, the serapes and the escape from winter! He was proud of his fish, we were proud of him and I was proud of my Mexican serape!

Mexico and everything Spanish had long been a love of mine since high school. Now years later my first serape was a simple treasure I kept close, just like Clint had said—in case I needed it sometime. It stayed in my apartment for weeks, then my car, then back to the apartment. Finally, I zipped it in a plastic case and put it in the trunk of my car where it stayed—a warm, waiting friend, just in case.

For years, it went with me everywhere, sometimes coming out of the trunk as a picnic blanket, sometimes keeping me warm as I gazed at the moon on a cold night. And it was with me when I returned to Nashville to pursue songwriting. There, I wrote and became a supporter of other friends who struggled to make a break into the Big Time. Fame and fortune were the only passwords for every wannabe, and we dropped in at various clubs to listen and cheer them on.

One Saturday night in late November, we met at a community bar south of Nashville, a nondescript joint like so many tucked off the side roads past the winding hollows through the woods. The musicians figured any opportunity to make music was worth it, regardless of how obscure it was. After all, someone might hear them and someone else might give them the big break. But driving to this place was a little creepier after darkness fell—a real Goldilocks path. Trees climbed high on either side of the road; no white lines existed on the shoulder; deep ditches waited just off the pavement. And, deep in the woods, this road was one more to get lost on.

When the show was over, I asked a friend for directions home through the some twenty mile maze of hilly roads. Careful and specific, he explained, saying finally, "Then follow the road to the stop sign and that's Old Hickory. Turn left; take it to the stoplight and that will be Murfreesboro Road. Go straight through the light; you'll know where you are and you'll be on the road to home." My watch said 2:30 AM. I stored away his words and headed home.

Quickly, the black road in the black night became a black menace. The lonesome waterhole I left behind became a fond memory I would have preferred re-visiting. Hills and curves prevented speeding as I struggled to see the shoulder of the road. The deep bedrock ditches waiting at the edge were enough to discourage any driver in a hurry.

Tennessee has only inches of topsoil on limestone bedrock—bedrock that often must be dynamited to build most roadways. It is a costly endeavor with thousands of miles of road in the offing. Consequently, many country roads are only as wide as needed, often dropping two and three feet into the gully. An unskilled driver could easily find themselves stranded in the middle of nowhere with only a long, nervous hike for help ahead.

The black night and scary road had my attention! Back at the joint the band wasn't the only bunch needing a lucky break—I needed one just as badly and began to pray to God and all the Angels for my safe deliverance home!

At long last after more than an hour of creeping through the woods, I reached the stop sign. Hallelujah! Old Hickory Boulevard! My trepidations dimmed as the road improved and, happily, a gleaming red stoplight appeared. No other vehicle was in sight as I approached the light; suddenly I was exhausted and ready to be home. But in the same

The Mexican Serape

moment, without warning, a terrible feeling of danger and dread flooded over me, shocking my senses with a fear that literally shook me. As I drew closer and closer to the red light, the terror increased. As I stopped at the light, shaking and desperate, I wished I didn't have to go straight. I waited for red to become green.

Really frightened, I muttered, "He said to go straight! I don't want to go straight! I don't want to go straight! He said go straight!" The terrible feeling stayed with me. Over and over I said, "I don't want to go straight! I don't want to go straight!"

Almost in tears, I struck the steering wheel and cried out in despair, "I don't want to go straight!!" The sound of my voice jolted me. Calm replaced fear as I reasoned out loud, "Well, Whitmer, you know what happens when you feel like this—you better not go straight."

The light turned green. I turned left, the wrong direction. As I drove away from the intersection into new darkness, the terror began to diminish just as suddenly as it had overwhelmed me. The farther I drove from the light, the more the fear ebbed until, in a few hundred yards, it was gone. I was alright.

Only God in Heaven knew what was going on! Now too tired to care about why or what, I was relieved to feel normal again. Restored to my comfort zone, I quickly turned the car around, drove back to the light and waited again for it to turn green. What a night! It sure was taking a long time to get home!

Old Hickory felt good again. This time I turned left and up the hill towards home still miles away. But the night wasn't done with me yet.

Seconds later headlights appeared in my mirrors out of nowhere. A split second later a vehicle roared around me, engine screaming as it disappeared in the darkness! He was going fast, too fast, easily eighty or ninety miles per hour! It was a sleek, old model vintage El Camino, tailpipes thundering as it charged past me only to expose another set of headlights. Coming up equally as fast, as loud, the second car, too, roared around me!! Yes, in that second I guessed their speeds were nearly one hundred miles per hour for they were out of sight over the hill in an instant!

Horrified at such foolish risks in the night, this time prayers tumbled from my lips not only for myself but also now for them. Then I remembered the construction project over the hill where concrete barriers narrowed the road to two lanes. There was barely space for two vehicles to pass--at such speeds, they would never make it if they met someone. They would never clear...there was no room...there would be a crash!

In a flash my priorities changed to help the people that may be ahead. If they met someone, if it happened, God help us all! I cried out loud, "Please, Lord, please don't let them crash! Please don't let them crash! Please, Lord, please keep them safe! Please don't let them die!" Heart pounding, I sped over the hill to help the victims I knew were waiting. Seconds later I saw my prayers were answered.

Two cars rested against the concrete barriers. Steam spewed from the crumbled hood of the second car shoved into the trunk of the first. It was the second car that had passed me. But the first car wasn't the El Camino--the El Camino was nowhere in sight. I skidded to a stop in a restaurant parking lot and jumped out as people ran from the restaurant. Two dazed young girls staggered from the front seat of the first car, an old Cordoba. Fearing the gas tanks would blow, we hurried them away from the cars just as the driver of the second car stumbled from the door and disappeared into the woods!

Shaking from shock and cold, the girls huddled together, tiny, frail and terrified as we all watched the awful scene before us. The explosion never came. It never blew...there was no fire, no flames, thank God. Only the radiators spewed steam. We stood thanking God it was no worse than it should have been. Suddenly I remembered the serape! Clint had said, "You might need it someday..." Yes...the day...the black night had come.

The Mexican Serape

Seconds later its long, soft cozy length was wrapped around the trembling girls. Each held an end and snuggled together into it like Siamese twins, its bright colors covering them to their ankles. Now comforted, warmer, they waited with all of us for their fathers to arrive. Minutes later, police officers were securing the area, questioning witnesses, calming us with their presence. Soon the facts unfolded. The ordeal became an astonishing list of unbelievable details.

The police agreed the speeders were traveling nearly a hundred miles per hour at the moment they roared around me just as the girls had pulled onto Old Hickory from an apartment complex. Trying to get out of their way, the driver pulled her Cordoba as close to the barriers as she could, slowing to a near stop to let them by. The El Camino made it by, roaring over the hill out of sight, but the second driver had not seen the Cordoba ahead of his friend. There was no time to swerve, no time to miss. He had only a second to press the brake, but it was enough…one second to bring the frame of his car down to meet the frame of the Cordoba. Instead of the two cars exploding into oblivion, the speeding car shoved the solid steel Cordoba into the barriers where the crash was absorbed by the concrete. All three people were unhurt, the second driver obviously nimble enough to dash into the woods.

What a night! The police completed their witness reports which included several restaurant patrons who said the first speeding car was not an El Camino. The girls and I, however, held to our truths that the first speeder was in the El Camino. But, at last it was over; the police said we could go. The girls and their fathers stayed behind as I drove away.

Dark night was fading into dawn as I started for the third time over the hill for home. My thankful prayers for deliverance fell from my lips with every mile. Would this terrible night ever end?! The long drive through the woods, the terror at the light, the racers, the accident? All

Angel Talk

I wanted was peace and safety. I just wanted to get home in one piece. But terror was not finished yet.

Minutes after leaving the scene where wreckers and police cars filled the road, headlights ahead of me showed a car coming, fast. Petrified of a repeat of the last two hours, I slowed in terror as the car roared past me—it was the El Camino! He was coming back to find his buddy!! Good Lord God Almighty! He was going so fast he could never stop in time to miss the police cars and the wreckers on the other side of the hill! He was going to zoom over that hill and crash straight into all of those innocent people!! It couldn't be! It couldn't happen—not again! Overwhelmed one more time, fear became desperate sobbing prayers as I spun my car around and raced, one more time, after the speeding El Camino, already out of sight!

Weeping and terrified at what I would find, I crested the hill, knowing the sight would be worse than the one I imagined earlier. And they were there. Flashing lights, police cars, wreckers, Cordoba, El Camino, all filling both lanes of the road. But this time they were safe. There was no second crash. But it had been close!

The El Camino was stopped sideways in front of them all. Indeed, he had flashed over the hill to see the terrible scene before him, and, like his buddy, had just enough time to slam on the brakes and skid sideways to a stop in front of the astonished policemen and bystanders!! When I pulled up, a policeman stared, stunned to see me again--the only credible witness to support our claim of the El Camino. He rushed to my car, shouting, "Is it him?!" I nodded sadly. My prayers had been answered again.

One more time, I waited for the policemen to dismiss me, but this time it took only minutes. One more time, I started down the narrow tree-lined road toward home, the fourth time! This time my tears flowed freely with relief, not terror. This time my grateful prayers were jumbled gratitude that the night was over at last. I felt pretty certain it was. Darkness was now lost in the lovely rainbows of dawn as I thanked God and all the Angels that we were all alive, still.

The Mexican Serape

As the miles passed behind me, I recounted the nightmare night. Then, suddenly, I remembered the stoplight! The stoplight and that terrible feeling of dread, the fear until I turned left and drove away the wrong direction! That lucky break I had prayed for wasn't a lucky break at all. It was God and all the Angels listening, watching...

The terrible wreck should have been with me! I would have been where the Cordoba was! When I approached the stoplight the first time, the two speeding cars were already bearing down on the intersection. My desperate decision to turn left instead of going straight changed what was written. My decision altered the outcome of the collision waiting to happen. Those few seconds of diversion delayed me on the road. I would have been at the construction zone...they should have crashed into me.

If I had not stopped at the red light, I would have driven past the girls where they were waiting to pull out on the road. They would have waited for me as I passed them. They would have seen the speeding cars thundering up behind me, waited, and they would have watched as the cars crashed into me. They would have been spectators instead of victims. Only because of the few seconds when I refused to go straight was I saved from this tragedy.

Respecting my intuition kept me out of harm's way. My fate was marked by seconds of decisions that only I controlled. Everything else was waiting for my decision, even the Mexican serape--waiting for years for the night I would need it. I held my destiny in my hands and no one knew except God and all the Angels.

The insurance man called the next day to thank me for helping the girls. He asked if there was anything I needed, and I said, "Well, I would like to have the serape back again if that is possible." He said he would make certain it was returned to me. It never was. Probably because I would never need it again.

Obviously, the girls needed to have the Mexican serape. Though they never knew the story of the serape, maybe it has been the friend to them that it was to me. Maybe one of them has it still, maybe she uses it for her children. Maybe they share it; maybe they look at it and tell the story of that black night of speeding cars. Or maybe one of them uses it for a picnic once in awhile. Or, maybe she keeps it in the trunk of her car, just in case she might need it someday...

18

The Rijksmuseum, 1990

PSALM 31

21 Blessed be the LORD; for he hath shewed me his marvelous kindness in a strong city.

Angel Talk

"Eve! Eve! Hurry! Hurry! Call this number in the next five minutes and you'll win a trip for two anywhere TWA flies in the world!! Hurry!! Hurry!!"

"What?! What do you mean?!"

"I'll explain later! Just call right now!"

So Eve called and won the trip! Later, I told her that a friend heard her name announced on a radio promotion, "Eve Burke, if you're out there, give us a call in the next five minutes and you'll win a trip for two anywhere TWA flies in the world!" It was true! When the friend called Eve's home to relay the radio announcer's invitation, I was a guest, answered the phone and only too happily relayed the message to Eve at work! She called and the rest was "Where do you want to go?!" Thrilled with her prize, Eve and her husband planned for Europe. But, at the last minute, he relinquished his seat to me over concerns for his diabetic condition. Now it was May and we were bound for Amsterdam!

Equally as excited as Eve with my first trip to Europe, I told my friend, Dwayne Warwick, artist extraordinaire, of my plans to visit the world-renowned Rijksmuseum. The Rijks is one of the greatest museums in the world, home of the renowned "Nightwatch," by Rembrandt. Dwayne had himself spent his life enamored of the Dutch Masters, and had developed a unique style reminiscent of theirs. Dwayne, however, produced in watercolor what the Masters produced in oils six hundred years before!!

Nashville's "Images" magazine had recently featured a story on Dwayne, displaying his beautiful paintings so similar to Ver Meer and de Hootch. Gazing at the article, I instantly decided the Direktor of the Rijsmuseum should know about Dwayne's talent! He needed to know there was an American in Tennessee who admired the Dutch Masters quite as much as the Dutchmen themselves! Confident of my success, I confidently stowed two copies of "Images" in my bag for my forthcoming visit with the Direktor.

Why should I not see him? Surely I would see him!! Undeterred by circumstances that would no doubt prevent

The Rijksmuseum

it, I informed Dwayne I was hand-carrying the magazine to Holland to introduce the Direktor to his work! Dwayne stammered at my announcement, reluctant to hope for such a possibility—the Direktor of the Rijsmuseum?! Impossible!! But, it would be nice if someone in Holland, maybe a gallery owner or two, could see the article...

Amsterdam was our point of arrival in Europe. A friend from N.V. Philips, Haan Waalvijk, drove across Holland to meet us at Skiphol Airport, then happily showed us his homeland. We drove past the famous dykes holding back the ocean, to The Hague, then back to Eindhoven. There he and his wife hosted us for a long evening of dinner, piano and stories of their lives. When talk ultimately came round to art, I showed our hosts Dwayne's magazine article. Confidently, I added that I would be delivering the magazines to the Direktor of the Rijksmuseum when we returned from Paris!

Shocked at my cheeky confidence, Haan exclaimed, "The Direktor of the Rijksmuseum?! Ree-tah, you think that you can take these magazines to the Direktor of the Rijksmuseum?!! Why he is a very busy man in Holland!! Not even important businessmen can see the Direktor of the Rijksmuseum when they want!!"

Unphased, I replied, "Oh, that's alright, Haan. Dwayne's art is too good—it is just like the Dutch Masters and the Direktor *must* see it! He *must* know about Dwayne's paintings. So, don't worry, I'll get to him somehow!"

Taken aback, Haan countered, "Ree-tah! You cannot just walk into the Rijsmuseum and think that you can see him! You cannot go there and say, 'Hello! My name is Ree-tah. I am from Amer-ee-cah. I am here to see the Direktor!' That is like going to the White House and saying, 'Hello. I am here to see the Vice President of the United States!'"

Unfazed by his warnings of failure, I replied, "Oh, that's alright, Haan—he'll be there, I know he will! You just wait and see!" Haan shook his head in disbelief at my casual determination, still telling me as he drove us to our hotel that I could never get to the Direktor. We said our goodbyes then, and I laughed, "Don't worry, Haan! I'll call you when I get home and tell you what the Direktor said!!"

Europe was nearly my undoing. Overcome by the countryside, World War II, perhaps old memories from another life, I became another person from another time. My eyes searched for soldiers on every street. Though I was a non-smoker, I longed for a cigarette as we waited at every train station. Making change with foreign money was easy. I flipped through coins from Germany, Holland, France as though I had done it all my life!

In the streets of Paris, I felt as though I knew exactly where I was going, always aware of my bearings. How could it be? What was this sense that allowed me to know these things in strange countries? World War II and strange, foggy memories crowded my mind. Nervous, sorrowful and uncommunicative, I was overwhelmed, completely unprepared for the distant past. Even at Notre Dame, the Monmarte, and walking through the cobblestone streets, I could not overcome my sadness.

Still Europe was everything I "knew" it would be. In Aachen, Germany, we plunged into the spectacular ancient world of Charlemagne's cathedral. Whispering with other tourists within the great stone walls, we knew the Angels walked there.

Our time in Europe passed swiftly. Too soon it was time to return to Amsterdam for three final days of sightseeing before returning home. We had just enough time to see "The Hiding Place", the Van Gogh Museum, and of course, the great Rijksmuseum.

A huge, magnificent brick building, the Rijks was constructed in the late 1880's solely as a museum to "preserve and display treasures from the past!" Rembrandt's "Nightwatch" and countless treasures from around the globe dazzled us in gigantic room after room, bringing back school lessons from literature, history classes and biographies. The Rijks surpassed my wildest dreams of ever seeing them in living color!!

The Rijksmuseum

Not forgetting my phantom appointment with the Direktor, I asked a docent if it would be possible somehow to meet with the Direktor. Like Haan and his confident protests, she firmly informed me he was a very busy man—it would be impossible to see him. With that stroke of finality, I walked away thinking how easy it was to fail at something one could want so badly...impossible to see him. Haan was right. It was useless to try.

With my hopes to see the Direktor vanquished, I focused on Holland, complete with real Hans Brinkers, but also a different world in another way. Unbeknownst to us, our visit coincided with the fifty-year anniversary of Hitler's invasion of The Netherlands during World War II. There in Amsterdam, memories of the war were everywhere. Re-printed war posters showed in windows, people stood sadly on the streets remembering beside memorials, flowers rested against street signs, on park benches, at front doors, in front of buildings. Everywhere were reminders of those last places where someone beloved had lived and died during the unspeakable horrors of the Occupation. Though long gone, the war was everywhere, far beyond forgetting. And it rekindled my determination to see the last refuge of Anne Frank.

On our last night in Europe, Eve and I discussed over dinner our plans for the next day, our last in Holland. We decided to separate as she wanted to see a museum; I wanted to see Anne Frank's hiding place. So we went our ways, Eve to see Dutch art and I filled with trepidation as I rode the tram to the little Dutch house beside the canal. I was completely unprepared for what I would see.

There in the rooms where the families had hidden from the Nazis, more morose memories overwhelmed me, holding me as I stepped from room to room in the hiding place. In an instant the tragic energies overtook my soul as I learned first-hand the horrific Nazi crimes.

The hiding place was a place which, upon seeing, forced its truth on the visitor. One lived the struggle of Anne, her family, and friends against sure death by the Germans. It was also the place where I lost some of the freedom most

Americans forget they have. Oddly, in those brief days of Amsterdam with memories of World War II everywhere, I gained a greater responsibility to guard freedom for all peoples everywhere, a responsibility I have never been able to ignore since.

But at Anne's hiding place, I was determined to see and feel every single thing displayed in the hideaway, that unsure haven where the desperate group held out for freedom. For more than two years they hid behind windows covered away from the world. Now I saw videos from Nazi archives never before released. Possessions, items from their life, their words written on papers—all of it left me sick, numb and revolted at the unconscionable inhumanity and cruelty of humans against humans. At last, hours later I stumbled out the door almost blinded by sorrow. Numb with shock I hurried past the cathedral bonging its hour of prayer and caught the tram to a coffee house.

Notes of the hideaway flew off my pen. Angry, sad, nauseous, regretful, I made a promise to never forget, never pretend our American freedom was anything except vulnerable, precious and threatened. Finally calmed with steaming Dutch coffee, I rested in the quiet coffee house, slowly pulling myself back from the abyss of terror the little group had endured. The war was long, long ago, wasn't it?

As I reflected, I suddenly sat up straight. Without explanation, I exclaimed to myself, "I've got to go! I've got to get to the Rijks! I've got to see the Direktor!" Shocked, my mind racing, I thought, "Maybe I can reach him! Just maybe, even if they say I can't!"

Only a couple of hours remained in the afternoon—our flight was in the morning, no free time then. I had today! Right now! Tossing all my Dutch money on the table to surprise the waitress with the huge tip, I dashed out the door, around the corner and down the street! Without a map, no bearings for north, south—not even knowing which direction the Rijks was—I rushed down the street! I had to hurry to get there, wherever it was!!

The Rijksmuseum

Two blocks from the coffee house I stopped on a corner, thought where the Rijks would be, said out loud, "I think I need to go this way," and dashed straight ahead down an obscure street. Never pausing, down I hurried several more blocks, deciding on the run, I better go this way, then that way! Another left, another decision, dashing, almost running through the streets of Amsterdam.

I didn't know where I was going but I knew where I wanted to be! Finally, breathless but happy, I turned a corner and Bingo! There it was! Its red brick walls a half block away! Hurrying to the girl at the tour window, I asked, "Can you tell me where the Direktor's office is, please?" Unlike the docent earlier, she smiled, pointing where the magnificent wrought iron fence bordered the property. "At the end of the block in the cottage in the center of the gardens, Room 21." Almost there!

Hurry! Hurry! Rushing past the wrought iron fence around the corner to the open gates, I saw the entrance of Room 21. I made it! A Mercedes car waited with the trunk lid open. A man paced beside the car, glancing impatiently from his watch to the door as I entered the building.

Looking something like the entry of the Von Trapp home in "The Sound of Music", the lobby was light colored, long and wide, with marble tile and a ceiling rising two full stories. At the end of the room, a staircase led to a full balcony around the lobby. Chairs were placed along the walls, as well as a small desk with a telephone where a little elderly man sat, the lobby attendant.

I approached him, asking if I could speak to the Direktor's secretary. Motioning that he understood no English, he dialed the telephone and handed me the receiver. A youthful female voice asked in careful English, "May I help you?"

Quickly I explained who I was and described my American mission. She replied slowly that she would have someone else call and hung up. A moment later the phone rang again. The little man handed me the receiver and another woman spoke. I reiterated that I wanted "to leave for the Direktor an example of American art in admiration of the Dutch Masters..." She said someone would be down to see me and hung up.

While I was on the telephone, the pacing man by the Mercedes entered the lobby where he paced up and down. Checking his watch over and over, he looked at me, talked to the little man obviously about me, and paced. Then he hurried up the stairs, returning moments later to continue pacing across the lobby. Now certain that surely at least the secretary would be down to see me, and I would really get my magazines to the Direktor, I removed the two magazines from my bag, put my finger at Dwayne's article, and waited.

I refused to sit. Sitting would imply to the pacing man and the little lobby attendant that this was a casual visit. I stood in one place. Serious and respectful, I was secretly pleased that I had at least gotten this far! I was in the man's office, for Heaven's sake! Regardless of whatever happened from here on out, at least my efforts were not in complete vain!

The secretary would be down soon—my magazines with Dwayne in them *would* get to the Direktor! So, I stood still holding my magazines. The pacing man paced, checked his watch. The little man watched both of us. All three of us waited.

Nearly fifteen minutes passed. Again the pacing man went up the stairs. Then, to my delight, a tall, handsome man in a suit and trench coat, carrying a briefcase, hurried down the stairs. He was followed by two, three secretaries. The man walked up to me. Immediately I decided he *had* to be the Direktor—he *had* to be!! But, he also very possibly was not. The secretary did not say he was in. She said "someone would be down..."

When he said, "May I help you?" the secretaries stood on the stairs watching. The pacing man came down the stairs carrying two suitcases and hurried toward the car. I smiled at the stranger. Taken aback, he, too, smiled as we stood, eye to eye. My moment had come! Carefully and fast, I flipped the magazine open and started talking,

The Rijksmuseum

delivering my speech and Dwayne's Dutch Master art to Holland!

He glanced at the page, gasping in radiant surprise, and exclaimed, "I love it!" I explained they were for the Direktor so he could know someone in America loved the Dutch Masters, too. The man declared, "Wonderful! I shall read them in the car!" He thanked me over and over, shaking my hand. Still not knowing to whom I was speaking, I asked for his card "so that I may know…"

An odd look of surprise passed over his face as he pulled out his wallet and handed me a card. Thanking him, I said, "Are you leaving? I'll walk you to your car!" At the car, I said goodbye and walked down the drive. When I turned to wave, he was still standing by the car, watching me with a happy, puzzled look on his face as I walked through the gates and out of sight.

I had done it! At least I had gotten to someone at the Rijks!! Almost floating, I looked down at the card, smooth and white in my hand…*Dr. H. W. van Os. Direktor General…!!* It was he! I had gotten to the Direktor himself!!

Amsterdam and flowers…Anne Frank and her hiding place…posters from the war in the windows…All of them became a gentler memory as I strolled slowly down the Kade toward the hotel. Overwhelmed that God had led this stranger through the strange city, right up to the front door of the Rijksmuseum, I thanked Him over and over again!

Contrary to what anyone may think, I decided the Direktor had been waiting for me! Why of course! God and all the Angels had kept the pacing man waiting and the Direktor General lingering in his office, Room 21, all because a girl from America had a magazine and was rushing from Anne Frank's hiding place to give it to him!

I gasped in amazement recalling how close I came to missing him!! Why, we had only minutes to spare—probably seconds, judging by the pacing man peering at his watch when I entered the lobby! How close can it get?!

Angel Talk

It is true! God manages life and time down to the wire, and He is always, always in control. Always.

When we landed in New York, I called Haan and told him what the Direktor said! Incredulous, he exclaimed, "No, Ree-tah! You did not see the Direktor!" "Yes, yes, I did, Haan!! And I have his card to prove it!!" As I laughed, he exclaimed over and over, "No, it is not possible! It is not possible!!"

Later, we would laugh again over the first stories of *Angel Talk* that I had left him. An admitted agnostic, he said solemnly, "It is a wonderful thing, this book, *Angel Talk*, that you have written." I think I made a believer out of my dear friend, Haan!

Back home in Nashville, I wrote the Direktor and thanked him for seeing me, suggesting he consider visiting Nashville someday. He wrote back saying that perhaps someday he would! Dwayne had the precious business card matted and framed where it hangs on his wall today, not only as a reminder of a great director in one of the world's greatest museums, but also as a token of God's wondrous works. After all, when everything was said and done, it would appear that God, the Great Master Himself, loves the Dutch Masters and those who love them as well!

The Rijksmuseum

HOOFDDIRECTIE

RIJKSMUSEUM amsterdam

POSTBUS 50673
1007 DD AMSTERDAM
TELEFOON 020 - 73 21 21

Miss Rita Whitmer
801 North Oaks Drive
NASHVILLE, Tennessee 37211
U.S.A.

Uw referentie	Uw brief van	Onze referentie	DATUM
	30.6.1990	hvo/nbs	18 juli 1990

Dear Miss Whitmer

I was very pleased to receive your kind letter of June 30, 1990. The pleasure was mine to be introduced to the work of Mr. Dwayne Warwick! I also thank you very much for the nice issue of the Nashville magazine, I read it with interest.

Looking forward to - once, I hope - a visit to Nashville and to see you again.

Sincerely yours,

Prof. Dr. H.W. van Os
Director General

Ingang museum: Stadhouderskade 42
Hoofddirectie, Hobbemastraat 21

POSTGIRO 425180
AMROBANK 43.30.66.006

19

The Cowboy, 1992

PSALM 20

7   Some trust in chariots, and some in horses; but we will remember the name of the LORD our God.

The Cowboy

Once again, Montana was home for my wandering soul. Since Nashville denied me the song contract I had coveted for years, I decided to return to Montana, get a job in Billings, have my beloved mother come live with me and settle down forever—without music. Good thought. Good intention. I knew good businesses always needed good executive secretaries, regardless of what part of the country they were in. Good things would come of my decisions—good enough that perhaps at last I could settle down. Abuse victims seldom believe in safety. Perhaps I could finally get far enough away from Tom so I could live in peace without fear of his attacks.

To say that Montana is different is an understatement. Every spectacular mountain range, sweeping green valley and sagebrush prairie controls every human that walks its magnificent, challenging expanse. It has been said that everything in Montana bites—rattlesnakes, mosquitoes, deer flies, hail, the cold, the sun. But the mortals who choose to live there accept the odds of survival with a courage and determination unique to westerners. Their grit is reflected in their eyes, the same clear-eyed, steely glances Zane Grey and Louis L'Amour wrote about in their romance novels.

Such stories are filled with cowboys braving and overcoming the worst only to glory in the best of the West! Always steady, ready for action, decisions, mistakes, misfortune, the luck of the draw, the cowboy heroes, and the real ones in Montana, are ready for anything that might thwart freedom in their unpredictable world.

My siblings and I knew what that was like. We learned it firsthand when we lived on Grandfather Calk's ranch west of Jordan. Riding the range on old Pinkie and Patches, chopping wood, hauling water, feeding cattle in forty below zero, it was all part of our own real cowboy life. Pretending to be Lewis and Clark, we rode through gullies and sagebrush and learned how to be ready for anything Fate or the weather threw our way.

Our Uncle Joe was the same when he was a cocky, teenage cowboy at Brockway Dairy Day Rodeo. Climbing atop a wild bronc in the bucking chute, Uncle Joe settled into the saddle, shoved his boots through the stirrups and gathered up the halter rope as the raging bronc thrashed and pawed. When the cowboys manning the chute hollered, "Are you ready?" Uncle Joe responded with three words, "I *COME* ready!!" As horse and rider burst into the arena, Uncle Joe surely had no idea his confident proclamation would carry him to a fame greater than the heaving bronc pitching him to the dirt! To this day, and as it has been at the Brockway Rodeo for decades since that first ride, cowboys sitting gingerly on broncs are asked, "Are you ready?" The brave reply is the same: "I *COME* ready!"

So, being ready for Montana meant to understand there is no lazy, tranquil look in the eye of a Montana man or beast. Being ready is a cowboy's willing courage, mirrored in his hats and boots and rugged clothing needed to endure the endless rigors created by the elements and creatures around him. Being ready is that famous "Code of the West" lived by pioneers struggling westward and cowboys driving trail herds north from Texas. It is a code repeated every day when strong, magnificent cowboys sweep their great hats off in front of white-haired grandmothers or deliver a well-directed swing at the drunken fool in a saloon who grabs for his untouchable headpiece.

That cowboy confidence is well-deserved, an arrogance honed by winning countless desperate battles against snowdrifts and inhuman cold, saving their cattle and sheep and surviving other seemingly endless tragedies and triumphs. Their intensity, recklessness and honesty are found often in places where few people and limited resources exist to support their survival. Cowboys simply don't have time to waste on fluff. They measure their lives according to the next priority that guarantees their freedom and readiness to survive.

Freedom. Montana is freedom to roam the range, the mountains. It is freedom to hunt, fish, ranch, farm—do just as one may want, and freedom is the life of the cowboy.

The Cowboy

In my mother's youth, horses were the mainstay that guaranteed freedom, but now today, cowboys have different chariots. Though horses still fill their lives, the powerful four-wheel drive pickup truck carries them through their rugged world with a recklessness no different than their forebears on horseback in another time.

So the question to Uncle Joe was the same for me on my return to Montana. I had been gone years—was I ready for what Montana had in store for me? Reaching far back in my memory to recall "the way it was", I told myself I had to be ready for anything—absolutely any crazy thing that might come along, indeed, even out of the blue.

Such a world would be a shock after the warm, slow, easy living I had enjoyed in the South. Few obstacles to life exist in those sunny climes. Contrary to the constant challenges of Mother Nature and simple survival in Montana, southern citizens enjoy different, more casual cultures and traditions, courtesies, manners and behaviour. Their everyday life is tempered by agreeable climate and constant influence of Bible-quoting preachers. Little did I know that soon I would learn that God's loving hands were as close as they had been to me in the South, close enough to save me and a few unsuspecting Montanans around me.

One Saturday afternoon, I wound my way across Billings, deciding to take Parkhill Drive home. It was a lovely street with older, beautiful homes not far from the Rimrocks. Driving slowly, I gazed at the great red sandstone cliffs where traces of old buffalo jumps still lingered. On those cliffs for hundreds of years the Indians had charged buffalo off the rims for an easy kill. Now brightly colored homes bordered the streets, so different from Nashville's brick homes.

Enjoying my drive, I soon approached a four-way stop and waited as other cars took their turns through the intersection. Three other cars were at the stop signs, the car on the left approaching just before I reached mine. As the others passed on their way, I waited for the car

Angel Talk

on the left, an old, dark green sedan with an elderly gentleman at the wheel.

The old man waited, almost as though he were asleep, seemingly oblivious to getting on with his driving. Long, slow seconds crept by as a car pulled in behind him, then another behind me, another across from me. I waited, saying to myself, "It is not my turn. I will not go; it is not my turn." We waited for the old man. And we waited.

I realized that what started as a leisurely drive across town had now become a stalemate with an old man at a four-way stop! Thirty. Forty. Forty-five seconds passed. I said out loud, "What is the matter with you, Mister? It's your turn!" Still he sat. Still I waited, and we all waited.

More cars pulled in behind me, across from me and behind the old man. I refused to be impolite; I refused to go before my turn. I would not break the law. I would not be rude. Where I was from, people had manners everywhere you went. Being rude was not part of my life and I wasn't going to start being different in Montana. I waited. The other drivers looked at the old man, then back at me. I waited.

By now, impatient and angry at the old man's failure to move forward, I struck the steering wheel and exclaimed, "It's *your* turn, Mister! Would you go, please?" Of course my explosion did nothing to change the stalemate. The old man still waited.

By now, over a minute—*more* than a long, minute—had passed. The other drivers sat, too, waiting for the old man, then me, to cross the intersection. Then in an instant our impatience changed to shock...

Out of the blue, over the hill on my right came a speeding four-wheel drive pickup truck with a cowboy at the wheel! Barreling down the hill toward us, the cowboy drove through the intersection where we sat. Stunned in disbelief, we watched frozen as he disappeared over the hill! Moving easily sixty miles an hour, he had blasted in and out of our lives in a second as we sat motionless in shock!

The Cowboy

Then, as though he knew the cowboy would be coming through, the old man in the green car slowly pulled forward, turned left ahead of me and drove out of sight.

None of the cars in the intersection moved. It was as though we all needed to comprehend for just another moment what had just happened! I was drained at the thought of what might have been, what had been, what now raced through my mind. Of course it was all understandable! Of course the stalemate was clear! I knew, and surely the other drivers knew, why we waited for the old man. I wondered, "Had he been an Angel? Was he the only one of us who knew that wild cowboy was on his way toward us, threatening our very lives?!"

None of us had honked; no one had rushed through the intersection out of turn. What had kept us still? If the old gentleman had paused, then started through the intersection, he would have been struck broadside by the cowboy. Or, if I had gone out of turn, I would have been in the intersection when the cowboy roared through. The truth was undeniable. If any car had started forward, someone would have been in the intersection, would have been hit. Cars would have been crashing off each other like bouncing balls at the tremendous speed the cowboy was traveling! If I had started the chain of cars moving out of turn, it would have been a lose-lose for everyone at the stop signs. Inevitably, all of us would have suffered an agony of injuries or death or the memory of something we would never have been able to forget. But God and all the Angels were ready for the cowboy...

Parkhill Drive was more beautiful as I finally drove slowly down the street. Shaking and grateful, I breathed thanks again to God and His Angels for delivering us safely past that reckless cowboy. He was no doubt a wonderful young cowboy, probably fresh off the range and hadn't seen a four-way stop in months. He was probably a cowboy who wasn't ready to die or to kill someone on a beautiful Saturday afternoon in town. Maybe he was just a cowboy who would have wanted, instead, to die with his boots on. Maybe he was thinking about doing something

Angel Talk

he liked better, like riding a bronc on a different trail than this city street. We did not know who he was, but we knew he was a cowboy who would never know I waited for an old man...and God waited for all of us.

So it was that God and all the Angels were ready for the cowboy, for the old gentleman and for all of us at the stop signs. We were supposed to live another day. They were ready to silently keep telling me to be polite as we all waited. They were ready to save our lives because we were not ready to die...we didn't even know our lives were in jeopardy.

Such, indeed, is the way with life...being ready for what we anticipate and also being ready for something out of the blue, something beyond our scope of imagination or anticipation. We are reminded that our trail of life is intended to be both what we make it, and what others make it. And, if we're lucky, if we make good decisions, if we have consideration for others and respect for the law, usually that behaviour results in a good life. But, just as the world has watched Americans become unique in the world, ready for almost anything, we must also remember that our trail of life is simply sometimes in the gentle, loving hands of God and His ever-watchful Angels!

20

Gladys Baker, 1994

PSALM 19

13 Keep back thy servant also from presumptuous sins; let them not have dominion over me; then shall I be upright, and I shall be innocent from the great transgression.

Angel Talk

It was time to go back to Nashville. Success was not mine yet. I had not kept my promise to God: "Please, Lord, please, if only I can make it to the dawn, I promise I'll do something with my music." Since December of 1974 it had consumed my thoughts night and day, unfinished business that would not go away. My heart and soul said I had not given it the chance I should. Now it was February, 1994, and I decided to try one last time to get my songs recorded in Nashville.

For three months I had stayed with Mother on her farm, safe in that snowy world but barred from travel by constant ice on the highways and blizzards sweeping in again and again. One break was promised by Valentine's Day with enough sunshine to warm the roads. I prepared to make a run for the border—the long happy weeks with my mother were coming to an end.

For endless hours, she had charmed me with reminisces of her own childhood on the ranch, riding the range and her father's ancestral home back in Kentucky. Her memories of life with my father and raising all nine of us were precious to me and I loved every minute we shared. Mother updated me on the local farmers nearby on Nickwall Road—those who had moved away, who had children, who had died, what they left behind. When it was time for me to leave on Valentine's Day, I wondered when I would be back. What did my future hold? Of course it would be different from hers, but only God knew the details. I knew for sure it would be interesting, more than a little bit of qué sera, qué sera!

As I drove slowly away from my beloved mother, the road bounced up to meet the car, just as rough and rugged and unchanged as thirty years before. I thought of Mother's life there, driving that road past the neighbors every day, her days intertwined with everyone else's through brutal winters, wet springs, dry summers. Seldom was there ever perfect weather in between.

As I passed Roy and Gladys Baker's old place, I remembered Gladys from the times as a young girl that I babysat for her and Roy. Sorrowfully I recalled that she was

Gladys Baker

a kind, tender-hearted soul with tragic eyes, undoubtedly because of the meanness Roy visited upon her during the grueling labors of raising pigs and farming. Back then, she had been about the same age as my mother, her hair gray and rolled in an old-fashioned bun. She wore dresses with anklets, seldom spoke, perhaps because several of her teeth were missing. Her silence could have been, too, because Roy seemed to do all the talking when they were out and about.

Like everyone in the country, Gladys and Roy worked endless hours on their farm, having little energy left to visit neighbors. When in town, Gladys was with Roy and was seldom seen visiting neighborhood women. She was alone on the pig farm with Roy. While men in the area surely knew more details about Roy and Gladys, it was known that Roy was an unkind man and Gladys' plight was pitied by many.

As Mother and I visited over countryside news, she said Roy and Gladys had moved away years before Roy passed on. Gladys now lived near her daughters somewhere around Glendive, more than a hundred miles away. But as I drove past the old buildings, memories of a terrible night there decades before came back. Gladys had saved me that night from a fate no human should ever know, but one that too many girls do.

When I was twelve years old, Gladys called Mother asking if one of her daughters could babysit the baby while she and Roy went to a movie. I am certain that Mother felt sorry for Gladys and was glad the poor woman had an opportunity to have something good to remember, even if it was a movie. She said that I was available. Roy picked me up and we returned to their tiny old homestead-style house.

As Gladys briefed me on the baby's needs, Roy blasted her with shouts to hurry, waving his arms and calling her names as she put on her coat. She picked up her purse, an old two-handled item, clasped her hands together through the handles and turned to face Roy at the door, just as I looked to the other end of the living room.

Angel Talk

To my horror, there in a corner, almost hidden in the darkness, stood a great tall, hulking young man perhaps eighteen, leering and drooling at the mouth. Obviously, he was mentally impaired. I had no idea anyone else would be at the house while Roy and Gladys were gone, and surely not someone like this person! I was petrified at the sight of him!

Though tall for my age, I knew I was nothing against the strength and intent of such a human being! Nothing! Anybody could guess what was lurking in his brain and what would happen when Gladys and Roy were gone. What could I say? What could I do? I was twelve years old, alone on a farm, miles from help if I needed.

Terrified that in minutes I would be alone with this person, I stared at Gladys. She stood calmly holding her purse, her toothless mouth puckered closed, chin raised. Roy shouted, "Hurry up! Hurry up! We're going to be late!" Then Gladys calmly replied, "He's going with us." Roy erupted! "He ain't goin' with us! He's stayin' here!"

Wild curses fired back at Gladys, jolting me in shock. I had never heard a man attack a woman before and certainly not in a little house with my parents far away. No doubt about it, Gladys and I were females alone against one raging man and another retarded one! Again she said calmly, "He's going with us." Again Roy blasted her with even angrier, uglier words. Still calm, she repeated, "He's going with us."

Throughout the entire assault, Gladys never moved, never flinched at Roy's foul insults. She never wavered, her hands folded calmly against her coat, holding her purse as though she were visiting with the parson after church. Finally, perhaps knowing his wife was capable of occasional stubbornness, Roy gave in. He put a coat on the fellow and they left me alone with the baby. When they returned, nothing was said. Roy drove me home without ado.

Those thirty-three-year-old memories were vivid as I drove down the Nickwall Road to the highway. Now in my forties, I knew well what would have happened if Gladys had not stood her ground against her awful husband. Back then, I was only a child and didn't know cruelties were committed against children. But I felt the danger! I knew intuitively I would be harmed at the hands of that person, and I was helpless to save myself...Gladys was my only savior.

As the miles passed, I sorted through the facts, remembering Gladys, so calm, so determined, so unafraid of Roy as he raged. I wondered if he beat her after I was gone. I wondered how many times he raged afterward and punished her with more ugly words and insults. Or worse, did he punish her for her "insubordination." The more I thought of the nightmare, the more grateful I was to Gladys for protecting me, for guarding my innocence, for saving my childhood.

Out loud I said, "Lord, I really wish I could see Gladys again so that I could thank her for what she did that night. I wish I could tell her how much it mattered to me then, and how much it matters to me today to know she had the courage to save me." But the road to Nashville was long, I was far away in northeastern Montana heading for Billings, and I knew I would never see Gladys again.

Nearly three hours later, I reached the freeway at Glendive. More anxious than ever to put miles behind me, I decided not to stop for lunch, but dashed into the side door of the McDonald's for a quick rest room stop before leaving town. Minutes later, I stepped to the sink where a woman stood, drying her hands. I glanced at her reflection in the mirror and saw Gladys Baker.

Of course she didn't recognize me. How could she know me, but how could I know her? Of course I knew her! She was the same!! I knew it was her!! I stared at her in disbelief! I had just asked God and the Angels to see her again, to have the chance to thank her again! What a blessing that she was beside me now!

Quickly I asked, "Excuse me, aren't you Gladys Baker?" She looked at me and smiled a little smile—she had teeth!!—and replied, "Yes." I said, "My name is Rita Whitmer. We lived on Nickwall Road, and I have just spent the last two hours thinking about you and something you did for me when I was twelve years old."

She looked at me, now a little old lady holding a million, million memories in her head. She did not reply as she tried to sort out who I was, what I was saying. Then the door opened and a young woman said, "Mom, are you ready?"

Gladys started toward her—she was leaving! Maybe she didn't hear me! Maybe she didn't believe me! Desperate to stop her, I said, "Excuse me, my name is Rita Whitmer. Are you her daughter?" The woman replied, "Yes." Again, I explained who I was, that I had just been wishing that I could see Gladys and thank her for something she did for me long ago. The woman responded happily, "Oh, I remember you! Your family lived right down the road from us! We were just leaving—we've been here over an hour and we were just going! My sister is here and two of our kids. Let's go sit down and you can tell all of us!"

So, flooded with warm, happy feelings of one more blessing in my very unique life, I sat down with Gladys Baker!! As her daughters and her grandchildren listened intently, I told them the story of that night when I was a child, a night that would have changed my life forever.

Gladys listened and finally said, "I don't remember that person. I don't know anyone like that." One of the daughters explained, "Oh, yes, Mom. That was Uncle Henry's** son. He used to stay with you and Dad a lot." Gladys looked off trying to find the memory in her mind, then discounted it with a shrug. The girls laughed at the incongruity of our chance meeting and we parted, surely never to see each other again.

I drove away from Glendive, exclaiming in glad astonishment. Crying soft, happy tears, I rejoiced to have a prayer answered again, and in such a place as the ladies' room of the McDonald's restaurant! What if I had slowed down on the highway?! What if I had decided to keep going?! What if her grandchildren had said, "Hurry up! Let's go!" I would have missed Gladys! I would have

---

**   Name has been changed.

missed telling her how much she mattered to me all those long, long years ago!

Seconds!! Seconds was all that was between Gladys and me! She was drying her hands! She would have been out the door moments later! Seconds later, she would have been gone and I would never have seen her! We would have missed. Missed. But we didn't.

Moments such as these are gigantic gifts from God and all the Angels to help us deal with our lives. They help us sort out the memories in our hearts, to satisfy the guilt, regrets, hopes and all the needs and wants we have as we grow. These moments are gifts so that we can live more complete lives, lives that are intended to be parts of the whole. When we are able to share and grow, our lives take on added value and enhanced meanings that in turn enhance the lives of others.

Seeing Gladys again remains one of the most special moments of my adult life. She was a wonderful gift from my past, a wish and hope that never became a regret. If I had not been able to see Gladys, a part of me would always have regretted not making an effort to find her, call her, write her. That need to thank her would never have gone away. I would always have wanted to tell her of my gratitude.

Not always as humans are we able to accomplish the end result we plan for, the goal we hope for. We do not always achieve the consequences we need from our decisions. Sometimes we need help to get there. And, sometimes if we ask for it, it comes to us...glorified and grand from the Highest Source, the Greatest One. After all, it is God who knows the past, the present and the future. It is He, who with all the Angels, knows what we need in our human lives to reach the goals of our souls. And it is up to us to always be grateful for receiving His Gift.

21

The National Cemetery, 1994

PSALM 28

7   The LORD is my strength and my shield; my heart trusted in him and I am helped; therefore my heart greatly rejoiceth; and with my song will I praise him.

The National Cemetery

Sometimes there are moments, times in our lives that we want to remember forever. We want to remember every detail, every word, every motion so those special moments will be with us completely whenever we think of them. Memorial Day weekend at the National Cemetery in Nashville was such a time for me. I share it now because it was one of the greatest joys of my life.

In March of that year, I gave a tape of my POW/MIA song, *Home Free*, to Fred Tucker, chairman of the Memorial Day ceremonies in Nashville. I gave him free license to do with it as he wished for the upcoming events at the National Cemetery.

Fred was a retired Marine and Viet Nam veteran. Meeting him and learning of his work on behalf of the veterans was a special time. He read the lyrics and wept, saying that he would present the song to the Committee for consideration.

A few days later, he surprised me, saying, "The Committee has decided that we want *you* to sing *your* song at the ceremonies. We have you on the program for Sunday at the State Veterans' Cemetery and Monday at the National Cemetery." So it was that I was on the program to sing my song, the first time I had sung in a formal public event. It would be one of the great honors of my life, but I had no idea how much of one it would be.

First order of the day was inviting my nephews in the Army to attend. Ross was at Fort Knox in Kentucky, and Warren and his wife, Tamberly, were stationed at Fort Bragg in North Carolina. Knowing the importance of Memorial Day to military personnel, I thought it would be a special occasion for them as well as myself. I asked Ross' sister, Kristi, in Montana to come; the cousins had not been together in over ten years and all agreed to meet in Nashville.

For the next two weeks, I practiced with the soundtrack. I had plenty of time, but wanted to get the song down early. To my distress, I caught a cold, which became near pneumonia and coughing spells that persisted day and night. I considered calling Fred to say I could not sing, but something stopped me. Something told me I would be

Angel Talk

alright. I had to do it for the POWs, for the MIAs, for their loved ones. I had to do it for the song, not for me.

Sunday morning at the State Veterans' Cemetery dawned clear and bright without rain. Ross and Warren sparkled in full dress uniform, tall, handsome and proud. Tamberly and Kristi were sweet and supportive, confident I would sing well, in spite of coughing. As we drove to the chapel along the winding road lined with flags, I swigged Robitussin, fought the cough and considered myself blessed to sing at such a lovely place.

A crowd of some 600 gathered on the little plaza beside the chapel as the sun rose, warmer and warmer. Fortunately, a steady breeze cooled the waiting guests seated facing the podium where nearby a chair draped with the POW/MIA flag was placed. It was the silent honor to America's missing soldiers. Soon it was time to start. The program participants were seated and the ceremony began.

As we stood in the brilliant sun waiting for the flyover, the magnanimity of the occasion filled my heart. No tears could stay away this day, especially with the lyrics I had written. I was so glad I was alive, that I had written the song. God had been in charge, had seen me through the tribulations in my life, and now I was part of one of the most important ceremonies in America. I had nothing to fear, not even a cough.

Soon the guest speaker, a tall handsome captain from the Corps of Engineers in Omaha, plied our hearts with thoughts of past wars, of America's soldiers. He closed his speech with remembrances of our boys missing in action. And then it was my turn.

Carried by the music, the pathos of the lyrics, I sang with all my heart. Across the audience, somebody's mother watched me, her head thrown back, almost defiant as her tears flowed unheeded down her face. Her sorrow made me choke as I looked away. A man removed his glasses to wipe away his tears. He never looked up again, sitting quietly in his chair sobbing, wiping his tears over and over as I sang. Overwhelmed, my voice cracked in sorrow—his grief was more than I could bear.

The National Cemetery

Struggling for control, I sang to the memories of those wonderful soldiers and to the ones who loved them. The drums beat slowly into silence; the crowd sat, silent.

Later as guests greeted me, I thought again how glad I was that my voice was restored enough to sing, that my hand worked well enough that I could play the piano. I thanked God that my brain worked well enough to write the song. Yes, all those years of trying to do right and live decently mattered, not only for my own responsibility to life, but also to others.

Then, a tall, distinguished gentleman walked toward me. His VFW cap was embroidered with "Normandy". With tears brimming his eyes, he clasped my hand, and said, "I cannot tell you enough how much it matters to hear your song. Thank you. Thank you." He looked so much like my father that I was overcome with sadness. I hugged him tightly; then he laid his head on my shoulder and we cried together. My life's agony was worth it to be able to comfort this wonderful old soldier, as he wept for his buddies lost in a war far away, long ago.

The four cousins and I drove to the 101st Airborne Restaurant, the place where I had seen the MIA bracelet that inspired the song. Surrounded by sandbags, memorabilia and photographs from the World War I, World War II, the Korean War and Viet Nam War, we visited, listening to Ross and Warren tell their own Army stories. When I left my special companions, I had no glimmer of a thought that in a few more hours I would see, before my eyes, a wink from God that would leave me awestruck for the rest of my life.

That night sleep evaded me, coughing spasms lasted too long, prayers were only to help me through the next day. Seeing people weep had nearly been my undoing so I vowed the next day I would look only at the sky, flags, the trees—no faces, no tears. It was going to be tough.

Time neared for the ceremonies. After watching Ross and Warren polish and shine brass and boots once already, I suggested the cousins spend the day together instead of sweltering in uniforms again. Relieved, they quickly made plans for the day and to meet me after the ceremonies. I left for the National Cemetery alone.

The great stone archway at the entrance spread high above the flag-lined driveway. Nearby, a giant American flag blew in the gusting wind, sentinel to the beautiful grounds where some 35,000 soldiers lay. A gray stone wall surrounded the cemetery, protecting the beautiful white marble markers precisely aligned in the green grass. An American flag was at each marker; others flew everywhere. Red white and blue bunting graced the magnificent granite rostrum where military unit banners stood. Hundreds of chairs waited for the guests in front of the rostrum where a single chair draped with the POW/MIA flag rested in the place of honor.

This was the place—this beautiful place—where I would sing for our soldiers lost somewhere back in time. It was overwhelming. The beauty, solemn grandeur, tranquility of this hallowed place humbled me to tears. As a cough jerked me out of my reverie, I despaired, how *ever* would I get through it? What was I to do? Silent prayers all night were now pleas out loud for help. The day, the weekend, the soldiers—it was too special to fail. I had to do it right. I had to.

Though I arrived early, hundreds and hundreds of flower-laden mourners moved slowly through the graves and sentinel trees, searching the markers for the names of their loved ones. Winds gusted fiercely, thrashing the magnificent tree branches up and down, flags whipped. Beyond the cemetery wall, traffic hurried in usual noisy fashion. A train roared nearby; police sirens screamed. It was mayhem in the serenity of the cemetery. Soon I found my friends, visited briefly, and walked to the rostrum to do a sound check. But there was no recorder...

Shocked at the prospect of singing with no music, I found an official who assured me a recorder would be coming. Soon Fred arrived to learn there was a glitch—the recorder had been left behind. There would be no soundtrack. No music.

But I was a novice singer—a writer, not a singer, a coughing singer! Dear God in Heaven, I would be singing

The National Cemetery

alone...a cappella. No music was any real entertainer's nightmare. I sat stunned with my friend, Katy, thinking. Yesterday I sang seriously for the first time in my life in front of a real audience. Today I would sing in an even more heart-wrenching place, against the wind, to perhaps a thousand or more people. The whole scenario had disaster written all over it. Yet, my heart beat calmly, my stomach didn't roll. I felt completely under control without a qualm. Somehow, it would be alright.

Undaunted, first order was to find my key in my mind—the ceremonies would start soon. Quickly I walked to the distant corner of the rostrum at the stone wall, plugged my ears and sang the first lines. Then the announcer asked for dignitaries to be seated. There was only time for prayers.

Nashville Mayor, Phil Bredesen, sat beside me with other guests. Fred began the ceremonies as the wind blasted through the microphones, roaring out the speakers. Coughing and praying, I watched the flags whipping, tipping in their stands and tree branches plunging up and down. There was nothing anyone could do. We were all in God's hands.

Mayor Bredesen delivered his poignant speech, holding his papers against the wind and contending for sovereignty of the mike. Then he finished. Fred made his introduction; it was time for me.

Remembering not to look at the somber faces below, I fastened my eyes on the giant flag at the cemetery entrance, lifted the microphone to my lips and began to sing. No cough. My voice was clear, more pure than yesterday. I sang with all my heart, and then God answered my prayers...

The wind stopped. Cold. As though someone threw a switch. It stopped. Beyond the graves, flags hung limply against the poles. Tree branches were still, no longer heaving. Banners before me stood limp in their stands. Stillness was everywhere. Yes. God had stopped the wind.

Angel Talk

Mayor Bredesen speaks against the wind.

The flags are still.

The National Cemetery

I looked at the crowd. They seemed frozen as they listened. In that instant, my whole being split—one part was singing the song; one part was hearing me sing, saying to myself, "I'm on key--I'm on key." One part was saying, "The wind has stopped! The wind has stopped!" and the other part was saying, "The flag isn't blowing!" My body seemed to become transparent, as though I were the air itself—mingling with every single living thing around me in that cemetery. I felt like I could fly away! Calm filled me. I knew my song was right. No one moved—no one said a word. No sirens sounded, no trains rumbled. The world was magical!

With the last line of the song, I looked at a uniformed officer in the first row, and sang the line to him. "Their memories will live free 'til we bring them home, and we greet them each morning or weep alone." And then, it was over.

Fred took the microphone as I turned toward my chair. Mayor Bredesen stood holding my chair, his eyes flooded with tears. His sadness was so overwhelming I couldn't look at him for fear I, too, would burst into tears. He seated me and we sat silent in our grief as echo *Taps* were played and Fred closed the ceremonies.

Then, people gathered on the rostrum and our attention turned to them. But there, coming toward me, was the officer from the front row—the one I had sung the last line to.

Taller than I, he looked me in the eyes, squared himself at attention, ramrod straight without saying a word. Never taking his eyes from mine, he reached for his gold braided hat and slowly, slowly, almost in slow motion, removed it. Slowly, slowly he placed it under his arm. Then, he reached for my hand and thanked me over and over for my song, saying how grateful he was that I had written it.

Speechless at his incredible salute, all I could think was, "Daddy said an officer never takes his hat off. Daddy said an officer never takes his hat off." Shocked at the significance of his action, I could only tell him I was so glad that I could write it. After all he had no idea what my life had been, what a milestone this day was. Then, he smiled, replaced his hat and turned away. Instantly, my friend, Katy, rushed up, showed her camera, and whispered, "I got him! I got him!"

The Colonel

Later, after Ross and Warren and Tamberly had started on their long drives home, Kristi and I were guests at my friends' home. As we reviewed the day's events, Beverly exclaimed, "I am completely exhausted from praying for you!" I asked, "Did you pray for my voice?" She replied, "I prayed for your voice! I prayed for your coughing! I prayed for the wind to stop! I prayed for the sirens and the trains and the traffic! I prayed for everything!!"

Her husband added, "You know, Rita, I said to God, 'Now God, you are going to have to ask the Angels to stop the wind, and I know that They can do that.'" Stunned at their words and their own utter belief in my Guardians, I said softly, "The wind did stop, didn't it?" They said, "Yes. It did."

What else is there to say?

The National Cemetery

HOME FREE

She told me the war
Was so long ago
But the chaplain
Never knocked on her door;

When she looked at his picture
She kept him alive
In her heart
And on the bracelet she wore...

Chorus:
His memory is home free
And she can't forget
The truths that he lived by
And the love that he left;
His memory will live free
'Til they bring him home
And she kisses him each morning
Or weeps alone.

His letters are wrapped
With the ribbons she saved
From his flowers
When they danced one last time;

When she touched every postmark
She prayed he'll come back
From the jungle
That never says he survived...

Refrain:
Their memories are home free
And we can't forget
The truths that they lived by
And the love that they left;
Their memories will live free
'Til we bring them home,
And we greet them each morning
Or weep...alone.

November, 1989

Angel Talk

MEMORIAL DAY
The National Cemetery

We have waited for this day now since the last one;
Our tears have touched your markers in the sun;
We've brought you flowers wrapped in all our memories,
For we've loved you still the same although you're gone.

We have set your names in stone from Nature's bosom;
Your banners cast their legends to the sky;
Our words remember you and what you fought for,
And our endless love will never let you die.

Today the sun has poured across your resting place;
The winds have wept their way through every tree;
The grass becomes the cloak around our heartache,
And we are left alone to grieve in harmony.

Back then your path was watched by waiting Angels,
But even God regrets the price you had to pay,
For time was meant to teach the heart of mankind
To gild his future with the growth of change.

But the guns of war still boom on far horizons,
And it seems the soul of man will never calm;
Yet today your spirits reach to brush our teardrops
And restore our hopes of peace as each tear falls.

So our songs today are whispers of your legacy;
Our prayers are all the dreams you tried to live,
So that every soul will meet in love and honesty
And our worlds will know the peace you tried to give.

Rita Whitmer
June, 1994

22

The Christmas Coconuts, 1994

PSALM 9

18 For the needy shall not alway be forgotten; the expectation of the poor shall not perish for ever.

Angel Talk

It was Christmas Eve. And on that bright, sunny Kentucky morning, no one in the world except me knew my world was not sunny and bright. Instead, it was different from anything I had known--a new brand of darkness and hopelessness.

No one knew I despaired that day. In a few hours it would be Christmas and I should be happy! Christmas was bringing families together, celebrating with thankfulness and joy! Christmas had friends and loved ones laughing at the door, ready to rejoice with the fresh promise of a new year! But today, only the coffee in my cup was warm and welcoming as I thought gloomily about the path that put me in this dark reality—I was broke on Christmas Day.

Months before, Kentucky had been one more place to rest in my long, long search for peace. An offer from friends to house-sit their deceased mother's home seemed like a solution, a place to write the songs and stories peering from the windows of my mind. My old promise to God "to do something with my music" still had hold of me and wouldn't let go.

Unfinished business in Nashville still haunted me but at least Kentucky put me only a couple of hours away from Nashville. It was the stepping stone I needed to keep my promise. Now being a stranger in a small coal town caused nagging trepidation and worries about surviving, but I took the chance on Kentucky. It was not going to be easy, not easy at all.

As we learn in life, things are not always as we think they are or will be. Other people's intent and perspective may be different from our own. Hidden agendas too often wreak a havoc all their own, and our goals can become lost in the goals of someone else. So it was with Kentucky.

But I set aside my worries and got a job at a dress shop. Minimum wage barely allowed survival but it was enough until I could decide how long I would stay. Surviving was enough only until I looked in the mirror on Christmas Eve and truth looked back...

The Christmas Coconuts

Six days before, the dress shop owner had called me to say she didn't need me anymore; she would mail my check. Fired seven days before Christmas without a prior word of discontent! But employers don't always need explanations, even if it was a week before Christmas, and no one in town was hiring. What does Christmas matter when a decent, hardworking girl has $23.00 to her name and no windfall in sight, no presents under the tree? Yes, I did have a tree, a lovely one, bought when I had money three weeks before. Now its lights brightened nothing except the dining room window and ghosts of my Christmases past, ghosts floundering in the brutal reality of this Christmas Eve and Christmas morning hours away. My money predicament also destroyed my plans to visit my nephew, Ross, at Fort Knox—how could I even buy gas to get there?

Furious at my decisions that led to such a miserable situation, I chastised myself over and over, re-thinking how and why and what I had done to wind up with a Christmas that was so wrong. Christmas was my time! I loved it for all of Heaven's reasons and a few more: my twin's birthday was the 21st, the car wreck had been in December, I survived; I had my 25th birthday in I.C.U.! For sure, I had more reasons to love Christmas than a lot of people and now here I was nearing that precious day with no money, no one to chorus my happiness for everything the day meant to Christianity, to the world and myself included. Depressed was an understatement for my heart.

A knock sounded at the door. I opened it to find the granny from across the street. She invited me to her daughter's home at five o'clock for their family Christmas Eve gathering. It would be informal, just sitting around the Christmas tree with a few refreshments—she was sure her daughter would love for me to join them. I thanked her for stopping, but instead of being happy at a chance to climb out of my Christmas doldrums, red flags sprouted in my mind. Be careful! Be careful!

Angel Talk

Though I had met the daughter who was nearly my age, saw her many times, the woman never spoke, was never cordial, not even when I was in her mother's driveway as she arrived to visit! Now to receive a left-handed invitation for Christmas Eve probably meant the daughter had no clue her mother was inviting a stranger to her door—hardly the kind of situation a hostess without the mostest would be pleased about. I told the granny I would see later if I could come by for a bit.

So, my bleak Christmas Eve morning moved into a bleaker Christmas Eve afternoon. Finally, I made my decision about my Christmas Eve and Christmas Day celebrations: I would spend $13.00 on gas to see Ross at Fort Knox; I would accept the granny's invitation to her daughter's house; after all, I had something to be happy about—I was alive, and healthy. And, perhaps meeting new people might be fun anyway. Determined to build some good memories, I called Ross and told him I was coming next day but I was poor and he might have to buy Christmas dinner.

Dressing up for any special occasion makes a person feel better, I thought, as I sprayed on perfume and headed out the door. Nagging doldrums drifted almost out of sight on the dark road to the daughter's house. A pretty tree waited, happy people, maybe Christmas carols; a good time was in store for certain!

Though night had fallen, my heart was light as I pulled into the drive, minutes after five o'clock. Several vehicles filled the drive where I parked. As I walked toward the front of the house, I thought, why, it would surely be a nice evening after all.

As I passed the front window toward the door, I glanced in for the shock of the season: the entire family was seated at a great long dining table, replete in Christmas splendor with candles burning, china, and crystal! This was no Christmas Eve by the tree! This was a formal, family dinner!

Stunned at the scene, I stopped cold, then backed quickly out of the light, praying no one had seen me.

The Christmas Coconuts

There was no place for me at that table. And I instantly knew that no one else knew I was coming. The daughter had no idea her mother had invited me. Shivering in the darkness, I thought of what would happen if I knocked. The daughter would come to the door to see a stranger—unwanted stranger. What would she say? What would the guests say? Do? No. I could not, absolutely would not, interrupt this family dinner just because I was alone on Christmas Eve.

One more misery on Christmas Eve? Nope. I had had enough terrible experiences in this coal town to last a lifetime and adding another one to my memory bank was not in the cards—nor Christmas lights.

Moments later I was out the drive, lights off, careful not to hit my brakes as I skidded onto the highway. Once again, black night surrounded me as the night became a new darkness, a new bleakness, a new gloom. How could it be?! Seconds before, I was looking forward to a happy evening with new people. Now I had one more thing to forget, put behind me. I was glad the road back to town was dark and empty and long. But it was the loneliest drive I had had in years.

Collecting happy Christmas memories from the sad cellar of my heart, I filled the darkness with old images, counting my many, many blessings of Christmas at home in Montana, at the ranch, the hospital, with my darling in New Mexico. They really weren't too long ago. After all, if you can remember, then it is as near as your heartbeat.

A thousand little old things now made me glad again to be part of our special world on Earth. I thanked God for my health, my mind, for the magic of life, for this Christmas Eve and tried to put away my sad thoughts.

The city Christmas lights appeared, I was restored—not completely—but I was not so terribly depressed as I was at 5:05. Thoughts of my trip next day came to mind. Christmas Day meant presents--I had to take Ross a present! But where would I find a present—something cheap—real cheap, at this hour?! By now it was nearing five thirty—the stores were closed or closing soon. What could I find quickly before it was too late?!

There! The grocery store lights were still on! They were open! Surely I could find a present there to take to him—why, even a Hershey bar wrapped in pretty paper would do!

Inside the grocery store entrance sat a huge crate filled with fresh coconuts—nice, hairy, three-eyed, healthy looking coconuts. Fifty cents apiece. Smiling, I thought, "The price is right! Why, Ross has never seen a coconut! I'll take him a coconut!" Choosing two, one for him and one for me to mark this special Christmas, I waited at the check-out stand as the clerk chattered happily about Christmas. Employees bustled about to close as she asked if my card was punched and took my dollar and change. I showed her the card, punched to her satisfaction, wished her "Merry Christmas!" and left with my Christmas coconuts.

But my cheery moment of Christmas shopping was just that—a moment. A few minutes later, I unlocked the door to the house waiting empty and dark, just like the road into the town. Inside, my perfume still lingered in the hall for the party I never went to. Gloomed out again, I left the lights off and sat, wretched to the bone, in the hall by the old telephone table. Christmas blues sang in my heart. Christmas was everything it wasn't supposed to be. Sad. Lonely. Dark. And then the telephone rang.

I answered slowly. A man's voice asked, "Is this Rita Whitmer?" I said, "Yes." He said, "This is the manager from the grocery store and we've drawn your name in our cash drawing. If you tell me what the last number is punched on your card, I'll tell you if you've won any money."

I didn't understand what he was talking about, but remembered the card the clerk had asked to see minutes earlier. Three weeks before, she and her co-worker had said, "Rita, you need a card for our drawing. Just bring it in every time you come in and we'll punch it for you." So, I had done as they instructed. But mine had only the last

The Christmas Coconuts

four punches on the card. I said, "Well, it looks like the last number punched is 52."

The store manager exclaimed, "Well, Rita, you've just won $400 dollars! If you come over here, I'll give it to you! You're really lucky, too, because we almost never have $400! It's usually only $100." I sat down.

"Four hundred dollars?! Four hundred dollars?! What do I have to do to get it?" He responded happily, "Just come over here and I'll give it to you!" I couldn't get his words in my mind. "You mean I just drive over there and you're going to give me four hundred dollars?" Again he replied happily, "That's right! And you'd better hurry because we're closing in fifteen minutes!"

Shocked beyond belief, I jammed the truth through my head—how could it be?! Seconds ago I was poor and now I was rich! Stumbling to my car in tears, I knew, one more time, that God and all the Angels took pity on me. God loved me, a lot. He and all His Angels had mercy on my poor broken heart, my wretched Christmas. They had given me a Christmas I would never, ever forget!!

Now the Christmas lights on the road back to the grocery store twinkled at me celebrating my Christmas miracle, so differently than a few minutes before!! Tingling all over with this new reality, humbled and diminutive in the loving embrace of God and His Angels, I wept soft new Christmas tears all the way to the store. There the manager happily counted out twenty brand new twenty-dollar bills.

Then he shook my hand, reached for his Polaroid camera and said, "Okay, Rita! Give me a four hundred dollar smile!" Still in shock, holding my new fortune, my astonishing gift from Heaven, I gave him his smile, thanked him again and drove back to the house!

Slowly, slowly, glory took over. What a brand, new sparkling Christmas unfolded before me! I was still living it, still happening, right now! And it was out-shining every flicker of misery and unhappiness and self-pity from those days, weeks, months in that town!

Angel Talk

Once again I sat in the dark empty house, this time with a candle burning, smiling in wonder at the crisp new twenty dollar bills before me. Four hundred dollars! What a Christmas! I thought of the Angels watching as the store employee reached in the basket to draw a card. Did They make him feel through the mass of cards, maybe stopping his hand when he started to remove one that wasn't mine? Did They make his hand go back in, searching until his fingers touched the one They wanted--mine?

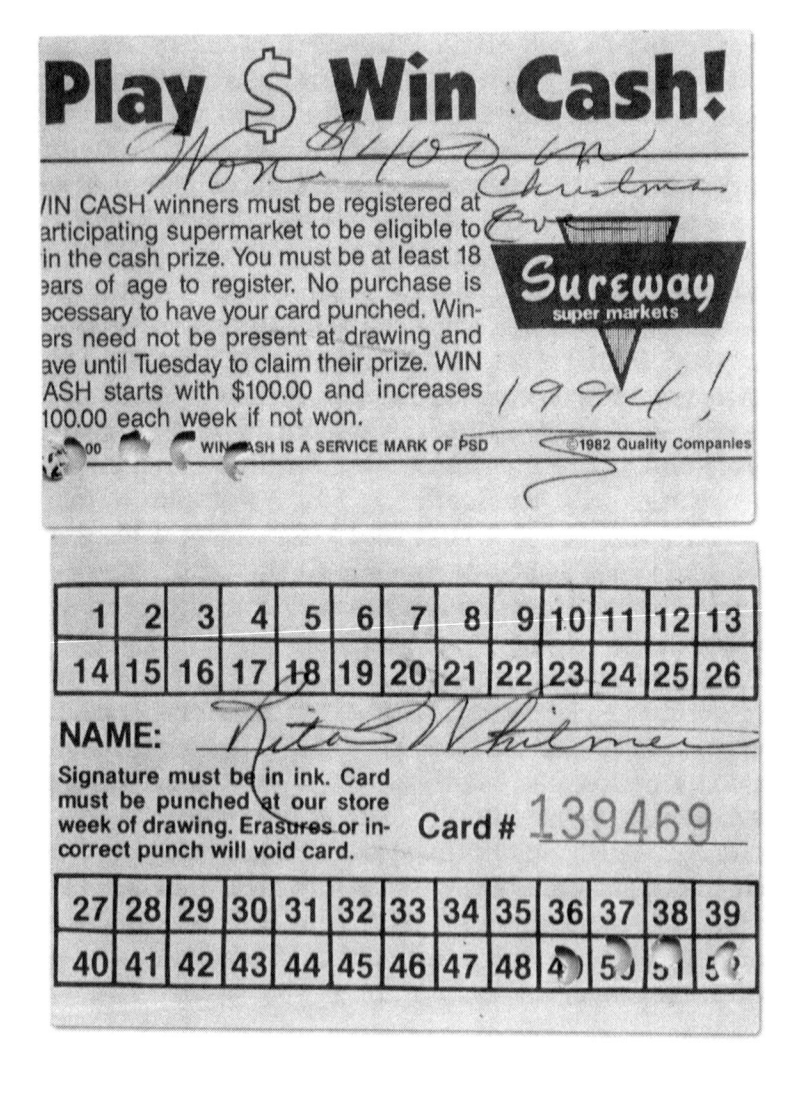

The Christmas Coconuts

Only God and all the Angels knew I was desperate, broken-hearted and shattered. Only God and all the Angels knew what I had been through, and only They could give me a moment that would change my life, just like They had so many times before! And change it, They did!

Later, when I was calm, I called Ross to tell him I was rich and Christmas dinner was on me! He exclaimed, "How can you be rich? You were poor just a little while ago?!" Listening in disbelief, he agreed I had added a Christmas miracle to my belt!

Next morning at church, I put the first crisp twenty-dollar bill in the offering plate. Then I drove across a quiet Kentucky to Fort Knox for Christmas with Ross. He held the Christmas coconut gingerly, frowning at its hairy ugliness. "What is it?" I was right! He had never seen a coconut!

We laughed and drove through the silent city for Christmas dinner, on me, at the Sheraton. We talked of many things and he told me he was going to college after the Army and "build speed, if you know what I mean." Then it was time to go and we parted with Christmas memories both of us would be remembering for a long, long time!

On the beautiful drive across Kentucky to the coal town, God and all the Angels winked down on my only Kentucky Christmas. With their Christmas miracle, They restored my trust in my decisions. In hindsight, I had certainly been right to not stay at the daughter's house. But it was *my* decision, *my* choice. The option was mine: stay or go. This time, the outcome was good. But as we know, sometimes our decisions don't always produce a win.

My Christmas miracle made me want to try harder than ever in life, to do more and better things. It made me want to never stop doing what feels right and best, to listen to my intuition. After all, if I had knocked on that door at the party, the daughter would somehow probably have accommodated me. But I would have missed the manager's call. Later I asked him how many times he would have phoned. He said simply, "Three. If there is no answer after three times, we draw another card."

Life was different in Kentucky after that, and I was different. Several months later, I returned to Nashville for one last try with my music. There I would meet more people who would change my life and make me glad I made the decisions I have.

Since Kentucky, I honor my personal values and standards more than ever and defend my time and energy against intrusions and infringements by others. Life is precious and fragile, a time of valuable learning, sharing and growing. We cannot reach the goals of our souls if we allow others to insult our precious time and essential resources, and demand that we entertain compromises denying us our goals.

My Christmas miracle became another reminder of our human tender hooks to Heaven—those loving strings connecting us to God. My Christmas miracle will remind me forever that we are truly puppets on the strings of Heaven and those wondrous strings will never ever be broken.

CHRISTMAS

Not often in our lifetimes
As we forge the chain of change,
Does that golden link of love
Connect our past and future days.

And if perhaps upon a lifetime
When those days are joined anew,
We treasure golden moments
When all life and love are true.

And if perchance upon a Christmas time
When all Creation bows to God,
He lets us glow like Christmas stars
That see His blessed nod.

Then Earth and Sky and all Mankind
Are linked in harmony;
The clock will stop while Angels wrought
What God has meant to be.

Then we know that Christmas time
Has gilded how we think;
Our chain of life is changed forever...
By one blessed golden link.

For Karen and Charlie Chase
Christmas Day, 1996

Epilogue

A lifetime has passed since my first star struck awareness of God and Divine Intervention. Thirty-nine years of dazzling surprises, experiences, people, have filled my life, astonishing me over and over again with unanticipated knowledge and change. Each one, of course, has added to my understanding of life and of myself.

Through these years I have come to believe we can rightfully call our beautiful planet "Paradise" and consider ourselves honored for the chance to live here, to see and breathe and feel the wonders it offers us. Every wonder to me is simple evidence of God, all the Angels and the magnificent power of Divine Intervention.

Since *Angel Talk* began finding its way to paper, my dedication to the manuscript was interrupted many times with sorrow, suffering, loss. I believe these events were part of the goals of my soul, things I had to endure so I could be enlightened further during my time on Earth.

Many of the people in *Angel Talk* are still alive, though I lost my beloved mother in Montana on December 4, 2005. Her absence has created a perpetual sadness in my life and void in my future. She was part of every day I lived. She was a participant, a listener about every event in this book. She knew many of the people and the places where the events occurred, even those outside Montana. Each time I told her of yet another astounding miracle, she listened rapt to the incredible details. She believed in God, she believed in prayer, she believed in love, and she mattered more to me than anyone in the world. Now as each of you share these moments of my life, I am sure she delights in knowing you are part of them now!

Mother lived on the farm with all her memories until several years before her death. Our neighbor, Ruth Harris, lives in Wolf Point. Her son, Larry, owns her farm, my brother owns Mother's farm and the fields still produce the greatest wheat in the world. The schoolhouse is still down the road.

My brother, Rex, had a dynamic career in real estate and lives and works in Fairbanks, Alaska, enjoying the wonders and wildlife of that great state.

In Helena, after nearly a century of sheltering young dreamers starting their own lives, the YWCA is still in the same beautiful old Victorian building, with the same magnificent oriental rugs, the same grand piano in the lobby! Last Chance Gulch was re-designed as a historic neighborhood and closed to traffic near the little chapel where the Angels began talking to me so long ago.

In Albuquerque not long ago, I returned to the ICU unit at Presbyterian Hospital to see the rooms where the doctors and nurses struggled to keep me alive. It was odd to feel the energy in the place, now used as an overflow trauma area for the Emergency Unit. The windows still opened to Heaven--everything was the same. I remembered so vividly lying in those rooms, and it was wonderful to see them again as a well, ever-grateful person.

After their ordeal with me, Dr. Spingola and Dr. Erickson became an organ transplant team until Dr. Spingola moved to California where he still practices in Santa Rosa. Dr. Erickson retired from surgery but works a few days a week with the Renal Medicine Group in Albuquerque where he lives. Still passionately committed to improving human life, he continues flying medical missions into Africa where he ministers to the natives isolated in the jungle.

Also retired from surgery, Dr. Maron recently returned to Albuquerque and, too, remains deeply committed to improving human lives. He is active in preventative medicine, nutrition and providing naturopathic treatment and awareness.

Bob Watson still lives in Albuquerque with his family, and though he is nearing a four-score birthday, still works half days! Just as my doctors stay on my mind, he, too, is a constant part of my prayers and gratitude.

Sister Beriswell passed away at St. Michaels in Gonad, Arizona, only a few years after her unforgettable visit to me. Though I saw her only once for those few minutes, her memory has remained an abiding light of love in my life, my beloved messenger from Heaven.

In 1992, I also had the good fortune to meet Dr. Perry Berg again in Billings, Montana. We met last when he operated on my shattered ankle in 1966. When I told him who I was, he stared hard at me through his Cary Grant glasses, his eyes lost in my face as he thought back through the years trying to recall. Suddenly he proclaimed, "Oh! I remember you!! I remember you! I used those slides in seminars for years!"

So my life has moved through the years. Though I was never able to be the nurse I dreamed of, I have participated in the medical profession in my own unique way. I was the someone on whom the great ones had to practice! Through it all, knowing my devoted doctors and nurses are still alive, still helping save lives, improve lives, their passion has helped me live my own dream vicariously, albeit from the opposite side of the bed.

One evening a few years ago, I had the "miraculous" good fortune to see a television documentary recounting the tragedy of the Lost Boys of the Sudan. One of the survivors gazed sadly into the camera, his sorrowful soul tormented as he told the heart-wrenching story of their flight across the desert. As he and thousands of others despaired of reaching safety, they slowly died of thirst, one by one. He said they stumbled on and on, praying for help from God...praying and stumbling and dying. And then the rain began to fall...but it fell only on the road...not across the desert dunes. It fell only on the long, narrow column of desperate children stretching more than a mile over the sand, its precious drops restoring their strength until they reached another haven. I thought, "I know, too, what God can do with a little rain...He can make it fall, one drop at a time, exactly where He wishes..."

In another book, *God and the Milkman*, I have written the story of the ex-husband's life and shocking death. In 1996, he was murdered by his bride of six months with a gun he had stolen from my brother when we returned to Montana in 1975. My vow to testify in her defense severed all ties with his family, but her case never went to trial. While going through my files, I found documents proving his cruelty and threats to me decades before. I sent them to her attorney in Dallas. She was given a deferred sentence of ten years; the case ended.

All of my siblings are still living and reside in various parts of the country. Clinton drilled water wells in Montana for years, taught high school physics and supervised drilling rigs in Oman. Patsy and her husband, Bud, live in Yakima where he is an orchardist; she earned her PhD in nutrition and they have two sons. My twin is a writer still living on the farm. Kristi is in finance and lives in New Jersey; Jeannie lives in Circle where we began our lives, and Ross did "build speed". He became a rocket engineer and lives in Salt Lake City.

Dwayne Warwick never met the Direktor of the Rijksmuseum in Amsterdam, but his magnificent artworks still dazzle admirers everywhere! Haan and Marga remained in touch, writing from places they traveled around the world. Less than two years after our visit, we lost Haan to an inoperable brain tumor; Marga remains in Holland.

Gladys Baker lived to be 91 years old and left this world in 2004, a kind gentle soul to her last breath.

And, my music, that endless commitment of keeping my promise to God? After twenty years of trying to get a song recorded, I never succeeded. Only my POW/MIA song has comforted many where I have performed it and hopefully will do so in the future. Today my writing time is focused on other books and movie scripts waiting to find paper. My songs, however, will always remain that testimony of my promise to God. He let me live. I kept my promise. I did something with my music.

So it is that these stories are simply moments of one person's life—stories of living, like people everywhere around the world. Many, many people have special experiences that are really miracles. When recognized, they are only reminders of Heaven's astounding constant participation in our daily lives. For me, regardless of pain and sorrow, there is not a day I would change, not a moment I would turn away from for the honor of living through this wondrous life on Earth!

With the rapture of knowing these truths, it is my wish that you, the reader, will also see your own stunning miracles and glory in your days. Then you will know how I have felt during these years of astonishing enlightenment. I hope that when you proclaim your joy to God and all the Angels, you will remember that They, too, rejoice even more in your life, the days you are so honored to live.

Acknowledgements

These stories would never have been told without the abiding love and support of my beloved friends, Sue and Pete Ettinger and Bob Hofeldt. For nearly forty years they have mused, wondered, pondered and protected me as I added another experience to my Life List. Their understanding and caring has steadied me through times that should have broken my faith and ended my courage to face another challenge. I will be forever indebted to them for their loving support and for staying by my side.

To my dear friend, Eve Wilson, I extend my gratitude for decades of encouragement, time and support of my values and my life, and for sharing the laughter, the tears and Amsterdam.

My dear friends, Karen and Wayne Bernard, a/k/a Mr. and Mrs. Charlie Chase, believed in my music and I thank them forever for the gift that let me write, and for making my dream worth living.

This road has been smoother by the guidance and faith of my dear friend, Vivian Pennington, whose mentoring and memories with Preach kept my own faith shining in the dark.

My dear cousins kept the latch string out, and my thanks to Bob, Jerry, Junie, Duane, C Ball, Tom and Nancy, Donna, Chuck and Lynn are as big as the Montana sky.

To Clinton, Patsy and Rex, and my friends, Dwayne Warwick, Patricia and Tommy Latham, Pam Gilliam, Cindy McGuire, Markley Pohlman, Mary Ann Montoya, Joe and Retta Beery, Lori Washburn and Jim 'Brad' Galloway, I thank you for the years, for listening, sharing wisdom and unselfish support during this incredible Earth journey.

Ann Rutherford, Sherwood McKay, Dot Dougherty and Frances Moen must be thanked for their time and thoughts in reviewing the final pages.

And, *Angel Talk* could not have gone from manuscript to book without the patient and devoted counsel and expertise of my dear cousin, Patrick James Whitmer.

Surely God and all the Angels thank you, too.

PSALM 30

12 To the end that my glory may sing praise to thee, and not be silent, O LORD my God, I will give thanks unto thee for ever.

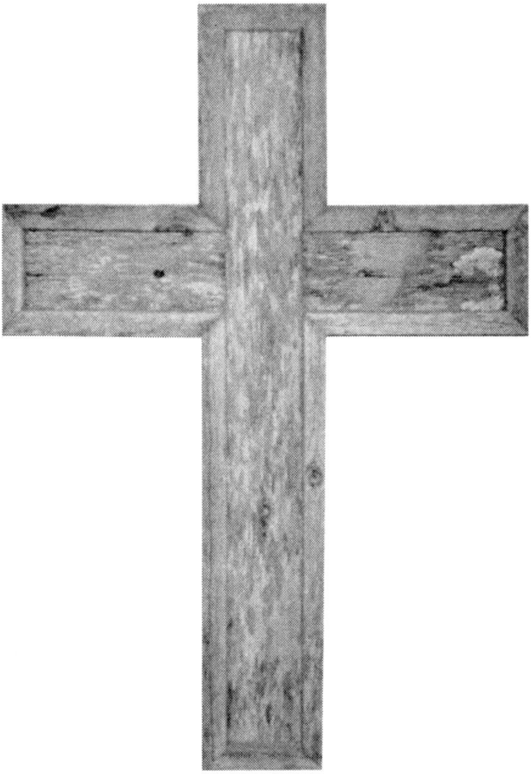

Printed in the United States
144887LV00004B/107/P